To Remain Vigilant
Book I of the Epic of Hotspur

Liz Sevchuk Armstrong

Print ISBNs
Amazon print 9780228631828
Ingram Spark 9780228631835
Barnes & Noble 9780228631842
BWL Print 9780228631859

Copyright 2024 by Elizabeth Schevtchuk Armstrong
Editor Victoria Chatham
Cover artist Pandora Designs

All rights reserved. Without limiting the rights under copyright reserved above, no part of this publication may be reproduced, stored in or introduced into a retrieval system, or transmitted, in any form, or by any means (electronic, mechanical, photocopying, recording, or otherwise) without the prior written permission of both the copyright owner and the publisher of this book.

Sir Harry Percy confronted the foe ... the man nicknamed 'Hotspur' for his conscientious resolve, for, while others surrendered to sleep, he strove to remain vigilant..."
    Henry Knighton, medieval chronicler

Table of Contents

Chapter I 7
Chapter II 15
Chapter III 27
Chapter IV 42
Chapter V 58
Chapter VI 79
Chapter VII 102
Chapter VIII 109
Chapter IX 124
Chapter X 140
Chapter XI 152
Chapter XII 170
Chapter XIII 196
Chapter XIV 208
Chapter XV 223
Chapter XVI 251
Chapter XVII 281
Chapter XVIII 305

Chapter I
February 1399 - Smithfield, London

His visor shut with sobering finality as he gripped his horse with his knees and gazed down the lists—toward eternity.

Sir Harry Percy's left hand flexed the reins while his right tightened on the lance, heavy and cumbersome but as familiar as a lover's hand. Beyond him, the audience settled in subdued expectation, waiting just as he did, as his opponent did at the other end of the field.

"Remember, Percy," he cautioned silently. "He's unseasoned but could kill you and seems to want to, not for anything you've done but because he would climb to glory on your broken back. And he's a fool, too reckless to know how foolish he really is."

Well, let him come...

"But be careful, for your sake and his."

Scenting the icy edge of mortality in the midwinter thaw, his horse tensed, and Harry patted him comfortingly. Otherwise, he remained immobile, with no outward anxiety betraying his deliberations or coiled, controlled nerves. He'd aim for the visor slits, and hard, he told himself. But not hard enough to kill or even blind his adversary. Though God knew, the idiot was blinded already by dreams of grandeur. Only spear him enough to unhelm and unhorse him. Then, let the rest fall out as it may.

"Lay on!" The tourney marshal sent the horses off as the crowd began a low roar.

They hurtled toward confrontation, and—as all knew—one probably raced toward his Maker, as well, for this contest featured not only England's best knight and an eager if untrained rival but real weapons, not the blunted "peace arms" typical at tournaments.

Metal gleaming, azure lions and grey fish prancing on his coat-of-arms, Harry watched the distance disappear under the horses' enormous strides. They would meet on the left, allowing maximum use of lances carried on the right. Shield couched against his shoulder, he guided his horse securely and invisibly.

His challenger, Sir Richard Arundel, was nephew to the great lord of that name who had died a traitor's death eighteen months earlier. Resplendent in silver armor with copper gilt, young Arundel hoped to restore his family's fortunes and boost his own by feats of prowess, or the nearest one could come to them in this year of truces. Hence his challenge to the thirty-eight-year-old Lord Henry Percy Junior, invariably known as Sir Harry, or by his nom-de-guerre, Hotspur.

As Harry realized, Arundel had nothing against him directly; the champion was only a means to an end: When Percy fell, so might Arundel rise.

Harry had other ideas. He chose a likely moment to feint diagonally right—not left, as might be expected, since they would pass on that side. Yet, as soon as he charged right, he veered sharply back again into Arundel's path.

Arundel's lance carved the air as Harry ducked low in the saddle, raising his own lance. Powered by his muscular right arm, its tip entered the eye slits of Arundel's helmet. As Harry exerted pressure, the helmet broke free of its straps, wrenching from Arundel's head. Raising it like a trophy on a stick, Harry tossed it across the field and turned back to his quarry.

Temporarily shocked, Arundel dropped his lance, wheeled his horse—and lost his shield. The side of Harry's lance thudded against him, stifling air to his lungs. Arundel stiffened. Harry hit him again, and Arundel fell to the ground.

The crowd went wild, foreseeing a fight on foot, with blood to be let. Already, a small stream splashed from Arundel's nose onto the turf. Gasping, he got up, unsuccessfully groped for his shield, and drew his broadsword, anticipating another onslaught.

But Harry trotted down the field, threw his own lance aside, jumped from his horse, and, unsheathing his sword, loped back to face his antagonist.

They squared off in the grass, warily dancing around each other. Long moments passed while the audience's yelling increased until Arundel opened the duel with a thrust. Harry parried it but sloppily deflected the follow-up. The edge of Arundel's sword jabbed through the chainmail at his left shoulder. As the mesh dug into his flesh, Harry abandoned his own shield, easing the burden on his upper arm, but lashed out with his sword.

Arundel met the cut and the two blades crossed and seemed to lock, motionless, as the men stood foot-to-foot, each straining to make the other drop his hand first, each seeking to strike decisively.

But it didn't happen.

They gritted their teeth and lunged against each other again until Arundel's footing began to slip. He kicked out, attempting to force Harry off balance as well. Warned by a sixth sense, Harry jerked his leg up, booting Arundel in the stomach. Head aching, ribs already sore from lance buffets, Arundel stumbled.

Pressing his advantage, Harry forced him over backward. Haphazardly, Arundel tried to raise his sword. But Harry was upon him, straddling him, wresting the sword away and pressing his own against Arundel's chin.

"Kill him!" A spectator urged.

"Do you yield, Sir?" Harry demanded, his words distorted into an ominous growl by his helmet. "Or shall I have to slit your throat?"

"Kill him!"

Other voices joined the heckler. "Kill him! Kill him!"

"Why not?" Harry mused, "Easy enough." Easy enough, too, to get away with it. He need only let up long enough to tease Arundel into another futile grab for his missing sword and then inflict vengeance, claiming self-defense.

Nor would anyone blame him.

He listened for Arundel's plea for mercy or acknowledgement of surrender. None came. But the young eyes were sallow and terrified in a face devoid of hope or color, while beneath Harry's sword, Arundel's throat quivered like a hare in the maw of a hound.

"Kill him!" The chant spread.

"I could well satisfy them," Harry thought again. "Most would say he deserves it. And had the outcome been other, he would have killed me. So why not?"

Still, he made no move.

Glancing down, he noticed their shadows: Dark figure of a knight, leaning over an enemy whose toes dug into the soil, as if trying to hold onto life itself. The shadows firmed, but Harry's vision momentarily wavered, and he saw not himself and Arundel but another triumphant warrior and another young man, brought low in part by his own hubris, thrashing on the bloody ground of Otterburn, a dirk at his throat. And in memory he watched a Scottish lord forsake the knife to extend a hand of deliverance to an anguished Harry Percy.

The refrain intensified. "Kill him!"

Harry no longer heard, though. Nonetheless, 'twouldn't hurt to teach Arundel a lesson about vanity and unnecessary combat, or magnanimity.

"Well, Sir?" His sword pushed harder against Arundel's chin.

"I ... yield," Arundel croaked.

"Good." Harry sheathed his sword. "That steel has tasted enough blood. No need to add yours." He reached down to help Arundel up. The younger man grasped his wrist and stood—only to slide back to his knees. Grabbing Harry's hands, Arundel kissed them as if in fealty. Once more, Harry pulled him up.

Forgetting its demands for death, the crowd scrambled to its feet, cheering this unexpected but welcome demonstration of chivalry. Buoyed, Harry and Arundel walked arm-in-arm to the reviewing stand.

There, for the first time all day, Harry noticed King Richard II next to the eleven-year-old girl who was his queen. Seeing her, a homesick French child, a pawn in the constant squabbles between England and France, Harry was relieved he hadn't succumbed to the temptation to slay Arundel. Queen Isabel had enough to frighten her in this alien land; there was no reason to expose her to more barbarism.

"Sir Harry Percy is declared victor," the marshal announced with appropriate fanfare.

Arundel stepped back.

Harry raised his arm, acknowledging the acclaim, and surveyed the lower boxes reserved for contestants' families. Remnants of the Arundel clan filled one front row, but the adjoining space was empty. A maternal cousin had joined his tourney team. Yet here among the spectators, there was no one: No father, wife or children, no Percies at all. But there never were, and he didn't expect any, not these days. He'd been too long immersed in knighthood and competitions; this was only one of many. His kin had stopped watching years earlier.

Turning back toward the royal box, he knelt.

King Richard, marvelous in gold robes and crown, sat as if in a trance, saying nothing. Isabel smiled brightly, however, and motioned Harry forward. Reaching over the reviewing stand, she gave him an exquisite pink rose, nurtured in a palace orangery and wrapped with a gold chain.

Harry held the flower to his lips and bent his knee to the girl before walking toward the edge of the field.

Midway, he turned to acknowledge the applause again before disappearing into the palisaded area reserved for contestants. From there, he hastened to his tent, ready to be free of his armor and London, though the stewards were loudly announcing music, dancing, and festivities extending into the next day.

For him, they held no attraction.

Nonetheless, he found his tent jammed with squires and knights intent on revelry. After all, earlier in the tourney he had led a team to triumph in two grand melees, mock battles, and gone on to win individual jousts. There was plenty to celebrate, and if he shied away, he was a minority of one. Lounging around the ember-burning braziers that transformed the tent into a cozy den, his teammates dispensed wine from a cask, toasting Harry and each other.

"You will join us, won't you?" His red-haired younger cousin, Sir Thomas Neville, Lord Furnival, asked as Harry found a bench and let a squire remove his leg armor. "We'll attend the king's musicale. And then my brother Ralph says he knows a tavern near Westminster where they cater only to lords and knights like us—and the elite of Parliament, no less. It's said the wenches who serve there are exquisite.

"But you don't have to chase the women if you don't want to," Furnival added, noting Harry's indifference. "There's very good meat and ale, too. And their wine is supposed to be from the best of Burgundy, not this cat-piss from Bordeaux you serve."

Harry laughed. "'Tis not of my choosing, the wine. Ask John Hardyng. He and the rest of my squires got the barrel somehow. Swiped it from other contenders, probably. I thought it best not to ask questions."

Outer armor gone, he stood and pulled his chainmail hauberk over his head and shed the tunic and leggings he wore below. Stripping off his underclothing, he reached for the basin on a stand. Sponge in hand, he began scrubbing the sweat from his clean-shaven face and lean body. The water ran in fine strands over his broad shoulders, falling in gentle drops onto the matted hair of his chest, over his oak-straight back and down his long legs.

Wincing as he touched the cut from Arundel's sword, he daubed it with wine and water and finished washing.

Furnival threw him a towel. "Well, Harry, Will you share our fortunes tonight? You ought to make merry, you know. Once again, you've shown all of London you're fucking good."

Harry's deep-blue eyes flashed mischief. "Fucking good?' No, Thom, I've never shown any of these folk I'm fucking good. Before a crowd? What kind of games did you think these were?"

Furnival grabbed the towel, hitting him. "You know what I meant. Anyway, you are the champion. And we'd be delighted if you'd deign to honor us with your presence—at least for supper. After that, be an old maid. Talk to your horse all night, for all I care. We'll invite Arundel, too, if you like, so he can finish mending fences with you."

Harry smiled, shaking his head. "I'm grateful. And by all means, take Arundel along. He owes me naught. He's probably lonely anyway. Bear him my compliments. But I'm away, to my father's house, to say farewell. Then I ride north. I've been in this damned town long enough."

In fact, he had only been in London several days, albeit after spending six weeks in Essex, on estate business his father had found no time to address. Duty there completed, he had ridden to London more to confer with his father than for the tourney, though after receiving Arundel's challenge he had been compelled to see it through. Now he was finished.

"I want to go home," he confessed. "Get back to hunting in the Cheviots. See what the Scots are up to. There've been rumors a border laird brags of going a-reiving soon."

He drew on fresh underwear and socks, a shirt, and goatskin leggings, topped by a thick woolen tunic. "My appreciation and apologies I can't join you." Feet again booted, he buckled his belt, adjusted his leather cloak and slung his saddlebags over his shoulder. "Please, enjoy the hospitality of my tent. My squires will be here another day or two, packing our gear." Then he was gone, out the back flap.

As he left, a blustering giant of a knight, known as "Herr Hans" for his Bohemian origins, pushed to the fore, wine cup in each hand. He had been on the melee team and frowned at his captain's departure. "Will he not join us? I've never known a man so unwilling to enjoy the fruits of victory."

"He rides north before nightfall." Furnival replaced his empty cup with one of Hans' brimming goblets.

"Must be anxious to be with his wife and children back north," Hans surmised, having seen none of Harry's family in the stands.

"No. They bide here, in London, with my Uncle Henry, Earl of Northumberland. At their mother's urging, the earl brought the little ones south to keep him company through the court season. Naturally, their mother, Harry's wife, came along. She stays on, too—quite happily without Harry, I believe."

Hans looked befuddled. "Then he must have a mistress in the North."

Arm around Hans, Furnival led him from the tent. "You're right. Harry does have a mistress. And he finds her most delectable parts in the North. So he races to enjoy them again."

Hans' eyes lit up. "Who is this enchantress?"

Furnival chuckled. "You're walking on her." He pointed to the packed, brown-green grass at their feet. "That's his love, this land, and woe betide any man who tries to harm her or separate him from her. England is his mistress. But to him, her heart beats strongest in the North. And so does his."

Chapter II
March 1399 - Alnwick Castle, Northumberland

Only the first dank traces of dawn edged the walls as Harry saw her crossing the yard, skirts and head held high, following a path in a ritual as timeless as footprints worn on ancient paving stones.

Yet he knew she came not for his sake but that of their five-year-old son, whose hand she clutched. "Good morrow, lady." He stepped away from his horse. "We hadn't expected anyone to grace our departure."

"For Young Henry," Elizabeth Mortimer Percy explained, her tone apathetic. "He heard the cock's crow, saw you outside, begged to come down."

Kneeling, Harry reached out to take the boy from his mother. For the briefest of pauses, his hand rested on her arm, his touch as soft and remote as the look in his eyes.

As he embraced the child, Harry glanced up at his wife—tall and as regal as any monarch, with a face with the exquisite oval symmetry glaziers used to depict the Madonna—and as impassive and brittle as glass.

He had not expected to see her at all. Journeying from Durham to Berwick, he had reached Alnwick the previous evening to discover that she and the youngsters had been there two days. When the court season waned, she said, she'd ridden from London with her father-in-law and, at the latter's request, stopped at the castle to supervise the late-winter inventory. As she had made clear in the few words she and Harry exchanged, she much preferred to be at Newburn, her own elegant manse near Newcastle, far from stony Percy bastions.

Harry had only nodded and enjoyed a skittles game with the children before their nursemaid hustled them off to bed. Soon, he, too, had retired, alone, as usual, until scouts disrupted slumber with an ominous alert: Raiders gathered along the border.

"So, with the Scots afoot, I must be to-horse." Harry hugged Young Henry again. "You can see me off and make sure this beast is awake." Swinging the boy into the saddle, he led the black gelding, Redesraven, toward the outer wall.

"I can ride him, too!" Young Henry gleefully tugged a rein. "Can I keep him?"

"No," Harry laughed. "But someday you'll have one even better." Below the portcullis, he lifted the boy down again and into his mother's waiting hands.

"Now, by your leave." He gave his son's locks a final tousle. "We'll away."

Mounting, he motioned to his men and headed into the mist. He was uncertain when he might return. Not that it mattered to him—or to Elizabeth.

With a similar background of noble birth and high rank, Sir Harry Percy and Lady Elizabeth Mortimer were well-paired socially and economically and totally mismatched in everything that counted most in marriage, sharing neither values nor conversations nor opportunities for time with one another. She adored the city and its gilded townhouses and ornate furniture; its shops and markets, well-stocked with fine silks, perfumes, and jewelry; the opulence of the king's court and glamorous courtiers, all whirling through a grand world known well to her sister, who had become a lady-in-waiting at a tender age and shared tantalizing gossip in letters.

More comfortable in cow pastures than palace precincts, Harry cared little for court ceremony, less for court intrigue, and still less again for idle courtiers and their chit-chat. And, in any case, he still spoke an "uncouth" Northumbrian-Scottish dialect that included aye and nay instead of yes and no; burns or becks for brooks; fechting not fighting, and stanes for stones or hame rather than home. Sometimes, he caught his pronunciation mid-sentence and corrected it; more often, he did not—more proof of the North's backwardness, court habitués tittered into their expansive and expensive sleeves.

But it mattered naught to him; his portion came elsewhere.

While Elizabeth favored London, Harry relished long gallops through the windswept Cheviots, wandering alone, seeking the year's first woodland flowers in a final dusting of snow, swimming in isolated lakes, or watching the sun stab itself on western peaks, to bleed crimson across the moors. The lures of Westminster paled in comparison.

Nonetheless, despite their differences, initially, he and Elizabeth had at least shared a marriage bed, hardly ignorant of the steamy pleasures of young, sleek bodies entwining as each found moments of keen, sweetly tormenting bliss. But their romps were only that, momentary, purely physical, no proof of emotional commitment or devotion. She had soon become pregnant, and after the birth of their daughter, and, a year later, a son, they had spun separate webs of existence, she embracing motherhood and genteel tenure at Newburn or London as hostess at her widowed father-in-law's manor there; Harry immersed in duty, often far from her hearth and always far from her heart. As she was from his.

It was his own fault.

He had taken up with Elizabeth only to accede to his father's admonitions that it was high time for the heir to Northumberland to get on with ensuring the survival of their vaunted line and simultaneously seal the pragmatic alliance arranged with Elizabeth's father when she was a baby and Harry a child. To the Mortimers, marriage with the Percies promised entry to the North, while, for the Percies, Mortimer connections offered standing on the Welsh border and at court, for Elizabeth was the great-granddaughter of Philippa, the late Edward III's queen.

But Harry and Elizabeth had long dawdled. Only after his father had remarried, and his stepmother, Maud, had produced no additional offspring, and a second of his brothers had died, had Harry acted. Equally non-enthusiastic, Elizabeth had acquiesced, pressured both by her own family and a growing personal desire for children (if not the husband having them required). Besides, the only man she had ever wanted, Robbie, a poor but promising squire, had long since perished at sea, banished after her elders had discovered their trysts in her sixteenth summer. With Robbie gone, if she must wed someone, she had reasoned, Harry probably was as good as any.

Only his stepmother had advised caution, a month before Harry ceremoniously escorted Elizabeth across Alnwick's threshold and they physically consummated the bond. "You needn't go ahead with this," Maud had remarked. "You and Elizabeth are as ill-matched as horse and heifer: They may share a paddock, but little can come of it."

"You think naught shall come of this?"

"Little except the fulfillment of an obligation you never chose freely, betrothed as a small boy. Also, unions made for youngsters are oft set aside. Elizabeth's father himself shunned a match long-intended by his family, and, as a grown man, instead wed the woman he loved, who became Elizabeth's mother."

Harry had only shrugged.

"Does Elizabeth love you?"

"No."

Maud hadn't needed to ask; she'd seen their indifference for too long.

"And do you love her?"

"No, but…" Harry had blushed, though Maud's directness encouraged his own. "I've known women enou'—enough—in flirtations or … carnal romps. But I never loved any. Nor any man, either, as some do, taking other knights abed."

Maud had smiled over her embroidery, brown eyes warm, kind. "Then ponder this well. Remember, if you proceed, you'll likely harm not only yourself and Elizabeth but others: the woman you may someday love but cannot marry, being already wed; and the man Elizabeth might love but cannot espouse, for the same reason. Beware of loveless marriage, Harry. I know whereof I speak. I, too, erred that way when young."

"Even so," he had scoffed, "I'm better off with *armor* than *amour*. I'm a soldier. What need have I of love?"

"Never slight love, Harry, nor its importance, especially to a man like you, compelled by duty to endure hardship. Don't make yourself forsake love as well. Would that I could make you understand! Someday, mayhap you shall…"

Too late, he did understand.

Even so, once, after months on far-off duty with few messages exchanged, he had attempted to renew at least a physical relationship with his wife—to no avail:

He reached Alnwick unannounced late one afternoon, drenched with rain, mud encrusting his boots. Anxious to see his children and thinking he also might seduce his wife, he found the youngsters with their nursemaid in the solar, playing on a rug, their babble becoming a gleeful torrent when they saw him. Catching them up in his arms, he rubbed their faces against his, pressed them to his chest, swept them, one after the other, overhead, his exuberance blending with theirs.

Through the rear door Elizabeth emerged in a swirl of azure silk, golden hair mantling behind her, complexion still fresh with the cherries-and-cream of youth, plump breasts made more enticing by cleavage.

Putting the youngsters down, he came forward, arms outstretched.

Looking aghast, she stepped back against the wall, grabbing at a tapestry hanging there, as if to retreat behind its folds.

Sensing tension, the maid departed with the children.

With a brash laugh, Harry flung himself at Elizabeth, his hands, slick with sweat and rain, tightening around her waist and pressing against her exquisite skirts.

"Stop!" She pulled back farther and wrinkled her face at his scent, all horse, wet wool and clay.

His hands slid away.

Looking down, she saw the stains from his damp palms, leached into her gown. "See what you've done!"

Shrugging, he wiped his hands on his tunic and approached again.

She slapped him, then shrank back as the imprint of her fingers shone white against his cheek. Twisting the wall-hanging around her, she stared, as if startled by—but not ruing—her fury. "You're running with muck and water, and I can scarce guess what else. Yet you barge in like a ruffian with no warning," she chastised. "This is not one of your Borders fortelets, Harry. It's my chambers and you're ... offensive, out of place. I deserve better. Just go!"

"Trouble yourself not, lady," he replied acerbically. "I decamp to the guardhouse. I ask only that you allow me time with my children—later."

Elizabeth nodded hesitantly. "They will be here whenever you wish."

She saw the calm appraisal in his eyes, even as he read the disdain within hers.

Silently, he turned and left.

After that, he never approached her again. Nor she him. And he could ride off to confront the Scots, no lover to await his return.

* * *

Rural Northumberland

The flames reached skyward as if to singe the very stars. With a grimace, the Scottish chieftain paused, the smoke acrid to his senses but perfume to his reiver's soul. Standing in his stirrups, he surveyed his men before cantering over to the house, where he scraped the wooden porch with his firebrand, watching in smug indulgence as fire leapt to the roof. Already bereft of barn, tools, food, and livestock, one more farmer soon would be homeless, too.

Milling on the road, sheep and cattle spooked and sought escape, eyes lolling, their bellows adding to the confusion.

The chieftain signaled a retreat. Like wraiths dancing free of hell, his men emerged from the opaqueness, laden with goods. Two reeked of excrement from a near-fatal plunge down a privy shaft in search of hidden treasure; others dawdled over the well in a similar, futile pursuit. Several more had discovered an ale cellar and came forth with jugs to their mouths and unsteadiness to their steps.

"Mount up," the chieftain yelled. "Plenty a-more down the road. Get your arses moving before they're smoked like hams." They obeyed, albeit reluctantly, even as several began to cough, eyes salty with tears.

Booty stuffed into saddlebags, they rode off. The chieftain led, ahead of the herds, while the others fanned out alongside. Trading ale jugs, they let their horses do most of the work, with a wan moon illuminating the blackness.

A taciturn Lowlander, the leader, Angus Douglas, was the son of the notorious Earl Archibald "the Grim" Douglas, patriarch of one of Scotland's mightiest clans.

Angus stemmed from a lesser branch, however, the product of Archibald's liaison, at age fourteen, with a shepherd girl. Earl Douglas had never officially acknowledged his early, irregular parentage but also never disavowed it, ensuring that Angus enjoyed the money, materiel, and men necessary for a middling lord. Now in his forties, Angus was portly, long-haired but groomed, and mostly unschooled, though cunning enough to keep his sometimes-ragged force intact.

Drawing his cloak against the chill, Angus evaluated their spoils: Twenty sheep. Thirty of the fat cattle or "kye" for which Northumberland was famous, as well as five tender milch cows. One young bull still too inept to know what to do with five tender milch cows. Two plough horses. As many bags of grain as they could carry (sorely needed as cold weather persisted and supplies dwindled), plus household and farm tools.

More opportunity lay ahead, too, since they had encountered no resistance. At this last stop, a widowed farmer and children had fled at the first hoofbeats.

"Where're the English?" a soldier wondered. "Umfraville and his ilk."

"The local laird? Hear he's with a whore in Carlisle," a sergeant answered.

"And this much-vaunted Hotspur?" a pikeman asked. "Isn't he captain here, like your Lord Father is on our side?"

"Aye," Angus affirmed. "He's warden of the East March. And his father's warden in the West March. But the East being the greater charge, Hotspur's got real command o'er both, from Berwick t' Solway Firth."

"Then where's he?"

"London, jousting, I heard," another man put in.

"Nay." Angus corrected. "He's back; doubtless in the Cheviots, hunting, befooled: 'Tis Holy Week, when the kirk bans fechting."

"Some say he's nocht man but half man, half horse, like centaurs of auld!" a lancer marveled.

"Lies!" Angus protested. "I've spied him many a March Day, presiding with my father, reading our Law o' the March, settling disputes of English against Scots and Scots against English. Percy gets off a horse on two legs like you or me."

"Why'd the English name him hot-spur, anyway?"

"They didn't. My father and others did that. Couldn't even steal a chicken without him knowing and riding hard to stop 'em, like his mind never rested and his spurs never cooled. But you'd best thank God that Percy's not prowling here!"

Angus looked up. The night might have been better—a full moon and brighter starlight—though he wasn't complaining. Long hours awaited. But feasting and frolicking would follow in Scotland. Lulled by the sure-footed gait of his Borders hobby, he let his eyelids fall. "A roast tomorrow, in the yard. Ought to have geese or ducks by then, too. Plus more ale..."

Suddenly thirsty, he stretched, turned to a man riding behind, and ordered up a couple of jugs. His followers handed them on, a few taking a swig or two just to be ornery. But Angus didn't care. They had plenty. His bearded chin sank to his chest as he drowsed, though it wasn't long before he felt the terrain change and cursed himself awake again. Rounding a bend, they ascended a knoll of boulders and evergreens and he thought he heard the whinny of a horse not their own. Angus glanced around, straining to listen.

Nothing.

Naught but silence colluded with the night.

A cloud gobbled up the half-moon and he was again at ease. Only when the cloud melted away did his eyes catch, first, the glint of metal against the inky green of the trees, and then the unmoving, ghostly form of a mounted knight, backed by apparitions in chainmail.

———

"Halt!" Sword drawn, Harry cantered forward. "Yield."

"No!" Angus yelled, signaling his men. "To arms."

"Surrender!" Harry warned again.

Angus only spurred toward him—as Harry nudged his horse into a gallop.

They met head on.

Awkwardly trying to maneuver his axe, Angus barely glimpsed the sword in Harry's hand before it descended with fatal, crashing blackness. His body pitched downward, his horse swerving into the underbrush.

Racing on, Harry plowed into more reivers, blade swinging. Careening past him, his soldiers confronted the remaining Scots, most of whom had managed to draw their weapons but were encumbered by their loot. Abandoned in the road, trapped by the hills, the sheep and cattle panicked, scrambling and trying to climb over each other, further hindering the Scots' escape.

Curses, shouts and screams of the dying competed with the animals' uproar. Sword thwacked against shield, iron hit iron, as hooves pounded the ground. Ultimately, Harry chased down a lone reiver, who wheeled his mount and sped back toward his adversary, spear to the fore. Dodging it, Harry thrust hard with his sword, cutting through leather and chainmail. The raider collapsed, scarlet spreading over his breast and onto his horse's lathered withers.

But he was the last.

Harry rode several yards more, then circled, reining in. Dismounting, he pushed his visor open and took tally: All the Scots and three Englishmen lay slain. Beyond that, his men had suffered little but bruises and scrapes.

"God be praised..."

Methodically, he issued orders for rounding up the animals, assignment of a later burial detail, and collection of the booty, which, like the livestock, had to be returned to rightful owners. Stumbling over something, he squatted down alongside the hulk of the dead Angus.

"One of Douglas' whelps," he saw, peering into the vacant eyes. "And I slew him and shall probably have `the Grim' himself to reckon with. But this one burnt and stole and had to deal with me, or I with him. Let Old Archibald go flail himself if he doesn't like it."

Letting the corpse roll into the shrubs, he sought the bodies of his men. None had he known well, recent additions to his force. Still, they were his soldiers, and he had led them to their deaths. "You fought bravely," he told each dead man in turn, taking their cooling hands in his. "And I am honored to have had you among my company. Nor will your bravery—or family—be forgotten."

On how many fields had he recited those words? Too many to number, too many dead, too much killing. But once his initial battle had brought the first taste of terror (his own and others') he had learned to move beyond it: beyond the grisly violence, the disemboweled or decapitated or dismembered remnants of friends, the jaws spewing blood and vomit in the throes of a brutal death, the battlements slippery with gore and tears.

No good soldier could dwell on the horror. Nor could a good commander ever become oblivious to it.

Tersely, he instructed his lieutenants to bind the fallen Englishmen to horses. They, at least, would get proper graves.

After dragging dead Scots off the road, he regrouped his force. In the morn, he would have to ride forth anew to get a better accounting of what had happened, here and beyond. "Damnation," he realized. "'Tis halfway till morning already..."

Yet again, the warden of the March had lost the better part of a night's sleep and, yet again, perhaps saved the better part of England, though doubtless, the better part of England would never know. He would report the incident, as usual. But King Richard gave slight thought to the North and was a year behind in payments to its guardians. Little acknowledgement was likely from the Crown for border heroics.

Not that Harry was feeling heroic anyway, only satisfied, duty fulfilled, and tired. Taking the vanguard as they got underway, he soon dropped back to check that all his men followed. As he did, he saw how weary they were, too.

Enough fighting tonight. Let there be no more reivers ahead, he prayed; no further threats; no hidden holes to catch a horse, throw a rider, and force him as leader to draw his knife and cut the veins of a good steed suddenly broken-legged. Let there be no more trouble...

Gently, he whistled a Celtic tune, both mournful and uplifting. After a couple of rounds, though, he broke off in an unmusical flourish. "Esperance!"

Trotting forward again, he quickened their pace toward their still-distant barracks, as his shout echoed down the line, cheering his men as it cheered him.

"Esperance! Esperance! Esperance!"

'Twas his Anglo-Norman ancestors' hallowed motto, adopted as his own, years earlier.

"Esperance."

Hope.

Not a bad word for riding out the night...

Chapter III
May 1399 - Tower of London

The summons came in that lovely season when fruit trees were flush with delicate blossoms and leaves, and wrens darted from branch to branch in an ecstasy of innocence. All England appeared eerily beautiful as Harry rode south, but the pastel-colored countryside disguised unsettling currents, coursing below the surface, only to rise in the wary looks of other travelers or tavernkeeps whenever someone mentioned the king.

With a palace guard as his unwanted "escort," Harry covered the three hundred and thirty miles from his Berwick headquarters to London in a week, to canter through the gate of the Tower not far behind the herald who had raced ahead to announce his arrival. He was said to be anxiously awaited by his liege, Richard, the Second of that Name since the Conquest, by the Grace of God ruler of England and Wales—and Scotland, France and Ireland, too (or so the Crown claimed).

Why he had been called to court remained a mystery. Doubtless, he'd soon learn, he told himself, surrendering his horse to a groom in the yard.

"Harry!" The greeting rang out as he walked toward the White Tower, source of the fortress' name. Ahead, string of fish in hand, his uncle ascended from the watergate, where the Thames slapped at the Tower's outer wall.

"Uncle!" Harry's affectionate arm reached out, snaring Thomas Percy in a hug. "'Tis happy to see you I am, especially if you can tell me why I'm here. What does Richard want?"

Dressed in green serge, Richard's white hart emblazoned on surcoat sleeves, Thomas looked both pleased and distracted. A Tower raven lunged out of nowhere toward his fish and he swept the line to safety, in silence.

With wide experience in Spain, France, and beyond, Thomas Percy, Earl of Worcester, was a tireless servant of the Crown: admiral, soldier, advisor, and diplomat. In his late fifties, with a square, well-shaped face; often-laughing grey eyes, and a neatly trimmed beard, he had a reputation for honesty and impartiality, traits that had earned him his present post as the king's most trustworthy aide, seneschal or manager of the royal household.

"What does he want of me?" Harry repeated.

"Who can say," Thomas began. "Richard oft keeps his own counsel. However, he spoke of you accompanying him to Ireland, given rumblings of revolt there. I'm to oversee a campaign, as Richard's lieutenant-in-chief. And no one'd make a better field commander than you."

"Ireland?" Harry queried, as they entered the keep. "What the hell do I know of Ireland?" They climbed a staircase, Harry's voice bouncing off the twining stones. "Richard pulled me from the Borders for that? Hell, I've already left a trail of dead, mostly Scots, up north. 'Tis quiet now, but summer looms, when reivers prowl and trouble brews. And beyond confronting it, I've got endless other duties, too."

"I know. I saw your most recent commission as warden."

"Yet I'm supposed to go to Eire?"

"Peace, lad. See what Richard intends." Thomas ushered Harry into an anteroom, its sole window reminding them of the daylight they'd left below. "It may be some time before he sends for us. But we best be nearby, or we'll annoy him. Which no one wants to do."

Harry flung himself into a carved chair—heavy and ornate but comfortable.

"I'll scare up refreshments." Thomas exited.

Confined to a narrow chamber after riding the length of England, Harry felt trapped, fingers tapping the chair's armrest in endless staccato. Outdoors, a raven cawed, and he smiled wryly. "Aye, I could well complain, too."

According to legend, when the ravens left the Tower, England would fall. Thus they never left—and couldn't. Keepers of the mews clipped their wing feathers, preventing flight. And like so many courtiers growing fat and sleek around the throne, they lingered in well-fed subjugation, trading freedom for security.

"Caw!"

Harry smiled again.

Thomas returned with a tray of cheese, fruit, bread, and a hot, steeped infusion of dried berries, preferable to wine at a morning hour.

"Don't be surprised at Richard's determination to go to Ireland, Harry." Thomas settled into a chair. "He's unpopular here; growing more so. Everyone sees him as vain, bent on his own power. He needs to plant his arse elsewhere else a while, cool things off." Thomas speared a marinated pear with his penknife, meditatively chewed, and poured cups of the steamy beverage. "Ever since he seized that fortune from Bolingbroke this spring, there's been unrest. Nobody can guess what he might do next. And Lord knows, what he's done so far is bad enough."

Recollections of ill-fated moves churned through Thomas' mind before he spoke: "Demanding taxes and more damn taxes, near to ruining us all, from lowliest tenant farmer to highest lord. Ignoring Parliament. Dismissing just about anyone who tries to give him sound advice while he lolls with his favorites and wastes the treasury on them. Confiscating property. Meddling with the church; exiling churchmen…"

Nodding, Harry washed down cheese with drink. "And that's not even half of it."

"I know," Thomas groaned. "The worst is this proscription of the counties and these blank charters he's started collecting."

"Started and not yet finished," Harry observed as his uncle lapsed into introspection.

Against Thomas' advice, Richard had placed seventeen counties, containing most of England's population, under interdict, facing punishment for undefined violations of the royal will. He had likewise issued "blank charters," carte blanche writs by which the supposed violators could buy back favor, at a steep price. "Insidious, those..." Thomas grumped. "Each charter has that blasted line Richard himself dictated." He quoted, voice mocking: "'Because we, before this time, grievously offended Your Majesty, we give unto you ourselves, and all of our goods, at your will.'

"Just below that," Thomas continued, "on every charter, the parchment remains blank, so Richard can write in whatever he chooses. At the bottom, though, a mayor or local leader must sign his name. Now those fake charters are arriving in London. And they give Richard unlimited opportunity to fill in all those empty spaces with anything he wishes."

Harry nodded. "Should anyone object, Richard need only haul out the documents—signed, sealed, and delivered—and claim everyone agreed to anything."

"Exactly."

"Towns, shires, churches, farmers, fishermen, merchantry, craftsmen, even lords, could be signing away their treasuries, their land, their boats and sea catch, their shops, their manors ... even their rights and freedoms, without knowing it. Jesu!" Harry swore.

Thomas frowned. "They might even be selling their children into quasi-slavery as royal serfs. Who knows where Richard might stop? The old forms of serfdom—to say nothing of the slavery still practiced in places in Europe—are long gone from here. In England, men bound as serfs to some lord for a croft or field are oft freemen otherwise, holding other land in their own names."

"Aye, and serving as under-reeves and more."

"Yea. Yet Richard seems wont to end all that."

"Could he?"

"Who knows?" Thomas drank slowly. "All in all, Ireland might be a good place to be, away from this cesspool. Besides, Eire looks much like Northumberland. I expect you'd like it. The Irish fight much like the Scots, too. You'd know how to handle them."

Harry shook his head. "I'll stick to the Scots. Anyway, Richard can barely rule England. How the hell does he think he can rule Ireland? And the Irish can never agree on their own kings for long; they always turn on each other. Why tolerate him? No. Let Richard have Ireland without me."

To change the subject, Thomas inquired of the journey south.

Harry chuckled. "It was hardly well begun."

As he explained, he had trotted into Berwick Castle one evening, eager to turn his horse over to his squire, accept a bracing drink, and immerse himself in a hot bath. He had hardly dismounted, however, before being beset by Richard's guards, led by a herald who had declared, ostentatiously, that the lord king of England demanded the immediate presence of his cousin and servant, Sir Harry Percy, Warden of the March, in London, forthwith.

"And on and on he went, until I nearly hit him to shut him up," Harry sighed. "I forbore. Though I did have a few choice words for him." Finally, he had agreed to go along, but only if they left at dawn rather than risk men and horses on rough roads overnight. "With that," he told Thomas, "I went inside, leaving the herald on the stairs. But," he smiled sheepishly, "then I brought him some wine and invited him to dine with me and my aides. And we gave him a fresh bed for the night. By then, I thought he'd perish in surprise. He'd doubtless thought I was ready to throttle him. I was, at first. But he can't help what Richard is.

"Amazingly, he later rode most of the way at my side and asked if he might join my ranks and leave the king's service. As insufferable as he erst seemed, I think that, once he's away from this frippery at court, we might see the making of a fine soldier."

Thomas smiled as he realized Harry's gestures had been part mollification, lest word get back that he had insulted King Richard by mistreating his emissary and part genuine friendliness, for it was inherently difficult for Harry to hold a grudge. "So what did you tell the herald about joining your company?"

"That I'd be pleased to have him but dare not offend Richard and that he must talk to you."

"Yea. He rode in, told Richard you'd follow soon, came to me, and said he wanted to quit the royal household and join you. I agreed, but only after Richard returns from Ireland and if you'd have him." Thomas shook his head, amused. "Would that Richard had your knack. He's likely to turn friends into foes. You turn foes into friends..."

Harry only laughed, and for a time, they talked of the North.

As the light outside the window emphasized the passing hours, though, Harry stretched, and his uncle promised to check on their audience.

But when Thomas entered the throne room and asked a servant how long he and Harry must wait, Richard overheard, answering peevishly himself: It was not the place of his seneschal, or anyone, to question "Our keeping of a holiday."

Frustrated, Thomas returned to the anteroom to find his nephew pacing.

"Christ, Harry. We may have to spend the entire day here. Richard is in one of his moods or some goddamn thing; he keeps the holiday, or 'holyday.'"

Harry whirled. "What holiday? The monks at Waltham, where I lodged last night and dined this morn, kept none!"

Thomas looked uncomfortable, aware that Richard's idiosyncrasies would only further aggravate one as unaccustomed to idleness as Harry. "Richard has his own schedule. On feast days and what he calls holidays—and by his calendar they arise oft—after his morning repast he reclines in his throne, in complete silence. It can go on until evensong or later. And he insists his courtiers stand below the throne. They hardly budge, either; the only time anyone does anything is when the king nods toward one or another. Then that man drops to his knees in obeisance. No one else dare move or speak. It can last hours."

Harry broke into rich laughter. "God only knows what they do if they have to piss. I'd be sorely tempted to relieve both my loins and the tedium by piddling all over the floor!"

He made for the door. "I'll wait outside." With that, he disappeared: visiting the mews, trying a new crossbow at the Bowyer's Tower, making himself popular with pages and squires by conducting an impromptu swordsmanship class on a castle green.

As time passed, Thomas fretted, dispatching a squire.

After searching, the squire spotted Harry amidst a throng of young men, cheerfully crossing blunted swords with three simultaneously. He had shed cloak and tunic and moved bare-chested in the dappled sunshine, arm and shoulder muscles meshing effortlessly, and no signs of exertion except a few damp locks on his forehead. It was three against one, but the youths were hard pressed. Red and dripping, all three lunged at him in futility, Easily taking on one, and then another, and then the third, he cheerfully called out advice:

"No, lad. Don't look at your friends. Keep your eyes on me and my sword. If this were a real fight, I'd have long since run you through!"

Mesmerized, Worcester's squire forgot his assignment and joined the next trio Harry took on.

Another hour passed and evening was not far off when Harry splashed happily in the lavatorium, superintending wash-ups by his young admirers. He had re-dressed and was grabbing his cloak when Richard's servitors found him.

Harry sensed the tension but didn't care.

Richard hardly bestirred himself when Harry entered the hall. Majestic in a purple gown, yellow hose showing above bejeweled shoes, golden chain circling royal waist and pendant around his neck, the king half-lay on his cushions.

Harry walked with his usual efficiency toward the dais, paused beneath the throne, and sank to his knees, hands offered in subjection.

For long moments Richard failed to respond, regarding his guest with half-closed, limpid-seeming but livid eyes, crown set in exemplary balance across his brow, pudgy face bland.

No boor, if no courtier either, Harry was fittingly attired in a plain, light-blue tunic neatly girded by a wide belt with a buckle in intricate Celtic silver. With it he wore black leggings, tucked into grey suede boots. He bore no sword, though he carried his knife in a leather sheath that matched his belt, and his dark blue cape fell in graceful folds around his feet as he knelt. He had come toward the throne humbly enough, although with head erect. But when Richard declined to accept his outstretched hands, he dropped them and bowed his head as well, in perfect submission.

Neither said anything, while an apprehensive Thomas Percy watched from the side of the room.

Ultimately, it was Harry who spoke first—improperly, under court protocol—but courteously, and in keeping with his usual direct approach to life.

"You sent for me from the North, on issues of urgency, My Liege?"

"Why, yes, cousin," Richard answered. "Though I did not expect to have to send for you again within my own walls. I would speak to you of important concerns: conditions in the North, matters of state, my forthcoming campaign in Eire, which your Lord Uncle has graciously agreed to lead. Only I fear I must assume from your disappearance today you are not so faithful to England as I thought." He smiled, but a glint of cunning, not warmth, shone in his eyes.

"I was wrong, My Lord. I apologize for forcing you to hunt me down." Again Harry extended his strong, lightly tanned hands.

This time, Richard took them between his own creamy palms, allowed Harry to kiss the back of his knuckles, and bade him rise.

"I fear I haven't Your Majesty's patience for hours in the throne-room," Harry remarked. "I regret that Your Majesty feels disserved by me."

"Though," he amended mentally, "if I regret aggrieving Richard so soon, I don't regret not having spent half the day trapped in some anteroom."

"And as for the other," he continued aloud, "I have ever been faithful to England and, until the moment I die, I will remain faithful, to England, above all else in this world. To England. As My Lord King, I trust, knows well."

Richard caught the unvoiced implications: "...faithful to England, above all else"; faithful to England, but not necessarily to the king who ruled England if the king's interests and those of the nation itself ever differed.

And so it went between them: two men, still young and blessed with the promise of long years, distant cousins, Plantagenets both, although Harry's royal blood flowed from a supposedly inferior female line; both educated and keen of mind. Yet one was short-haired, physically vigorous, carrying his good looks with unpretentious masculine ease, endowed with a superb athlete's fitness and bearing and grace, yet sometimes shy and pensive. The other was all gilt and flamboyance, from the light-brown of his eyes to the long, honey-hued locks of his hair, a stranger to war and the land's ruggedness, pampered and sleek, not so much handsome as attractive in a soft, almost-seraphic way, given to flights of fancy and yet adept at political intrigue. King and knight, Richard and Harry, sunlight and storm.

"No diptych artist could make it more obvious," Thomas Percy thought, "the Light and the Dark ... it looks so simple. Yet, inside their souls, it's really the other way around..."

Their words covered the usual politenesses.

The king commended Harry for keeping the peace, neither aggravating the Scots nor letting them get away with anything; Harry was properly grateful.

They spoke inconsequentially, until Richard lamented that his subjects seemed to care so little for him. He received such a minute portion of the support warranted a monarch who truly loved his people—as he did love them, Richard averred; he suffered deeply, an unappreciated, neglected king who could not even count on his cousin to appear when summoned; a king thus ignored by even this, his old friend...

And so on.

("*Ad infinitum, ad infinitum, et ceteri, et ceteri*, as my Latin masters at Alnwick Abbey used to say," Harry later would recount to his father. "Twas like listening to a litany, except a litany is usually less monotonous.")

"Nonetheless," the king was continuing, "I'm expecting much to change. My loyal subjects are sending me word of their endearments and fealty, vying to see which town, which abbey, which lordship, can serve me best. Loyal men are sending me charters, which they have signed in advance, admitting their past failings, promising to give me whatever I specify.

"Truly though..." A slim finger flicked an unusual speck of dust from his gown, as his eyes half closed again. "I haven't heard much from the North. Such a shame—it's one of my favorite parts of the realm, you know. I should think my sentiments would be returned by the North, in a most meaningful way; don't you, cousin?"

Harry said nothing and uneasiness enveloped the room, as men-at-arms at the doors shifted their feet and servants slipping into the hall backed out again.

"Why is Richard doing this?" Thomas Percy lamented silently. "He need not have mentioned these damned charters. Yet he persists. He's baiting Harry—or trying to—because he fancies it amusing to afflict others. He picked no easy, wilting target this time, though. He should know that."

"Very soon, I should think, my charters will reach northern towns and shires as well," Richard added. "Then, cousin, your personal support will be most necessary. And most forthcoming, I doubt not—since you are, as you say, faithful to the realm." He dazzled Harry with another smile, his eyes now open and brilliant, though with the glee of malice, not friendship.

"My Liege knows of my loyalties," Harry replied. "Never will that change. I am faithful to England, as I have said; moreover, as I have proven, since I was eighteen or twenty or younger. Never will I shirk my responsibility, nor evade an order honorably given. Neither will I abandon my duties toward my people—your subjects, My Liege. I could not and will not misuse them."

Momentarily, he wondered whether he should leave it at that; just as quickly he decided to continue, to resolve this now. The northerners he both served and led deserved forthrightness. So, in a way, did Richard.

Already, though, a vein in the royal cheek twitched.

His own anger stirring, Harry felt his voice slipping into the stutter that had plagued him in childhood and occasionally still vexed him. "In all d-d-due respect to you, My Lord, n-n-nei... neither on behalf of the people in the North, n...nor on my own behalf, n-nor that of any of the Percies, will I personally endorse any documents whose c-con... contents ... I cannot know."

Pausing to get his voice back into rhythm with his thoughts, he knelt again deferentially. "The Crown ... the Crown and Parliament may send me copies of laws and decrees. And ... and even if I personally disagree with these, I will post them, and enforce them, in my capacity as lord or warden, to the best of my abilities, and with my own discretion. But those are acts of the Crown and Parliament rightfully enacted. They're not actions taken in the name of Harry Percy when Harry Percy does not even know what acts are intended. I do not sign anything I cannot read. And since I cannot read what has yet to be written, I won't sign any blank charters. Nor will I advise others to do so, in the North, or anywhere."

Richard remained mum, so Harry went on.

"'Tis madness! Surely you must see that. No good can come of this. Those who urged you to do this—they're mad. They're the disloyal ones, if anyone is. They would separate their king from the love of his people. 'Tis happening, by God! Can you not see it, cousin?"

Still Richard said nothing.

"No," Harry shook his head. "If any of these so-called charters reach me, I'll assume an egregious error occurred. I'll not distribute them. And, to repeat, I'll certainly never sign any. In conscience, I could not. But since my king would never wish me to do anything dishonorable, anything that could harm England, I trust I'll never have to worry.

"I am sorry, My Lord, if I give offense to you," he added, tone moderating. "But you called me here to speak to you. And so I have had to speak..."

Snapping into alertness from his half-recumbent position, Richard clung to the sides of his throne with both hands. His face transfused from pink to red to frosty ire as he spoke, his simpering voice sweet, sarcastic, menacing. "Offense is not the word. Try treason. It is treasonous words you speak!"

Harry leapt to his feet, stepping forward unbidden, even as the king's bodyguards likewise advanced, gripping their pikes. He stopped short of the throne, but his own hand nearly strayed to his dagger. Without even trying, he could sense the cool, reassuring touch of the hilt, imagine the blade slipping from the sheath. But he caught himself in time, willing his arms to remain at his sides, to not give anyone cause for alarm, or to seize him, or make a charge of treason stick.

"'Tis strange, if it be disloyal for a man to speak his mind." He began quietly, continued passionately. "If it be treason to speak truth, then I shudder for this realm!"

Richard, too, rose. "Get out of here! Get out of my sight, and never return. You are banished. Leave. Now, before I change my mind, and have you beheaded instead!"

Just as suddenly, the king slumped into his throne, buried his face in his upraised arm, and sobbed, while Harry strode back through the hall, pushing past the guards at the doorway.

No one pursued him, but his uncle wrenched at his elbow as he tried to make his way down the stairs, to his horse and the yards and his escape from this royal madhouse.

"Sweet Jesu, Harry!" Thomas exploded. "Could you not hold your tongue? You'll be lucky to get out of London intact. Do you know what you've done? We could all be proscribed for life."

Which, to be sure, might not be for long at all...

But the admiral saw the fire return to Harry's face and knew his nephew's anger was not misplaced. Moreover, it was no more than what Thomas and others, somewhat more diplomatically, had tried to tell

Richard, unsuccessfully. So Thomas could not really be angry. It was fruitless. Besides, there had already been too much wrath this day.

"'Twill soon be dark," he whispered, guiding Harry to the stables. "Go now, though I don't think you're in immediate danger of death, banished though you may be. Still, stay on your guard."

Harry listened stoically.

"Take one of my signets," Thomas proposed. "Use it if they won't let you through the town gates. Avoid giving your name, though. Say you're Henry of Bardewell-in-Essex, on an errand for the royal seneschal. You were christened 'Henry' and our family has holdings in Bardewell; 'tis no lie." He fished in his belt purse, found his extra ring, and pressed it into Harry's hand.

"Head north, as far as you can. Wait this out there. Richard won't really banish you, I think. He did intend to send you to Ireland, after all. And he needs you on the Borders. He'd never find another man as capable as warden. And he knows it damn well. Besides you provide him with entertainment, keep him from having to reserve all his tantrums for his servants, or me." Thomas' smoky grey eyes filled uncharacteristically.

As the lanterns on the stable wall cast somber shadows in the dusk, Thomas Percy reached out, embracing his nephew with an iron-sinewed affection. "I'm sorry, Harry. Go now. And may God go with you."

So they parted.

As Harry's horse pranced through the outer wards, Thomas Percy watched until his eyes blurred. "Godspeed," he murmured, as an old quote about sons, from Cicero by way of Augustine, flitted across his mind: "You alone among men would I wish to surpass me, in all things..."

Harry made it through London's gates before they were barred against him, disappearing into the inky night of the countryside.

Within hours, Richard calmed down, although only after decreeing that Harry's banishment be proclaimed throughout the land, causing many to shake their heads.

Declining to attempt Harry's immediate deportation, however, Richard instead fired off missives to the Earl of Northumberland, demanding that father and son attend upon him to explain the latter's perfidiousness.

Experienced in handling regal tempests, the earl responded politely but firmly: With the imminent departure of the royal army to Eire, any able-bodied men staying behind, including himself and his son—who was of course, northern commander—were behooved to remain at their posts, lest the Scots skip across the border and wreak havoc.

In time, begrudgingly, Richard gave up.

Meanwhile, Harry rode deep into Northumberland, to obscure properties in his care, spending his days much as an ordinary farm steward: checking accounts; rounding up stray livestock; meeting with tenants; ensuring that houses, barns and sheepfolds were maintained, purchasing supplies. Eventually, he returned to Berwick Castle, though he kept ready to move at a moment's notice. There was nothing new in that, however. As warden of the March he was always ready to move at a moment's notice.

He himself heard nothing further from the Crown.

Thus a troublesome spring slipped into summer and Richard turned his face to Ireland, sailing from Wales with a fleet under Admiral Thomas Percy.

Yet, if the king looked West, others looked East, as another ship lifted anchor in France, preparing to drop its contraband cargo on the winding coast of England. And throughout the land a scattering of men watched the roads at dawn, wondering, waiting.

Chapter IV
July 1399

Part prodigal son, part conquering hero, the exile waded ashore on the wind-scarred coast of Yorkshire, only a fraction of his once-huge retinue clustering around him as he took his first, confident steps back onto his native land. Henry Bolingbroke, Duke of Lancaster, Earl of Hereford, and Lord of Derby, had come home.

The unheralded nature of his arrival scarcely mattered. Tall and majestic, bronze-gold, with all the bearded virility of a Saxon god, within days he began drawing attention to himself and his cause: reclaiming his inheritance, unjustly seized by the Crown on the death of his father, John of Gaunt, mightiest noble in the realm. Moving inland under blue skies, his tiny band became a small force, increasing ten-fold, then ten-fold again.

Remarkable, chroniclers concluded, updating their ongoing logs. Utterly remarkable.

Or perhaps not...

Even before sailing from Europe, Bolingbroke had received messages from his countrymen, chafing under misrule, urging him to act. After all, like Richard, he claimed descent from princes. More to the point, he had a role to fulfill as High Steward of England, quasi-regent and first-among-peers, like his forebears. Thus he had crossed the Channel.

Soon, at every hamlet and crossroads the English were welcoming him: commons and knights, archers, foresters and fishermen, yeomen, prelates—magnates too. Never had he known its like. The only thing vaguely comparable had occurred at Richard's coronation twenty-two years earlier, when multitudes had cheered raucously, mindlessly, for their newly minted boy-king. Always the memory had fanned flames of envy in Henry Bolingbroke, every inch the match of his royal cousin except luck of birth. Always too, he had ignored the flames and gone about his own richly appointed life. Yet now the hosannas familiar to kings sang in his ears, when he'd done nothing but return...

With each mile, the outcry increased, dulling his political instincts and the realization that the crowds were infatuated less because he was worthy than because he simply *was*. He existed, embodiment of their longings, personification of their anger. He was there and theirs, revered like the relics they paraded on saints' days.

Nearly tangible, hopelessly intoxicating, fame dangled fresh dreams before his freshly-opened eyes. He sensed the hope his presence kindled, drank of his countrymen's praise and tasted their excitement as readily as he sipped their finest wine, pressed in his hands and raised to his lips. Their belief became his, and perhaps not only his belief but his destiny. Imperceptibly, the lines separating his patrimony from the rest of England blurred in his mind and on his maps, until even the vast expanse of his duchy seemed unable to hold all God intended for him...

———

White against meadow green, the tent stood like a proud bastion as Bolingbroke conferred with allies, new and newly reacquainted. They had been at it all morning, debating his rights. Several barons emphasized he had best restrict himself to his House of Lancaster. Others argued that, given Richard's despotism, it was time not only to restore Bolingbroke to his possessions but to revitalize the high stewardship, aptly filled during earlier crises by his father, Gaunt. If almost the same age as thirty-three-year-old Bolingbroke, they maintained, Richard indulged childish caprices that had sent more than one innocent to the block; he had to be stopped, by a council headed by someone of Bolingbroke's calibre. Still others suggested Richard might be eased from the throne outright, that, indeed, he might prefer a life of leisure to pursue his inane pastimes, while someone more suitable wielded the scepter.

Talk went one way, then another, though by noon consensus seemed to be coalescing around the middle proposal: Bolingbroke as high steward.

They drifted from the tent, led by the Earl of Northumberland, Henry Percy Senior, a straight-backed old campaigner with muscles bulging on his calves and gnarling his arms. His moss-green eyes, pale skin and thick black brows hinted at Celtic antecedents among his hallowed Anglo-Norman forebears, while his slightly aquiline nose and short, silvery curls evoked an ageing eagle. Like an eagle, too, he had long soared on the wings of success, ever since Richard had made him an earl. Now perhaps the winds of change could carry him farther still...

Running a bony hand through his beard, he awaited Bolingbroke, and, when the latter emerged, pointed toward rows of men. "If you could spare a moment, My Lord. Those knights and infantry wish to pay their respects. Most are from my own jurisdictions."

"Absolutely!" Bolingbroke boomed, always ready to oblige an audience.

They proceeded through the ranks, Bolingbroke taking stock in turn. "God's blood, but this is a fine array," he complimented the earl, almost enviously, as they finally paused, on the sidelines. "I can see you've brought them from nearly all your holdings." With a marshal's flair, he counted the standards. "But there's one I did not see." His eyes narrowed. "Where is my noble second cousin, your hot-spurred firstborn?"

"Harry? On his way, would've been here already, but for detouring to collect a few more levies. And he started from Berwick. That's a fair piece of riding, even for him."

"He doesn't doubt the righteousness of my cause?"

"Never! He remained outraged long after your exile." The earl paused. "And Richard complains he oft finds Harry's bluntness insufferable, even treasonous. In May, they nearly had each other by the throat. Harry was forced to flee almost into Scotland. He's no delusions about Richard."

They were still engrossed in conversation when a haze of dust and a low roar arose from the nearest troops. A lone knight, helmetless in chainmail, cantered through the lines, leaning down to shake one's hand, slap another's shoulder and raise his palm in salute to a third. Cries of "Harry!" and "Hotspur's come!" greeted him as he made his way, halting before the earl.

"Regards to you, Father," he slid from the saddle, warmly clasping the older man's hand. Turning to Bolingbroke, he grinned. "You old jouster's nemesis, Henry—welcome home."

"Harry Percy. I can't think of a better man to have at my side."

They embraced with the relaxed affection of the companions-in-arms they once had been. Harry was older by six years, though with a face largely unlined, dark hair just starting to turn grey at the temples, supple strength rippling through his every movement. In contrast, Bolingbroke's shoulders had begun to sag, while tiny creases webbed his eyes and spidered across his cheeks. Silver shot through the long, red-gold hair, receding from his forehead, and his neck appeared to be slowly shrinking into his broad chest. Despite his wealth, in subtle ways he almost seemed impoverished, a supplicant to time itself, discreetly massaging one hand in the other, as if to eradicate hidden pain. Yet few men would have noticed, awed by his presence as he exuded the supreme self-confidence that high birth, affluence, and prominent rank bestowed. Nine years earlier, he and Harry had astounded Europe by defeating all adversaries in the lists. Now, side by side, they wandered off to review Harry's contributions to the army, Harry's face open and animated, Bolingbroke's more stolid but wreathed in smile.

At first they bantered, joking of fame won and lost since they last shared the field, reminiscing, assessing the strengths and weaknesses of each other silently, and those of the army aloud.

Finally, Bolingbroke pulled Harry aside. "God, but I'm glad to see you. I was more than happy to see your father, too, but your support counts more than that of any man here. Heaven knows, too: Better to have you with me than ever against me. I saw too oft on the tourney ground what you can do!" A touch of emotion floated into his eyes and he slapped Harry's shoulder. "Even so, why are you here? You're northern commander, but you've left your Borders; spent much time, probably spent more money; ridden harder than anyone. Why?"

Harry answered quickly. "Why? Because of what happened to you and to help you reclaim what is yours, your inheritance. And bec..." With a self-deprecatory shrug, he interrupted himself. It wasn't just Henry's plight that motivated him, but his own fears: That on his father's death he could be similarly stripped of his greatest treasure, Northumberland, and all he had ever loved and bled for and protected; that if Richard weren't curbed, the next royal desire to banish Harry Percy might involve force and precipitate terrible bloodshed. "I say I came because of your inheritance," he continued. "But I'm here for me, also. I had to act. We—everyone here—had to act."

Bolingbroke nodded vigorously. "And mark my words, you, me, all of these"—he gestured toward the troops—"will act. `Vengeance is mine,' saith this lord. I'll have Richard by his heels. Nor is that all of him I'll have!" A throaty growl followed.

"I understand your anger." Harry paused, taken aback. "I share it. But you'd best not overstep. Use our force only if we're threatened. Seek your lawful patrimony, not unlawful retribution, or anything else not yours."

Bolingbroke stared, then chuckled genially. "I know my own." Playfully punching Harry, he pointed toward the soldiers inching toward them. "They want more of us. We'd best give them their fill."

They submerged themselves in the pack.

Watching from a distance, Earl Henry smiled, even as he felt a twinge of uneasiness, wondering how far bonds of old friendship could be stretched in remaking a reign.

———

Spluttering, the younger Percy faced the elder. "But h-he ... he c-c... he can't be king. W-we already have one. Aye, that king is the source of much misery. But Bolingbroke can't possibly think to climb on the throne himself! 'Tis not right. 'Twould go against God. 'Twould question everything this nation has stood for." Harry paced energetically. "And I've spent too much time in the North trying to uphold the law, trying to prevent one man from stealing his neighbor's possessions and hieing away across the border, to stomach high-ranking reivery by our leading lords."

They'd ridden some distance, for Earl Henry hesitated to talk in camp, fearful both of eavesdroppers and the outspokenness of this, his oldest and only surviving child.

"Peace, Harry. I'm not saying that Bolingbroke himself says any such thing. I'm only telling you this idea is being tossed around. And it's not just Lancastrians who're saying it or thinking it even if they don't say it. There are more than a few jaws wagging that maybe it's time to forget Richard, to let him retire to a Bordeaux monastery: with or without taking religious vows, with or without his little queen, but certainly without notions of coming back. Maybe it's time, some say, to have someone else as king." He paused. " It's happened afore. Henry I leap-frogged to the throne over his older brother. Stephen triumphed over Matilda, but her son ruled upon Stephen's death. And in your great-grandfather's day, Edward III was crowned while still a youth after his father, Edward II, was deposed with Parliament's help. And if we look to—"

"I ken my history," Harry broke in, pacing halted. "This is different. Bolingbroke can't expect to claim the crown. His patrimony and all it entails: Aye. Anything else: Nay! When we spoke, I told him as much."

"Told him?"

"Aye. It seemed he might want Richard's head on a pike. I advised him not to over-reach." His voice dropped ruefully. "I feared unbridled vengeance. Had I known of this other..."

The earl shrugged. "You know now."

"And find the knowledge distressing!" Harry's right fist slammed into his left hand in frustration. "I, and probably most of this army, joined him to help regain his rights. If that includes being high steward of England and foremost counselor to Richard, with aid from `our lords spiritual and temporal,' then fine. The country needs it. Richard needs it. By heritage and competence, 'tis Bolingbroke's due. If in redeeming those rights for him we can convince Richard to change, all the better. I'd risk my life for that. God only knows I've risked it already with Richard."

Striding back and forth again, Harry shook his head sadly. "I want to see England governed properly— with Parliament's involvement. I loathe having to explain to our men, and villagers, and the Scots when I seal Borders matters, that I disagree with much

Richard does, but still believe in our rule of law. I want what's right, for Bolingbroke and all of us."

The earl glanced over his shoulder nervously.

Undeterred, Harry continued. "Henry will never have a more loyal soldier if that's his aim, too. But seizing the throne himself? Never!"

Like his speech, his pacing abruptly halted. "Now I've probably irked My Lord Pater again," he thought. "He likes Bolingbroke tremendously. Cast from the same mold, they are. Sometimes I think Bolingbroke must really be his son, and I spawned by some reckless renegade my mother took to bed one night."

His gaze focused on the scudding clouds before returning to his father.

But the earl spoke first. "In truth, Harry, what you propose is what's in my mind and the minds of the leading men here—and in Bolingbroke's."

"Anyone reminded Bolingbroke of that lately?"

"He and I discussed it today, afore you got here. And he gave me his word."

"Aye, his word!" Harry nearly spat. "His word, indeed. Listen, Father, I'm fond of Bolingbroke. We were knighted together, along with Richard, by King Edward, years ago, remember? We competed in jousts together. He seems to excel in nearly everything he does. But one thing at which he does not excel is keeping his word."

His quick eyes caught the flash of doubt in the older man's face before the earl started to answer: "I'm not—"

"'Tis true," Harry interrupted. "If you don't believe me, ask Thomas Mowbray. Ask the elder Richard Arundel. Ask the Duke of Gloucester. But we cannot ask them, can we? No, because they're gone: One dead at the executioner's block, one murdered in prison, one dying or already dead in exile, all because my old friend Bolingbroke betrayed them. Oh, not single-handedly, mind you, but betrayed them all the same. Now you'd have me take his word. Christ-sakes, I wish I could. But until he swears to me on the Gospel itself, I fear I cannot."

Half-expecting another lecture, he was met by silence.

"In truth, you're right, Harry," The earl finally admitted. "You give me much to consider and I'd best do it here. You'll wait for me?"

"Aye," Harry said simply, as if there were no reason to ask. Yawning, he settled under an elm, long legs sprawled in front, thoughts circling back to the years when he'd been too busy in the North and France to bother about the court affairs that had so preoccupied Bolingbroke, Mowbray and Arundel...

―――――

Trouble started in 1386, when a handful of young lords took it upon themselves to improve Richard's governance. While they gathered under a banner of reform, their agenda remained imprecise. Their pedigrees did not. Led by Richard Arundel Senior, the "Lords Appellant" (as they styled themselves) included some of England's most prominent peers: Thomas Woodstock, Duke of Gloucester, uncle to both Bolingbroke and Richard; Thomas Mowbray, Earl of Nottingham; and Henry Bolingbroke. The apparent nobility of their purpose notwithstanding, their campaign soon degenerated into brutal executions and widespread intimidation as they seized control. For months even the king feared for his life as the "Appellants" ruled in his name. Eventually, though, he regained power. Royal pardons and reconciliations followed.

Then the court found a new diversion: John of Gaunt's love life.

Maud, Harry's stepmother, explained the latter "scandal" when Harry returned from service in France.

"Married her, Gaunt did, his `lady par amour,' Katharine, the only woman he's ever loved—even all that time he was married to that Spanish princess for reasons of state," Maud confided. "What's more, he had his and Katharine's grown children, those Beauforts, declared legitimate, despite their out-of-wedlock births. They're truly tight with his son Henry, too.

"Gaunt also took Katherine to court," Maud continued, "but nobles there called her 'concubine' and `harlot' and more. One of the worst was Arundel's wife, your sister-in-law. You know how foolish and shallow Philippa is. But Arundel encouraged her, complaining that Gaunt disgraced the court. Others said the same."

"They're all used to bedding, not wedding, their mistresses, and shunning their bastards," Harry commented, raising a goblet. "Here's to Gaunt for defying them!"

"Elizabeth didn't feel that way. She took her sister's part."

Harry shook his head. "Just one more thing where I differ with my wife and her kin. 'Tis baffling about Arundel, though. He unwisely gave Gaunt cause to despise him."

"Yea. That could bode ill."

Indeed...

In 1397, Richard struck back, not just at Arundel but all the Lords Appellant, inducing Mowbray and Bolingbroke to turn on their former allies. With Mowbray as jailer, Gloucester was bundled off to prison and slain under strange circumstances. Arundel was dragged to a showy trial at Westminster and prosecuted by Gaunt, assisted by Bolingbroke and two other rising lords—Ralph Neville and William Scrope.

"Did you not say, years ago, when first we plotted treason—and yea, that was what we plotted—we should capture the king?" Bolingbroke accused Arundel. "You betrayed him!"

"Never!" Arundel retorted. "You lie, lie at your own peril, Bolingbroke! Never did I hold any intentions at all regarding King Richard except to safeguard his honor and well-being!"

His protests failed. Without further ado he was formally denounced as a traitor by Sir John Bushey, who was Speaker of the House, though more inclined to do Richard's bidding than that of his Commons. The king joined the lords and clergy in dooming Arundel, who was beheaded.

But neither time nor the thin wash of legality brushed over the proceedings could make the realm rest easier. Nor were the Percies left untainted, for Harry's uncle, Thomas, had been tapped as the churchmen's proxy at the trial and concurred in the judgment. Whether he had acted independently, or at the behest of the bishops he represented, was unclear. While harboring private misgivings, Earl Henry, too, never objected to Arundel's fate.

In the aftermath, the king elevated his 'friends.' Mowbray became Duke of Norfolk; Scrope, Earl of Wiltshire; Ralph Neville, Earl of Westmorland; Thomas Percy, Earl of Worcester, and Henry Bolingbroke, Duke of Hereford.

Months later, though, the sordid drama resumed, as ex-Lords Appellant again turned against one another. Dabbling in intrigue, Mowbray learned that Richard supposedly sought to kill him and Bolingbroke, their new titles notwithstanding. He secretly warned Bolingbroke—who promptly informed Richard, alleging that Mowbray was slandering the Crown. Charges and countercharges followed, until Henry and Mowbray vowed to duel to the death. They were well on their way when Richard intervened, exiling both instead.

Mowbray fell mysteriously ill in Italy, while Bolingbroke charmed his way through Europe. So *things stood until Gaunt unexpectedly died. Eager to enrich himself while further denigrating Henry, Richard stole Gaunt's fortune, Henry Bolingbroke's inheritance.*

Now, outraged, thousands marched to help Henry recover it.

As long as it was all that he wanted...

———

Sensing his father looming overhead, Harry roused himself.

"You're right, son—about Bolingbroke not keeping his word, I mean," the older man began. "But you've also touched upon the solution."

"Aye?"

"Henry means what he says—at the time," the earl explained. "Then events change, opportunity arises, and he feels little compulsion about old promises. Probably it seems wiser and better not to honor them. So we'll bind him, get him to officially swear he's only pursuing his inheritance and role as high steward; that he'll respect Richard's crown."

Harry's eyes lit up. "Let's do it ere we leave Doncaster."

"On the morrow, at the White Friars' chapel." Pleased, Earl Henry slung his arm around the higher shoulder of his son as they returned to their horses. "Dine with me, tonight? I'd most pleased for your company, Harry."

"'Twould be an honor to share your table, Father. Let me tend to some chores first. Then I'll be there—gladly. You always have the better wine!"

———

That evening, he faded quickly, however. Finishing a private meal with the earl, he waved off a refill of his cup. "I'm sorry, Father, but I can hardly stay awake. Do you mind if I sleep here? I'm too tired to find my way to my own lines or face the hundred demands that probably await me if I do."

"My tent is yours, son, you know that. Take the bed. I've messages to deal with, anyway."

The earl straightened the bedding on his cot.

But Harry could hardly deprive his father of his own couch. So the younger Percy threw a sheepskin rug on the floor, shucked his clothes, and pulled a coverlet over his nakedness. Within moments, he was out. Yet his actions in sleep were nearly as vigorous as those when awake and it wasn't long before he had kicked off his cover and, without waking, begun to shiver. Catching the movement as he looked up from a letter, the earl retrieved the coverlet, found a blanket as well, and tucked them around his sleeping son. The lantern on his table glowed as he came back, but he shoved his correspondence aside, contemplating his eldest:

"How very different we are," he realized. "Flesh of my flesh, blood of my blood, he is; my first-born and heir, the one of all the children I begot to whom I should be the closest. And yet the one, since the beginning, whom I've understood the least, and been the least close to, the one, in truth, with whom I've ever seemed to spar.

"Always has he dared to question, to challenge me when convinced of the right of it. Yet he has always challenged himself, far more, in ways most men would not comprehend. Even as a child. Even then he surprised me."

He recalled his son's struggle with stuttering, for as a boy Harry had scarcely seemed to open his mouth without stumbling over his words. "I considered him stupid," the earl acknowledged, "thought he'd shame me with his lack of grace. So I began pinning my hopes on his brothers, sending Harry to Thomas for months on end. And when he was around, his brothers and the other lads in my castles would belittle him and I hardly tried to stop it. Yet, through it all, he was pushing himself, far beyond most youths.

"Suddenly, he was grown, renowned for his feats. His mind, far from being dull, proved swift and keen. Except when he's too excited or exhausted, he overcame his stutter, too, learning to converse in three languages. Men said I'd spawned the greatest knight in England since the Black Prince, or even the Lionheart. And I could scarce believe it. But in truth, I had so very little to do with it."

Not that Harry was perfect.

"Oft he's still too impulsive, and too direct. He says what he means and means what he says, with very little doubt about it, and such traits do not fare well at court. Someday, though, like it or not, he'll be earl and have to tend to court affairs.

"But he has a strong love of justice—mayhap too strong, for it leads to scrapes he could otherwise avoid. Nor did he ever forget his limitations as a boy, so he never lost his sense of humility—also rare among those who move in high circles. And he never asks his men to do anything he can't do, or wouldn't do, himself. They seem to love him for it and be ready to follow him to the ends of the earth. How many men could boast of that? I, for one, cannot..."

He swirled the contents of his cup.

"They say blood is thicker than water. Yet there are currents washing through Harry that are thicker than blood itself, that take him to depths I cannot fathom. But one might as well, like Canute, try to turn back the sea as try to thwart Harry when he's following his convictions. The Lord alone might stop him then. No man single-handedly ever could."

———

White Friars Chapel

Father Paul looked out from his vestry at armed men in the churchyard.

"Oh Holy Jesu, it's Henry Bolingbroke and his nobles, terribly serious for so new a morn. Doubtless they've caught some poor churl stealing supplies and want to hang him, and for me to offer prayers for the dying. Well, I suppose I must. Unless, sweet Savior," he implored optimistically, but with scant true belief, "they only want to hear Mass."

But when they assembled, it became clear they came neither because they planned to hang anyone, nor for Mass, but for another reason entirely, something about a sacred oath. However, being good Christian, God-fearing men, they'd be happy to hear Mass first, which pleased Father Paul immensely. Rarely for his early service did he have such strong attendance, much less such wealthy attendance, and there was always the chance of a fine contribution from this lot before they departed.

So it was that after the liturgy they gathered around the altar and he lifted the leather-bound Gospels.

Clad in buckskin leggings and a close-fitting, red-gold gambeson that skimmed his hips and revealed his handsome legs, Bolingbroke came forward. Kissing the book, he placed a hand on it.

As he watched, Harry's eyes were large and hopeful, his clean-shaven face pale. But his close-visaged father displayed no hint of emotion.

Slowly, Bolingbroke began:

"I, Henry, Duke of Lancaster, High Steward of England, swear that I come with pure intent to seek my patrimony, and support the royal authority of this land, and with recognition that King Richard reigneth until the end of his natural life. Also I swear to assist the king in good governance and void all malfeasance and wrong, and exact taxes only in conjunction with Parliament and when necessary to defend the realm, as it is a matter for all to assent to. Further, I pledge

to maintain the laws of England. All this I shall do, as God is my witness."

As he relinquished the Gospels, cheers broke out. Relief obvious, men clapped Bolingbroke on the back as they filed from church. Within moments, they had trotted away, leaving the friar pleased but puzzled. He wasn't too bewildered, however, to overlook the two gold coins he found on the altar after they had gone.

Chapter V
July 1399 - Bristol, England

For more than two weeks, the army snaked across the country, seeking its quarry, the king.

With each step the question of restoring Bolingbroke's property became less relevant, as one by one family fortresses fell into his hands, most without dispute, as their bailiffs greeted their rightful lord and more of England shook off Richard's onerous grasp.

Traveling at the incredible pace of fifteen miles a day, in late July Henry's force reached Berkeley, where the vanguard skirmished with men under Bishop Henry Despenser and Sir William Elmham, long loyal to Richard. No real battle ensued, though, and Berkeley resumed its peaceful pastimes with scant interruption. Taken into custody, Elmham and Despenser suffered no harm, arrest serving less as punishment than protection from those with grudges against Richard or his favorites. In Berkeley, too, no less a lord than Edmund, Duke of York, went over to Bolingbroke. Given his role as regent in Richard's absence, his capitulation would have seemed dishonorable had a viable alternative existed.

But it didn't. No one even knew where the king was.

Surely, he had left Ireland, had reached Wales, gone into seclusion, perhaps in Pembroke or Carmarthen, or North Wales. Even Edmund of York couldn't say. Nor could anyone gauge Richard's strength, so rumors abounded: He had left troops in Eire but landed with thirty-two thousand, only to lose all but six thousand; no, all but five hundred. William Montague, Earl of Salisbury, was trying to rally

Cheshire, with little luck even there, where Richard had showered largesse. The king was dismissing soldiers and those not harmed by Welsh marauders were making their way home or turning up in Henry's own lines.

And turn up they did: Some proclaiming they'd long sought redress against Richard, lavish favors to Cheshire or Wales notwithstanding; others admitting they were uncertain and had been swept along by their comrades' passion, right into Bolingbroke's camp. Whatever their motives, though, they came, until it seemed that only Richard himself declined to enlist under his cousin's banner.

Not yet, anyhow.

"We'll smoke him out," Bolingbroke predicted. "After Bristol."

* * *

As he stamped the gooey wax with his signet, Sir John Bushey smiled dourly, the only hint of hope or humor from him all day. He knew what was happening outside Bristol Castle; knew, too, it wouldn't be long before he probably was in chains. Bristol town had surrendered, if that was the right term, the city fathers seeing little choice: They had a couple hundred armed civilians, supplemented by hundred men-at-arms in the castle, against the sixty thousand milling outside the town. Besides, most sympathized with Bolingbroke, anyway.

From his room in the keep, Bushey had marked the enthusiastic shouts that had followed the army through the town foregate. Bolingbroke had yet to appear, but already Bushey could hear celebrations—thirsty soldiers, accommodating tavernkeeps, and residents well into their cups.

So much the better. It would only make it easier for his courier to slip out to a nearby mill and meet a loyal squire, to carry the message in search of King Richard.

Bushey rose, beckoning to the woman in the next chamber.

Tall, lean and spare, her hairline grey under her wimple scarf, she came quickly, moving from one arm to the other a basket piled with used jars and kitchen utensils. Her plain dark brown apparel marked her as a simple rural woman, but her slate-colored eyes showed intelligence and her face, though having seen some sixty years and bearing the lines to prove it, still radiated a glowing country beauty. A baker, she often sold honey and pastries to the castle, occasionally lending a hand in the kitchens or running errands. Her name was Agnes, and decades earlier Edward III himself had loved her, disappearing in the woods while hunting near Bristol to appear at her cottage, finding her rustic grace, good heart and sharp if unschooled mind a welcome change from his sophisticated if selfish London mistresses and his comely if dull-witted queen. Agnes had borne him a son, dead soon after birth, but despite this sorrow and her lover's irregular visits she had never lost her commitment to him, or to his royal house, including his grandson, Richard.

Thus she would undertake this mission.

"You know what to do." Bushey handed her the parchment "Give this only to the squire. If he's not there, and hasn't come within another day, burn it. And if you're waylaid by Bolingbroke's men..."

"I'll give them naught!" She tucked the note under the lining of her basket, beneath the dirty dishes. "Not those scoundrels!"

"But don't die for it, either. I'd rather not have you on my conscience. It's heavily laden already. Now, off!" He dismissed her abruptly, but with a friendliness mindful of her dignity. Her sturdy shoes echoed as she passed through the buttery door before proceeding, across baileys, and out the postern gate. Bushey sighed and wondered how many moments of freedom were left him and his equally trapped companions: William Scrope, royal treasurer and Earl of Wiltshire; and Sir

Henry Green, a long-time friend of the king. "An unholy trinity," he thought glumly.

A slightly portly man with a reddish-brown beard and eyebrows like a bundle of twigs, aptly mimicking his name, he had in his fifty-odd years experienced two reigns, several rebellions, assorted squabbles in Parliament, and numerous intrigues—and played roles in much of it. Former sheriff of Lincoln, he had been elected to Parliament and risen to Speaker of the Commons. With Gaunt, Bolingbroke, and Wiltshire, he had helped Richard orchestrate Arundel's downfall. Now, only two years later, Bolingbroke chased after Richard himself. And who knew, when the dust settled, what might await Wiltshire and himself, old allies of Bolingbroke or not...

Bushey didn't have time to speculate as Peter Courtenay, commander of the castle garrison, stuck his balding head through the doorway.

Though sympathetic to Richard, Courtenay had remained officially neutral and was prepared to defend the castle only if attacked first. "You'd best come and look outside, John. I've been offered terms, through the Earl of Northumberland and Edmund of York. I'm going to surrender. It's hopeless." A trace of sweat stained Courtenay's cheek and he wiped it absently with his arm. "I'm sorry. I don't know what this means for you. But certainly Henry will be lenient; he hasn't harmed any of Richard's followers yet."

Bushey sighed. "He's never caught up to anyone as close to the king as I. Or Wiltshire and Green."

They proceeded through castle halls, climbed a tower stairs and walked onto the parapet, shielded by massive crenellated walls. Bushey gazed toward the horizon, paled, and put his hand onto cool stone to steady himself. "Oh My God..."

Bolingbroke's forces filled the streets, manned the town defenses; filled the green, and spread to the Avon quays. In all directions they massed, division upon division. Too disorganized for a real military formation, they nonetheless remained grimly formidable. Among them, Bushey recognized numerous standards: the lion rampant and crescent, two emblems of the Earl of Northumberland; Cobham's fleur-de-lis; both Archbishop Arundel's ecclesiastical insignia and the Arundel family's bird motif; Willoughby's stylized cross and a Neville version of St. Andrew's Cross; Bolingbroke's greyhound, swan and antelope; and yea—*mirabile dictu*—even the pennant of Edmund of York.

Past the town walls, more men stretched out, including a battalion noticeable for its order. The flag waving above it caught Bushey's eye: Blue lions on gold, quartered with trios of silver-grey fish on deep red, with a red cadency bar across the top, denoting a lord's son who had not yet inherited. "Percy junior, too, is outside the gate. Even Hotspur has left his North and those damned reivers across the border. I once urged King Richard to ransom him back from the Scots, you know..."

Dispirited, he began picking his way back downstairs, Courtenay following silently.

"Yes, you'd best send out the word," Bushey agreed. "The castle yields. There're too many men out there, and too many damn good ones. Inform Bolingbroke that Green, Wiltshire, and I await his pleasure anon..."

Agnes made it to the outer town gate before two burly young soldiers barred her way with spears, demanding to know where she was going and what was in the basket she gripped so tightly.

Neither surprised nor particularly frightened, she stood her ground. "I'm bound for my mill. And if you'd be using the eyes God put in your heads, you'd see what I've got in the basket: Dirty dishes. I'm taking them so's I can wash and use them again, for more of my honey and cakes. Unless you'd be offering to wash them up for me, son." Her dusky eyes glinted with humor. "That'd be most kind..."

From their speech and appearance she guessed that they were northerners and probably new to this job of soldiering.

Sharing the boxy brawn and large-boned, ruddy looks of many descended from Vikings in the old Danelaw, they exchanged uncertain glances.

"We'll have to look ourselves." The slightly older one grabbed her basket.

Agnes let him take it. To protest would have aroused suspicion, whereas cooperation might ensure only a cursory check. But having little better to do, the young man was thorough and it wasn't long before his fingers pulled out the parchment. He hooted triumphantly. "What's this? What were you thinking to smuggle out under our watch?"

She took a cautious step sideways.

"Speak up, or I'll be more'n happy to let my spear convince you." He rested the spearhead at her bosom.

She moved it away calmly, as if brushing aside a pesky fly. "Just a note some fellow at the castle asked me to take to some friend of his, out by the mill."

"Then why were you hiding it beneath all that stuff?"

She looked at him as if he were daft. "Are you truly blind, and stupid, too? 'Tis a perfectly fine piece of parchment. Should I be letting it get mussed from dirty dishes? Don't be a fool; your own ma would do the same with someone's letter!"

He couldn't refute the common sense of that, and as he paused his companion finally spoke.

"Best take it to the guardhouse," the second said, touching the note gingerly. "Looks to be from someone important. 'Tis nay matter for us to chaw o'er. Let the sergeant or captains decide what to do with it. Best bring the old mother along, too." The first man nodded, and with their spears too close to allow escape she fell into step with them. Entering the guardhouse, they climbed the stairs.

When they reached the uppermost level, Agnes saw their uncertainty. They encountered no sergeant or captain but an obvious commander, clad in chainmail topped by a T-shaped coat of arms: azure lions diagonally on gold, quartered against silver-grey fish on red, all embroidered on dark cloth. He was alone in the room, which had apparently been requisitioned as a headquarters. Maps and charts lapped over the table while gear and saddlebags filled corners.

"My Lord Harry," the older guard began as the commander looked up, regarding Agnes with a hint of curiosity. "We've ... we've..."

"We've caught a spy!" the second guard blurted out.

"Ahhh, have you?" Harry chuckled. "What makes you think so?"

These were Northerners all right, attached to Sir Robert Umfraville, a Percy vassal and friend, who had sent his levies off with Harry's.

"We found a note, My Lord, hidden in her basket," the older one swaggered a little. "From someone in the castle. She was trying to win her way out with it. One of the king's crones, nay doubt."

"Shall we hang her?" the younger asked. "It'd take the fire out of any others who dare spy against us. Then see what Richard's friends think!" He spoke casually, as if unaware of what he really proposed.

"We could see to it right quick," his companion interjected. "Rope, a tall beam, and—*hizzap*—she's dead and gone!"

Harry flushed and left his desk. Grabbing the two by the scruff of the neck, he pushed them into the vestibule atop the stairs, barking out a gruff "by your leave, Mistress," to Agnes.

Releasing them as soon as he had slammed the door, he cut loose. " Since when might we be hanging folks on suspicion alone, or worse yet, for holding loyal to the king? Are we here to fight our own folk—or fight for the good of everyone? Should we be condemning old wives to death like cows to slaughter? On whose complaint? By whose right? Is that English justice? Shall it be so?"

They stood mutely, cowed by the questions tumbling out mostly in the Northumbrian dialect he shared with them but not with their captive.

Immobile beyond the door, unable to escape since the only exit led to the stairs where they conferred, Agnes strained to listen, but could only guess they were discussing her fate.

"Sorry, My Lord. I meant only to help. I'd be meaning no harm." The younger guard's discomfort was evident.

"`No harm,`" Harry repeated. "But to her." Leaning against the stair post, he regarded them sternly. "Never be eager to hang anyone, lad. 'Tis a loathsome thing, to be avoided unless law and justice provide no other recourse."

Their shoulders slumped.

"Now, what's this all about?"

The first guard handed over the parchment. "'Tis what we discovered, in her basket."

Harry fingered Bushey's seal before slitting it open.

"My Lord Sovereign: Bristol Castle is likely to yield to Bolingbroke. The town has already surrendered. Battle was impossible. If we can, Green, Wiltshire and I will try to find you. Do not leave the safety of Wales. Bolingbroke is said to have nearly seventy thousand men. Godspeed, until I may rejoice in seeing you again."

Bushey had signed it "your humble servant," name scrawled almost illegibly.

Harry deliberated briefly. "Well done." He smiled at the guards. "You have indeed intercepted a message to the king. I suspect that your `spy' knows not what she carried, though. And I'll wager she acted out of no malice toward us but devotion to the Crown and her customers at the castle."

He motioned them back to the guardroom. Barely in time, Agnes abandoned her position behind the door and stood silently and calmly at the table. Regaining his seat, Harry scrounged amid the maps, found a worn but clean piece of parchment, and dipped a quill into ink, penning a couple of lines with a quick, careful hand. He thrust it in front of Agnes. "Here."

She took it, casting her eyes upon the letters. "Do not cross me," Harry had written, "for if you lie, you will be hanged, drawn, and quartered. Without delay." The words were harsh, but as she looked at them her expression never changed; she registered no alarm, nor anger, nor any feeling at all except puzzlement. "My Lord has a most neat and stylish handwriting." She returned it to him.

He regarded her with both pity and respect. "'Tis as I thought. You can't read, can you, good mistress? You couldn't read my note, nor Bushey's, nor any other documents you might have seen scattered about the castle."

"No, My Lord," she answered, not with shame but acceptance. "I cannot read. Nor write. And I don't know what that message said. He didn't tell me."

"Bushey's no fool," Harry nodded. "He knows better than to risk telling you, and have you fall into the wrong hands, with his message beaten out of you. Well, no matter, we won't beat you, or let anyone else do so, either. You might tell me, though, to whom you were to deliver this."

"To no one I know. Some man, some squire, was to call at the mill. If he made it that far. Everyone for miles around must know your army's taken the town." She spoke willingly, beginning to trust him.

In turn, he sought to reassure her. "Where are you bound now? And what's your name?"

"Where I was always bound. To the mill—my cottage is nearby—to wash my jars and dishes; and fill them again, and bake, and help the miller. We'll be busy these next few days, feeding this army, I've little doubt. I just hope your Lord Bolingbroke pays for what he takes.

"My name is Agnes," she continued, "though folk call me Agnes Bymiller, because of what I do, and where I dwell. I married the son of the man who was once the miller. But my husband was killed in an accident. His younger brother and wife took over when the father grew old. But I had no place to go, so I stayed and all these years have worked hard and gathered honey from my bees."

She had no idea why she was telling him all this, except that he seemed kind and something in his eyes and bearing reminded her of King Edward, all those years ago. Embarrassed, she said no more.

"Well then, Mistress Agnes…" Harry deftly cut off the unused half of the parchment. On it he scribbled in English and Latin and then dropped a blob of candle wax at the bottom, stamping it with the ring on his hand. Tying it with a bit of leather, he passed it to her.

"Take it. You don't need to be able to read it, I'll tell you. 'Tis a safe-conduct pass, to get you through the lines, as long as you promise to bear no more missives for King Richard or his minions. Don't betray me on that. For if you do, 'twill be my neck as well as yours that you're hanging. And Harry Percy has no desire to feed the crows at such a tender age!"

"I promise, young man—My Lord Percy. I thank you, too."

"You can thank me better on the morrow. Come back then, with your honey and some oatcakes, or pies. I haven't had any decent oatcakes, and certainly no pies, in weeks. Fear not," he added. "I'll pay. In fact, I'm probably hungry enough to pay you double!"

"You'll be seeing me on the morrow." She stepped lightly through the doorway. "To be sure!"

He remembered the brothers, standing silently at the side of the room: "Well, look to it, lads. Haven't you got a gate to guard? You don't know who else may be trying to sneak by under our chins.

"I'm grateful to you," he called out, as they scrambled down the stairs.

"Now," he told himself. "I'd best hunt down Bolingbroke, or my father, or the archbishop."

He eventually located Arundel, in a cozy chamber of the abbot's house. "So, Harry..." The archbishop offered a cup of wine. "What brings you?"

"My men turned up a messenger, with a note to Richard from Bushey," Harry handed over the parchment. "In substance, it reports little. But it does suggest that even Bushey didn't know where to find Richard, and that Richard isn't aware of the size of the army moving against him."

Arundel read the note and slipped it inside his robes. "You're right. Nothing of real significance; no mention of any resistance being mounted; no palace secrets, either. But your men were good to discover it, and you to bring it. Bolingbroke will be most interested in anything Bushey has to say."

The abbot approached the doorway but bustled off again and the archbishop leaned back in his chair. Motioning his visitor to sit down, Arundel took another sip of wine while Harry accepted the invitation. In his middle years, Arundel was of moderate height and size, with ear-length greying brown hair, light brown eyes and an oblong, smoothly shaved face. Of all the recruits to Bolingbroke's cause, he was perhaps the most unexpected, for he was the brother of the man Henry had helped send to the block. Indeed, he had barely escaped doom himself. Fleeing to Europe, he had crossed paths with Henry, forgiven him, and, as the situation in England deteriorated, urged him to act.

Now, months later, he was one of Henry's most influential advisors. "You'll find out soon enough, so I might as well tell you," he confided. "Henry had Bushey, Green, and Wiltshire arrested. Your father was delegated to inform them. They're jailed in the castle and Henry says he plans to arraign them in the morn."

Harry whistled. "On what charges?" He steepled his fingertips against his forehead. "So soon he moves against the king's favorites... But it had to happen sooner or later, and better sooner. 'Twill show we intend to restore justice. That means holding Richard's men accountable and demanding changes from him, too—once we return him to Westminster, and he calls Parliament, and we resolve all these issues: his conduct, and Bolingbroke's patrimony, and everything else."

"Yea."

"And whether arraigned here or not, those three will doubtless be sent to London, for trial, after Parliament convenes—rather like your brother," Harry added. "Only this time, it should be fair and honest. Your brother didn't deserve to die. Neither, I think, do these three." The archbishop said nothing, and Harry continued, absently dangling an arm over one side of his chair and wedging his legs over the other. "Once convicted, they should forfeit anything illicitly leeched from this country and perhaps be imprisoned or exiled. But that'll depend on individual guilt and the charges brought."

Arundel took another draught of wine, avoiding Harry's eyes. "I'm not certain what the charges might be. I'm bidden to confer with Henry and your father and others tonight. Perhaps we'll consider it then. I do know Henry says he means to be firm. And it is the high steward's prerogative to initiate such proceedings."

"True enough." Harry mentally dismissed the matter. "I need to get back to my men. Some aren't used to cities and may go wild or be easy marks for dishonest alehouses and whore-mongers." He laughed lightly. "In fact, I intend to spend the morrow drilling my force and any others who wish to join us. 'Tis easier to avoid the temptations of town when you're in the field. Besides, they can use the practice, and so can I. Anyway, you doubtless have plenty to do here. By your leave, My Lord." He stood before Arundel, bowing his head slightly. "And with your episcopal blessing…"

The sudden delve into the spiritual caught Arundel by surprise. But he recovered quickly, extended his hand and delivered the words of the ancient benediction. Then he, too, paused, as if flustered but wishing to say something further. Seizing the younger man's hand, he looked up hard, into the dark-blue eyes. "Never change, Harry. England needs the likes of you too badly."

Startled, Harry merely shrugged and smiled, turning away. "Pray for me then. And for England, too."

He spent the rest of the day with his captains and those of the other levies, hoping to coax more unity from their chaos. But as twilight deepened he returned to the guardhouse, exchanged his chainmail for his usual tunic and leggings and dug into his saddlebags. Finding his leather-bound Psalter and Book of the Gospels, he made his way to the castle through streets full of revelers, including drunken soldiers.

"Nary a Northumbrian yet, so far as I can see," he told himself. "Either they've followed my orders about moderation, or they can hold their drink better and haven't yet fallen into the gutters."

Admitted to the castle precincts, he found Courtenay atop the walls and asked to be taken to the prisoners. "I thought they might like some reading. When I was captured by the Scots, locked up for the first time ever, I nearly went out of my head with worry and wounds. Then an Ayreshire knight brought me his Psalter. I found great consolation in it. I thought I might do likewise for these men here…"

Courtenay seemed a little nonplussed but could find no harm in the request and led Harry around the parapet to the keep. "If you visit with any of them, I'll have to take your knife, and lock you in, and post a guard outside. Sorry: Bolingbroke's orders."

"I think my fair cousin need not be so concerned about security inside. Better he pay more heed to what's outside." Harry gestured over the wall. "Look down there: mostly Henry's retainers, lurching out of taverns right and left, others crazed and brawling already. He'll be lucky if half the men of Lancashire aren't in a stupor by morn."

Courtenay nodded. "Yea, but Henry's got matters on his mind other than drunken soldiery."

"Where is he, anyway? I asked to see him earlier and was told he would not be disturbed."

"He's been hiding away. Right now he's holding some privy session, with Arundel, and Neville and your lord father and a few others at the abbot's house. Lesser men were not invited, I guess. I certainly have no right to be there... But I would think you might." Courtenay couldn't resist needling Harry. After all, this was England's leading knight, and the son of an earl, no less.

"Me?" Harry laughed. "I'm only a knight, remember, no earl and no archbishop. I'm well out of it—unless they're discussing military questions. In that case, however, I think my father would have had me be there too; he has that much respect for my abilities, anyway."

They entered the keep through a tower and wound their way down dark passages to a series of small, barred rooms. "Best wait, whilst I talk to them," Courtenay cautioned.

As it turned out, Green and Wiltshire were in no mood to see Harry, or make use of his books, or have anything to do with any of Bolingbroke's followers. Bushey, though, welcomed the visit.

Courtenay relieved Harry of his knife and waved a guard aside. Taking a key from his belt, he creaked the door open. The room was better than a dungeon, but much bleaker than the chamber upstairs where Bushey had spent the afternoon.

Harry grabbed a lantern from a peg in the passage as he entered, ducking under the low doorway.

"Stay as long as you like," Courtenay told him. "Just have the guard fetch me when you're ready to leave; I'll come and get you."

"Might we have some wine?" Harry asked, in sudden inclination.

"Why not? It's Bushey's wine we've been drinking upstairs, anyway. I'll send some down."

The door slammed and the scratch of the key in the lock followed. Bushey roused himself from a bench against the opposite wall, grasping Harry's hands warmly. They had met previously but were acquainted casually at best.

"It's good of you to come, Lord Harry. You're the only one who's asked to see us. I feel like a leper now, an outcast. But—welcome!" He pointed to his sparse surroundings. "I'm afraid this isn't very luxurious." The room contained only a small table adjacent to Bushey's bench and another low bench against a side wall.

Harry brought the second bench over to rest near the first, hung the lantern on a hook in the wall above, the only place he could find, and put the books on the table. "Some reading. It may help pass the time till morning."

Picking up the Psalter and Gospels in turn, Bushey noted both were in carefully lettered English.

"A legacy from Wycliffe. My father and Gaunt defended him, when I was young," Harry explained. "I never cared much for Wycliffe myself: Too fixed in his own beliefs, which seemed strange. I still don't understand his attack on the Eucharist. He was haughty, too, as oppressive as Rome at its worst. And his God—his God only seemed judgmental, vindictive even."

"Yea..." Bushey recalled.

"But Wycliffe was right about a couple of things," Harry added: "That the word of God should be easier for all to read, in our own language, and that God can be approached by everyone, without a bevy of priests to intervene."

"He gave you these?"

"Aye." Harry laughed lightly. "I suppose Wycliffe thought me in particular need of Scripture's chastisement! Howe'er 'twas, I've carried them with me for years—not because of Wycliffe, but because they comfort me."

Bushey leafed through the Gospel of Matthew. "You could get in trouble, you know." His eyes met Harry's. "A bishop or two banned and burnt Bibles like this, four or five years ago. Said they're the spawn of heretics. And that was long after your father and Duke John stood up for Wycliffe."

"Aye, so I learned," Harry agreed. "'Twas when I was in Aquitaine. But, to burn these, some idiot of a bishop would have to wrest them from my hands. That wouldn't be easy, either, since he'd be attempting it at the point of my sword!"

Bushey chuckled. Thumbing ahead another several pages, he stopped at the fifteenth chapter of Mark, reading aloud: "`And next, in the morning, the chief priests took counsel with the elders and scribes and all of the council, and they bound Jesus and carried him away... .'"

He closed the book, holding it momentarily before laying it aside. "Thank you. 'Twill be a comfort, indeed. It was good of you to think of such a thing. Most men wouldn't."

"Most men haven't been thrown into a dungeon, wondering if they'll live or die," Harry replied. "I have been imprisoned; I know... Besides, I owe you. You were in that Parliament, in 1389, that supplied money and implored Richard to get me back from the Scots, after Otterburn. I might not have been released otherwise. I'm grateful. I've never really thanked you."

"I remember," Bushey smiled. "We demanded that Richard do something. I always hoped your ransom would be worth it. I know now it was, even if it has taken you all these years to express appreciation."

The guard rapped at the door, unlocked it briefly, and set something on the floor. Harry retrieved the wine and goblets, pouring out two portions. They saluted one other and drank.

"It was a long time ago: Otterburn, and the `Merciless Parliament' and the attacks on Richard's friends, and all that," Bushey said. "I've done much wrong since then. I shall pay for it shortly, I expect."

"I can't condone many things you and Richard have done," Harry acknowledged. "The country's been wronged. You'll have to be ready to answer for that. But what's right will prevail. I believe that. I wouldn't be here if I didn't." He took a sip of wine. "Incidentally, we caught your delivery-woman, Agnes Bymiller. I passed your note to Arundel. It didn't tell us much…"

"The old woman?" Consternation filled Bushey's face. "Is she all right? You holding her?"

"Hold her? Why? Because she—God knows why—still admires our king, and was willing to do a favor for you? 'Twould make no sense. She knew nothing. She can't even read. I sent her off, with a safe-conduct pass. Two of my guards *did* want to hang her, but I put an end to that nonsense soon enough."

Bushey regarded him quietly, then lowered his eyes, lost in thought. Slowly, he looked up again. "Bolingbroke and his men plan to kill me on the morrow; Green and Wiltshire, too."

"Never! You were Henry's friend recently enough, at Richard Arundel's trial. So was Wiltshire."

"And because of that, because I know exactly what transpired regarding Arundel, Henry may play rough. He may regret we still remember."

Harry frowned.

"What's more, I subsequently advised Richard that it was acceptable to exile Henry, that at least for a time neither he nor Mowbray could be trusted."

"True. But others gave like counsel. Some say that even John of Gaunt, ere he died, said 'twas best that Henry leave England. Of course, once Gaunt died, Richard got even more reckless, seizing Henry's inheritance and committing all those other misdeeds."

Bushey smiled sadly. "For those I may pay with my life, in the morn."

"Scarce that! Remember Bishop Despenser and Elmham. They raised arms against Henry and he sent them off for London, quite comfortably. You gave up peaceably. There will probably have to be a trial, though, of many of Richard's ministers, including you." Harry readjusted his long legs before the bench. "But naught worse. You make too much of this, too much."

Bushey flared, as if to knock the goblet from Harry's hand. "For God sakes, mock me not. If that's what you want, go sport elsewhere."

Harry pulled back, stung. "I ... I don't know what you mean. I'd never sport with you. I don't understand. God's truth, I don't..." His head drooped.

Watching him closely, Bushey was amazed. "Truly, Lord Harry is an innocent, a naif," he thought. "He genuinely doesn't know. He actually thinks that nothing untoward will happen tomorrow. He believes that the rule of law, and what's right, mean something, even now."

Bushey's thoughts ran on, as Harry continued to retreat onto his bench, slowly sipping wine.

"He's not so thick-headed as to think that just because decent folk wish it, justice 'twill be done, or that it can come at the snap of his fingers," Bushey told himself. "He's no simpleton, or mooning idiot of a philosopher. But it's almost worse. He thinks that by struggling for justice and the greater good, they will prevail, if not immediately, then ultimately, if he just fights bravely enough, long enough. He's seen something of evil, but he doesn't know how strong it can be: Evil inside men, and evil in the world, unleashed when men come together and give in to it as one and begin to enjoy inflicting it on others. He thinks truth will ultimately triumph. And, in the end, obstinate as he is, he'll probably die trying to prove it. God help him..."

Bushey shut his eyes again, prayed, and then picked up his wine and turned back to Harry. "I'm sorry, My Lord. I was overwrought. I apologize."

"Apologies accepted. You've been under duress; any man would lash out. And don't bother to call me your `Lord.' God knows, there's already a surfeit of lords in this town tonight. Let's not add another."

Bushey smiled, in spite of himself, and they drank in affable silence.

"You're not the only one Richard has placed in a difficult position," Harry observed. "I think oft of my lord uncle. He's with Richard somewhere. I'd like to send word to him, but don't know where he is. I fear he may be cast into some jail, too. Or, worse, that it will come to battle and we might have to kill each other. I don't know that I could do it—kill him," he admitted. "That man cradled me in his arms when I was a babe; walked beside me erst I learnt to straddle a pony; picked me up from the dirt more times than I care to recall after besting me in swordplay. I'm the stronger, better fighter now, though, even allowing for his difference of age. If we met in battle, sans doubt I'd be able to slay him, if I wanted. But could I ever want to?" His eyes darkened with emotion. "I'd rather fall on my own sword first. And he'd feel the same about me. So in the end, 'twouldn't matter. We'd both be struck down by others, while we stood there refusing to lift our arms against each other. Would to God it never comes to that." He drank, blushing. "'Pay me no heed; I don't normally speak freely of such things. The wine must've loosened my tongue."

"Would that I had such a kinsman to worry over me!" Bushey exclaimed. "Yet Richard is no fighter. You may discover he's run off to Bordeaux or some other hidey-hole, but I don't think you'll find him leading his host in battle. So I doubt you need trouble yourself about your uncle. Besides, Thomas Percy is a man who knows how to take care of himself. As does his nephew."

Harry smiled sheepishly, and they drank in friendly silence again.

It was Bushey who finally called a halt to the evening, on the pretext of his own exhaustion, when he saw Harry stifling a yawn. "I'm sending you off, my friend. I grow weary, and I would have a little time to be alone, to read your books ere I sleep."

Harry stretched and reached for his goblet as Bushey's eyes closed.

In reality, Bushey was wide awake and, even with the solace of Harry's books, dreaded being alone. Moreover, he found himself enjoying this younger man's company and wishing they might have further evenings together. "I could teach him more about the real ways of the world and perhaps spare him a few pitfalls," he thought. "And he could help me remember that there are things worth fighting for; that honor and courage and justice do mean something, or should mean something... Passing strange, that I should only come to know him now, on what's likely my last night on earth. Yet perhaps God sent him for a reason, that I might remember that goodness really does exist, to die—if I must—with that knowledge..."

He turned to Harry in mock annoyance. "Begone, lad! Leave an old man to his slumber!"

Harry grinned, walked the few steps to the door, and summoned the guard.

"Keep the books as long as you like," he told Bushey. "I'll get them back from you in London." He drained his wine and was setting the goblet down when Courtenay arrived at the door.

Bushey placed both hands on Harry's shoulders. "I hope I do meet you again. But if not, farewell. And I appreciate your kindness." Slowly, he released his hold. "You've been rather an emissary of heaven tonight."

"That's a relief!" Harry quipped as he left. "Usually I'm considered a denizen of the Other Place!"

Chapter VI
Tuesday, 29 July 1399 - Outside Bristol

Sweat streamed down his spine and rolled off his tailbone, as other beads on his brow merged into a large drop, streaking his face, stinging the nicks where he had too quickly wielded his habitual morning razor. Astride his dapple-grey warhorse, Valdus, Harry shoved his visor up. Scanning the field, he smiled. This amorphous army seemed to be learning its stuff and by evening would have reached an imperfect but promising level of proficiency, to be refined in days to come. Already they'd been at it for hours, though the sun had yet to reach zenith in the heavens.

Before leading them across the river he had risen early to don armor: Helmet atop mesh cowl or aventail, plate-metal cuisses and greaves protecting upper and lower legs; armguard vambraces; chainmail hauberk, cuirass-breastplate over it, and, topping all, tabard-tunic, a T-shaped, thigh-length "coat-of-arms" emblazoned with his lions-and-fish, preferable to the ankle-clinging surcoat or confining, waist-nipping jupon beloved by courtiers who only dallied in arms. At his side rested his favorite sword, its three-foot steel blade inscribed with *Esperance*; hilt wrapped in black leather and capped by a roundel, likewise bearing his insignia, in colored enamel. The most-prized item in his gear, it weighed two pounds.

His force consisted of his own troops and a surprising number from other lords and locales, all spreading out like industrious ants. To spare the delicate crops rising in fields, whenever possible he had directed the men into fallow meadows, though he had evicted several flocks of sheep and given his squires some brisk riding, chasing a recalcitrant bull from his turf. Now archers sent volleys toward makeshift targets, infantrymen sparred with quarter-staves, spearmen competed to see who could throw the fastest, farthest and most accurately.

Retrieving a rag from his saddlebag, he wiped his forehead and trotted Valdus into a pasture of riders: Knights, men-at-arms, squires, young urban gentlemen, and youths from the far corners of England, aspiring to earn their spurs alongside the illustrious Hotspur. They cheered his arrival, anxious to show off in jousts or swordplay. But he bade them dismount, form squads, and choose ham-sized stones from a nearby field pile, one for each hand or as ballast in rucksacks. Then he had them run between their horses and the field, a dozen times. When, pink and panting, they began to stagger, he called them back together. "Doubtless, you're wondering the meaning of that..."

A couple Northumbrians, accustomed to such antics, nudged each other, winking, but he ignored them.

"Twas to help you learn to move quickly when you're weighted down. More on which anon." Surveying them, he frowned. "Most of you are here without armor. Some of you probably have it but left it in camp, thinking it too heavy for a warm day. Others lack it but hope to acquire it. Do so. Soon. You'll need it as horsemen. And once you've got it, by God, you'd better wear it when you take the field, or you won't live long enough to regret it. You see me in mine," he added, prisms of sunlight glancing off the metal. "Some of you likely thought: 'What an arrogant ass this Percy is, riding out in full plate, like a puffed-up prig on parade.' Others probably thought me less a proud ass than a daft one, too foolish to know how I'd roast on such a day. Well, no man knows better than I how uncomfortable armor can be. That's why you'll never see me with a beard or long locks—'tis already too damn hot inside a bascinet, or any helmet, without scratchy whiskers and hair down your neck. Yet I wear my armor, because it could save my life. It *has* saved my life, though it can also slow a man on foot."

He smiled mischievously. "Now, you're probably thinking: `Wouldn't slow me at all, because I'll fight from horseback.' Except oft it doesn't work that way in battle. And so our English codes of conduct demand that commanders be ready to fight on foot and forbid them to cry `to horse' for their knights while leaving common troops behind." He paused for emphasis. "A knight or man-at-arms must know how to fight on foot as well as on horseback, if he hopes to fight again."

He saw a couple of men dig their fingers into their fellows' sides, heard the whispered jokes that broke off when they became aware of his gaze. "All right, lads: Has the sun addled my wits? Some bird been shitting all over my helm? Or have I sprouted horns up there?"

Reluctantly, a burgher's son commented. "Some say, My Lord, that 'twas because you were fighting afoot at Otterburn, like some low-born serf, that the Scots captured you."

"Aye, they say that," Harry acknowledged. "I was seized at Otterburn—after hand-to-hand fighting, after my prior wounds re-opened—because I was fighting on foot. Had I been on horseback, I could have escaped, ridden off when I was hard-pressed, saved myself. And left my men without their leader, to meet defeat and death; and been derelict in my duty." Pacing a few steps in either direction, he looked directly into any questioning faces. "True, we suffered much defeat and death anyway. But so did the Scots. And had I not fought alongside my men, with every knight and lieutenant doing the same, 'twould've been much worse. But don't rely on me."

His tone lightened. "Talk to the French. Bid them tell you about Crecy. Many French *chevaliers* wouldn't fight on foot and couldn't fight on foot. All they could think to do was charge, on horseback—right into our arrows. Too proud to fight like ordinary men, they died like dogs."

Agreement rippled through the crowd.

"Poitiers, My Lord!" a Shropshireman yelled. "My father fought alongside the Black Prince. He said the like happened there; in 1356, 'twas."

"Aye, Poitiers," Hotspur added. "By then, ten years after Crecy, at least some French knew they couldn't always fight mounted. So what did they do? Attacked right into our arrows anyway. Again! They also had another whole division, dismounted, with many nobles. But the nobles refused to fight afoot and fled the field, abandoning their comrades. I don't intend to act that way. Nor will I allow my men to act that way. Hence, I make you run with stones, so you learn to maneuver on foot, even when heavily laden."

He let that much sink in.

"Remember this, too," he cautioned. 'Tis not just the weight of your own armor and weapons you must be willing to bear, but that of your wounded neighbor. You've got to be ready to carry him to safety. It's especially important in the North, where I come from, where we have bloody chases along the border far more frequently than we have major battles. Even if we triumph, I can't afford to leave a wounded man behind. Good soldiers are too wanting. I must carry him to horse and get us all home safely. Our success next time may depend on it. Also remember this: The life saved could be yours, when your friend hoists you on his back."

They guessed what was coming: Their next challenge was to carry each other while running and trying to fend off "enemies." Scuffling, yelling and cursing ensued, accompanied by the thud of crashing bodies, as dirt rose in shimmers, casting a sheen upon all.

Visor closed, Harry joined in. Grabbing Hardyng, he leaned over while his armored squire climbed on his back. At age twenty-one Hardyng was slightly above average in height, slim but strong—like his lord, whom he emulated in his clean-shaven chin and the short cut to his light-brown hair. Eagerly taking up his part as injured comrade, he draped himself across Harry's back, though he knew the roles would soon reverse.

Using one hand to hold the "wounded" Hardyng's arms around his neck, sword in his other, Harry cut a path through the mass of pretend opponents. Sweat flooded his eyes and bascinet, his calf muscles throbbed, and shoulders ached. Constantly balancing his own and his squire's weight, boots boring deep with every step, he raced to the sidelines. Hardyng slid to the ground, and they rested a moment before trading places.

To decrease the burden, despite the risks, Harry shed helmet, vambraces, greaves and gauntlets, though Hardyng still sank under his weight. They charged back across the field, dodging onslaughts as Hardyng slashed with his battle-axe. Head sagging on Hardyng's shoulder, legs locked around his squire's waist, Harry found his teeth jarring inside his skull; felt Hardyng falter and nearly lose him more than once, caught a mouthful of grit when an "enemy" suddenly loomed before them, sword bared. He would have "slain" them both had Harry not kicked out at the last moment and sent man and weapon tumbling.

"Well done, My Lord!" Hardyng staggered the last few paces to their lines. Dumping Harry in an undignified heap, he collapsed on the grass.

"For God's sake, John—you didn't have to make it *that* real." Harry gingerly picked himself up. "You dropped me as if I already were cold dead!"

Scrambling up, Hardyng turned his freckled face toward his lord and friend, hazel eyes bright. "You had it coming. You've done it to me often enough. And 'tis no disrespect for me to be reminding you of it."

"Well taken," Harry smiled. "And now we'd better call a halt, before everyone gets weary and careless, and someone truly gets injured."

Retrieving his armor, he stopped the melee, groaning inwardly as he noticed men nursing twisted ankles or severe bruises and saw that others dragged themselves in excruciating slowness, clearly lacking the stamina for real warfare. Well, that was why he'd brought them out here, to learn and improve, or face the consequences.

Turning to his horse, he untied his canteen, drinking gratefully. Then he reassembled everyone, leading Valdus into their midst. "How many know how to get on a horse quickly?"

Nearly every hand shot up.

"And how many can actually do it?"

Hands went up again, amidst laughter and bragging.

"Well now," Harry responded, with a trace of amusement. "We'll soon find out. You there, and you, and you, and you in the back, and you, lad." He picked five of the most vocal. "Bring your horses over."

The horses stood obediently before the crowd, while Harry kept their owners back, pending his signal. "When I give it, you'll run to your horse, mount, turn around, and ride as far as yon." He pointed to a hedgerow in the opposite direction. "'Tis not a real race, just a chance to see how well you do." Silently counting down, he made them wait, as they impatiently flexed their legs, like greyhounds straining at the leash.

"Now!"

The dash was on.

Two men quickly had a foot in the stirrup, swung the other leg aloft for the briefest of seconds, landed in the saddle, and galloped away. A third was nearly as fast. But he threw himself too far forward as his foot reached the stirrup and his crotch slammed onto the pommel of the saddle. Deeply pained and annoyed, he ignored the guffaws and stalwartly got himself astride properly, chasing after the first two. The fourth found his stirrups higher to reach than expected from a running start and halted abruptly, to mount while standing; the other botched the job entirely, skidding on foot right past his horse's head. More derision followed before Harry reclaimed their attention.

"Excellent, in at least a couple cases! As you saw, 'tis not as easy as it looks. You need to practice, constantly. I still practice constantly. Now I'm going to make it harder, show you how to do it without stirrups and a real running start."

A few disbelievers scoffed; Harry merely proceeded. Leaving Valdus a short distance away, he stood motionless, as if quick movement were the furthest thing from his mind. Then he strode forward, hastened his pace into a smooth lope, and, as he neared his horse, reached out, placing one hand on Valdus' withers and the other on his haunch, vaulting into the saddle, through the strength of his arms and the momentum of his feet leaving the ground. His boots didn't slip into the stirrups until, reins in hand, he was riding down the field. Trotting back to applause, he grinned. "See, 'tis possible."

"Then do it again," a wag shouted.

"Again?" He deliberated. "Aye, you might have to do it more than once, or twice or thrice, when fighting for your life and your men's lives. All right, I *will* do it again—or try."

His performance was as flawless the second time as the first, and every bit as good the third and fourth times. Finally, he refused another encore. "It's your turn to practice now."

So they did, drilling over and over: How to mount from a running start, with a quick foot in the stirrup. How, then, to mount sans stirrups. Few could accomplish the latter at all, and none could equal Harry's ease or speed.

Some voiced frustration as he walked among them.

"Eventually you will match me, if you keep at it," he told a disconsolate young Yorkshireman, one of many who'd failed despite otherwise accomplished horsemanship. "Once I wasn't any better than you. But

I kept at it. I also learned a few things from our old friend, Jean de Maingre, Sire de Boucicaut. The `greatest knight in France,' they call him—and not one of those Frenchmen who refuses to get off his horse. I met him at a tourney and managed to best him in swordplay, on horseback and afoot. But he could do a few things better than I, and mounting a horse this way was one.

"He showed me what I was doing wrong—exactly what you're doing, lad: Trying too hard to rely on my feet, to kick myself up and into the saddle, instead of mostly using my arms and almost gliding off the ground. Try it again. I'll help you. And don't worry. We're all here to train, including me." Good-naturedly, he cuffed the young man, a lanky, sandy-haired seventeen-year-old, with soft brown eyes and a shy, wind-reddened face. "Have you a name?"

"John, by my christening. But mostly Sean, after my mother, she bein' Irish and all. That is, Sean Irby," the youth hastily amended.

"Well, whate'er name you go by, lad, failure has no part of it. You only need patience and practice, and you'll be able to do this and lots more, too. It's hard, I know," Harry went on, when Sean still looked discouraged. "Being patient while you learn, I mean. Patience has never been one of my better virtues, either. It's much easier to give up, if you can't master something immediately, than to keep working, until you can do it. But alas, working at it is what life seems to require most. This your horse?"

"Yea." Sean patted a spirited bay mare.

"You've a good eye for horseflesh," Harry nodded. "May I try it with her? Good. Now, watch, and I'll attempt this again, more slowly, so you can understand."

Once more, he began ... and was suddenly in the saddle, in one unhindered motion.

Sean's eyes shone.

"See, if I can do it, so many times of a morn, and I much older than you, you can do it, too."

"And you, in full armor," Sean added in awe.

"So shall you move someday, in full armor. Now, you try again."

Sean set about it self-consciously but hopefully. He paused, then began to walk quickly, broke into a run, and reached out, placing his hands on his horse. Swinging into the air, he vaulted easily and effortlessly—right over the mare's back. He hit the earth with a dull crash, no movement coming from the limp body when Harry reached him. But as Harry knelt there, Sean rolled over and looked up, blinking back tears. Harry brushed a clump of dirt from the sandy hair and extended a hand. Taking it, Sean slowly arose, heartsick.

Harry cuffed him again. "Cheer up, lad. Until that last moment when you sailed too far, you were doing well. You're just ahead of everybody else. By vaulting right over your horse, you jumped right into my next exercise. Now, let's go through it slowly, together. But don't try anything further for a moment, just listen."

Methodically, he led the youth through the steps. And Sean took it all in, hero-worship burning in quiet eyes, until Harry sent him off to practice alone, leaving him with a clap on the back and a firm handshake.

By now Harry was beginning to tire, though still far from exhausted. "I should try the longbow, next, been a long time since I've had serious practice with that. At least then I can stand in one spot."

But first he had one more lesson to impart to this cavalry. He reconvened it. "You all saw me leaping into the saddle. Most of you've tried it yourselves; some have succeeded. Those who haven't"—he noticed a somewhat happier-looking Sean rejoining the group—"don't give up. It just takes lots of effort. As you can see, I'm sweating like a stuck pig. Better to lose sweat here, though, than blood in battle, elsewhere.

"Anyway, here's something else to learn: To leap right over your horse. Now, again you're wondering: 'Why would I want to vault over my horse?' Here's why: You're fighting on foot, on one side of a horse. But you're needed badly by your comrades on the other side. It's hard to get to them unless you go over the horse. If you try to make your way around him, on foot, it'll take more time and be more perilous. If you try to mount and dismount quickly, you'll expose yourself to arrows. If you spring right over the horse, though, you'll have a better chance of avoiding both arrows and at least some of the enemy pressing near. And you'll land on the other side, on your feet, with the element of surprise."

Several men seemed incredulous, though by now they knew better than to doubt aloud.

"There may also be a time when you have no choice but to use a horse as a shield, to save your life. To some of you, 'tis a horrid thought, I know. You love your horses. You live with your horses. You sleep with your horses!"

They laughed.

"I, too, am fond of mine," Harry continued. "But there may come a day when, if I would live, he might have to die. That's one of the realities of war—and there are far worse things in war, believe me. So you must be prepared to allow your horse to die, even as I, reluctantly, would sacrifice Valdus."

Hearing his name, the destrier ambled over, sniffed, and slurped his owner's uncovered cheek, licking salt from dried sweat. "Go away!" Harry merrily pushed him aside. "I'm about to consign you to slaughter, remember?"

The men laughed again, and Harry went on. "Suffice to say there are good reasons why you might need to get from one side of your horse to the other, leaving him at your back, like a shield. So, how to proceed? First, you act the instant there's an opportunity. Then you try something like this."

Once more, he left his horse several yards away and, from a standing position, began to stride and then run forward. Reaching Valdus, Harry put his right hand on the saddle and his left atop Valdus' neck, fingers in a hank of mane. As the horse automatically lowered his head, Harry lifted his legs off the ground and vaulted into the air, this time, right over his mount. He landed upright, treading lightly on his feet as he drew his sword and confronted imaginary foes.

"Thus 'tis done. And thus you must practice, until you've perfected it, and your horse never balks. And once knowing it, God willing, may you never have to use it."

He dismissed them to practice on their own and eased himself to the ground on a knoll, unknotting the ties that bound his helmet to his chainmail so he could pull it from his head. The touch of the wind tickled his face and brought blessed coolness. Hair plastered into lank sprigs, forehead gleaming, he closed his eyes. It had been a good day so far.

Arms crossed upon knees, chin resting on wrists, he idly watched Valdus, appreciating again the straight, lean length of the horse's legs and the well-shaped head. He had named him after one of his favorite saints, Oswald—or in the North, Osvaldus or Osvaldt—the brave young king of the Northumbrians, who, seven hundred and fifty years earlier, had loved God and justice and died far to the West, near what became Shrewsbury, battling a murderous interloper king. Buried as a saint, Oswald had been ripped from his tomb by his vanquisher, his body dismembered, and bones scattered. But the Northumbrians had never forgotten him.

Blissfully, Harry rested. But with responsibility weighing his mind no less than Hardyng's weight had burdened his shoulders, after several minutes he rose, in search of the archers and rest of this motley army.

And still it was only noon.

Metallic hisses cut the air, followed by the whack of arrows hitting home. A moment later Harry spotted Thomas Knayton, his senior squire, and Elyot MacKerny, master-of-bow, at opposite ends of a long row of archers.

Disengaging himself from a knot of men, Knayton came over, a teasing look in his ice-blue eyes. "Behold, one of the chevalerie joins us!"

"One of the chivalry could've been here all along, if you'd ever let me dub you!" Harry replied. "But carry on."

As cool and unflappable as always, despite hours of exertion, Knayton returned to his drills. Above medium height, with an archer's potent chest and arms, he had a square, beardless face and a cap of pale blond hair nearly as white as his colorless brows. Having earned his battle stripes in border clashes as a youth, he was as adept with lance and axe as he was with the longbow on which he first trained. Now in his thirties, he often captained troops on his own but had always refused Harry's offers to be knighted. "What need have I of knighthood?" he would ask. "Under your command, I've already become as able on the field as any belted knight, and as well-respected, too. And you welcome me not just as liegeman but as friend. Adding `Sir' to my name would change naught.

"Besides," he would shrug, if Harry persisted. "'Tis a distinction I can ill afford, making me liable for scutage and other taxes to the Crown. I know: You said you'd pay them, at least to begin. But you've better things to do with your money. So unless you order me to accept knighthood, I'll stay as I am, and be pleased to be a man of your company."

At first Harry had been disappointed, mostly because he himself valued knighthood so highly, regarding it as less as a prestigious status, or even an occupation, than a sacred vocation to which God summoned a man no less than others received calls to the priesthood. Sealed by vows, with quasi-sacramental dignity, it was to be earned, and, once earned, prized. Nonetheless he knew his ideals were hardly universal. If there were men like Knayton who merited knighthood but eschewed it, there were others, far less worthy, who attained it anyway, through preferment or purchase.

"Hell, my own father bought a knighthood that way: For me," Harry had once acknowledged to Knayton and his uncle. "More than a year afore I first bore arms in battle, 'twas, and me still five years shy of twenty-one, the customary age."

"Henry Bolingbroke and Richard were yet younger, but knighted the same day," Thomas Percy had reminded him.

"And King Edward got coffers of money, `manifestations of esteem' from Gaunt and my father for bestirring his gouty old bones to do the honors!" Harry had pointed out.

"But it served your father, too, did it not?" Knayton had asked. "After that, he became an earl."

"Oh, Father made out well enou'. I understand *why* he acted as he did. I just wish he *hadn't* acted as he did."

Thomas Percy had smiled. "Which is why, Harry, you spent so much time proving you deserved a knight's sword. 'Twas a decade before you convinced the last skeptic: You. To everyone else, it had long since been apparent!"

Eventually, just as Harry had come to grips with his tainted acquisition of knighthood, he had accepted Knayton's decision to forgo it entirely. Knayton was still a brave, chivalrous man; 'twas enough.

After a few minutes of observing the practice, Harry approached MacKerny.

Although almost a runt, MacKerny likewise had wide shoulders and well-developed upper arms, welded to a torso as unyielding as a barrel of bricks. With his silver, neck-length hair and drooping moustaches, he could have been an apparition on a fog-draped moor, a druid capable of invoking the wrath of a thousand gods. Though he had been raised in Scotland, his lineage was vague. "Part McAlpin, of the old royal blood," he would assert, "and part Ker, I am. And proud as hell of it."

"Part cur, you mean," Harry would tease.

Though well into his career, MacKerny could dispatch a dozen arrows with flawless ease, in less time than it took to count to forty. But Harry often jested that it was a close call as to which represented the more phenomenal span: the draw of MacKerny's bow under arrow, or the gap of his mouth in the boasting and yarn-telling that was his other notable trait.

In his earlier days, MacKerny had changed sides more often in endless Scottish feuds than even he could remember. Then one wintry night he had banged on the gate at Warkworth, a Scots price on his head and angry Grahams on his tail. For some reason, perhaps pity, Harry's father had admitted him, and he'd been staunchly in the Percy fold ever since.

Now his voice resounded in as inventive a round of invective as Harry had ever heard. As Harry approached, MacKerny broke off with a laugh, but more from having exhausted his profane vocabulary than in deference to his commander.

"Someday, MacKerny, I'm going to turn you loose against a whole army of Scots, alone, without your quiver," Harry joshed. "You don't need arrows; your words are barbed enough!"

"Harry, m'boy," MacKerny greeted him happily. "Want to try some shots at a few hundred paces? Or care to watch us beat the shit out o' the South? Or make a wager? We've got a wee bit of competition on, y'see, o'er who's better, those that be from south o' the Humber, or those on the north. Losers, begging your pardon, My Lord only with your permission—have to stake the winners to ale, in town tonight."

He looked both hopeful and doubtful, knowing that Harry gave his blessing to moderate, off-duty drinking but frowned on excesses that led to public inebriation or impaired abilities. "With your approval, of course," MacKerny repeated.

"Of course!" Harry realized he was being humored. "Well, permission is not given. It's too early in the day to talk of drink. And what men not of my levies do this eve, when they're back under their own lords' authority, is up to those lords. Now, who's winning your `wee bit' of competition?"

"Achhh—God damn—'tis a fair toss-up." MacKerny wrung his hands. "The North should be winning, seeing as how we're better men. But our lads seem to have lead in their arms. And these lads from the South, well to be sure, I think they've all been cheating, only so's I can't prove it. Which is to be expected, when you're dealing with good cheaters. So we've been evenly matched, round for round. And 'tis a sorry day for me, being from the North."

"Oh hell," someone with a southern accent shouted. "He's just pissed because we wouldn't wager for the amounts he wanted, and 'cause we're better bowmen, too!"

"And better looking," someone else yelled. "Better'n him, anyway!"

"Och, pay nay mind to MacKerny," a Northumbrian retorted. "He always sounds like he's got an arrow up his arse!"

Harry tolerated a few more coarse comments and then brought them together, thanking them for their service. As he finished, MacKerny slapped a longbow into his hand. Archery had never been Harry's choice. Still, he could hardly refuse.

From a bundle of arrows he selected seven that approximated the measure from his forearm to his palm. Lining them up at his feet, tips in the dirt, shafts rising to the sky, he turned to the group. "I'll try. But if

I shoot wide as the wold or shaky as a palsied pissant, I beg your indulgence."

Notching the first shaft, he raised the bow and pulled the cord back nearly to his ear. The arrow hit the target just off center. Aware of all eyes upon him, he plucked the second from the ground, pulled and released: A bullseye. Smiling almost shyly at the accompanying cheers, he reached for the third and quickly dispatched it. Skimming high, it disappeared into the meadow, eliciting hoots, which increased when his fourth shot went astray as well. The fifth hit the target, albeit askew. He loosed the sixth, cursing when it, too, went off-center. Steadying himself, he tried the last, knowing when he scored another dead-center hit that luck as much as skill was responsible.

It was hardly a flawless performance, but an acceptable one, and the archers offered both praise and suggestions, which he duly noted. Someone retrieved the shafts and he agreed to try three more. The first hit the target, off-side, and the second was hardly better. But the third thudded, hard and true, right into the middle: Another bullseye. Cheers swelled, and so did his sense of vindication.

"You can see why we all need practice. No. Why I need practice," he laughed. "May your arrows, and MacKerny's wagers, never go as wild as my shots. As for me: I quit the field, the day is obviously yours!"

A red-tinted sun cast its last warmth on the meadows when Harry accompanied the army back to camp. Bringing up the rear to watch for stragglers and assess the damage they had inflicted on the countryside, he rode easy, stained by perspiration and mud, with small clumps of manure clinging to his boots, tired but content.

Once the troops were restored to their bivouac, he shook off the worst of the muck and glanced overhead.

Still time for a foray into town to learn what the morrow might bring. They'd be moving on, doubtless.

The bells in the abbey church rang out for prayers as he made his way through streets nearly as choked as the previous evening. Something seemed different, though, as if frenzied desperation had replaced the carefree revelry.

Leading his horse, he crossed the green, wondering why it was so empty—until he nearly kicked a bouquet of flowers, lying at a crude cross, imbedded in the ground. A few paces beyond, his boots scuffed the edge of a well-trod patch of earth, curdled in the center by a reddish blotch, abuzz with flies. Though he squatted down to examine it, he knew what it was: Blood, shed in quantities, hours earlier. There was no mistaking what had occurred here. Distaste rose hot and thick in his throat.

Clench-jawed, he set off for the castle.

"Where's Courtenay?" Discharging Valdus to a groom, Harry strode toward the keep, shouting again. "Where's Courtenay?"

The door below a tower opened and Courtenay hurried out, worry creasing his forehead and exhaustion girding his eyes. "Harry!"

Harry ignored the proffered hand. "What the hell happened here?" But he already knew; the castellan's look merely affirmed it.

"They arraigned Bushey, Green and Wiltshire, not long after you took the army off," Courtenay said, dismally. "Then they had a trial, and found them guilty, and sentenced them to die. They did it out there—beheaded them on the green. It ... it was all over in half a morning."

He grabbed at Hotspur's arm, as if to restrain the latter and steady himself. "Harry, they *were* adjudged guilty. I liked them well enough and would have spared them, had I been adjudicating. But I was not. Still, they were found guilty of high treason, or something very akin. We know the penalty for that."

"Wh-wh... Who did this?" Harry demanded. "Bolingbroke? Who were these judges? What court was this that arraigned and tried and sentenced them with such ... such alacrity? Would that justice always moved so swiftly! Goddamn! 'Tis not right, Peter, no matter how many judges Bolingbroke found to preside!" His voice softened. "But 'tis not your fault. I'm sorry. You had naught to do with this, doubtless. You were too close to those men the last few days. These `judges' wouldn't have let you have anything to do with it, except stand and watch, with your castle guard."

"Yea, I was there. Would to God that I hadn't been." Courtenay's tone was low. "Let's go within. I have something for you, from ... this morning." He led Harry to the castellan's quarters in the keep, closing its heavy wooden door and retrieving a couple of chairs.

A decanter stood on the table, and he poured two goblets of wine, giving the first to his guest. "We could both use this now, I think." Taking a couple of quick gulps, he looked at Harry, whose own cup remained unquaffed. "You asked who the judges were."

"Bolingbroke himself, I fear."

"He was one, yea..." Courtenay hesitated. "There were two others, Harry. One was your cousin Neville. The other was your father."

The silence in the room seemed to spin around them. "Jesu." A look both stunned and knowing crossed Harry's face, and his eyes closed in a kind of weary resignation. Reaching for his wine, he downed a mouthful. "I'd like to be able to say I don't believe it. But it's true, I'm sure. I know my father and cousin. Good men, both. But so taken with this power Bolingbroke tosses them that they can act without thinking. Or, at least, they don't think enough. Maybe it's easier for them if they don't."

"And Bolingbroke?"

"No better and probably no more to blame than anyone here," Harry replied. "He's high steward of England now. He burns with desire to let all and sundry know there's a strong man to answer to, not just a whimpering excuse for a king. So he jumps into action—and error, perhaps. He would serve as check upon a corrupt ruler. But who shall serve as check upon him?"

There was no answer, and he expected none as he lifted his cup.

Courtenay removed something from an ambry. "Bushey asked me to give you these and make his farewells for him." He extended Harry's Gospel Book and Psalter. "He asked me to thank you, said they had been much succor through his last hours. Also, he said: `Tell young Percy that almost as much for his sake as mine do I regret that he was so wrong about their plans for me. Tell him I wish I could have returned his books myself, on happier terms.' And, he said: `Tell him also that I respect him as a truly good man, one of the most honorable I've chanced to meet, and that even as I prepare to die, in all honesty, I can say that of too few.'

"He held these, until his very last moments," Courtenay revealed. "Then he beckoned to me among the guard and gave them to me and spoke as I've said."

Harry took the books, almost caressing them, noticing the smudges on the leather covers where Bushey's sweaty and perhaps trembling hands had held them as he awaited death. Cradling them under one arm, he rose. "Thank you for your hospitality. But I'd best find my father."

"Still angry?"

"At you? No. At my father and Bolingbroke? I know not. At what happened today? Aye."

He climbed the steps to the great hall, where a pair of guards on the other side of the door answered his rap and barred entry. But his father promptly emerged.

"Harry! I was hoping you'd return soon." The earl leaned over to place an arm around his son's shoulder. Harry's stony expression stopped him short. "What's the matter?" the earl said. "And could you not come in from the field sooner? I sought you."

"What's the matter?" Harry repeated loudly. "Ask me whose blood I've been trudging through, crossing the green. Tell me what happened, and why. Then ask me what's the matter. No, tell me what's the matter with you, that such a thing *should* happen!"

"Good God, Harry!" The earl looked around in embarrassment. Nonetheless, with the guards back inside the hall they were alone. "We'll talk elsewhere," he directed, propelling his son down a side corridor to an empty chamber. "Now, for God's sake, what are you nattering about?"

"They killed Bushey and his friends this morning. Without due process or proper trial, 'twould seem. Isn't that enough to `matter'?"

"What, pray tell, did you think would happen? You knew they had to be brought to justice."

"Aye, to justice!" Harry paced. "To justice! Not to some sham trial. Not to summary execution. Why weren't they arrested but safeguarded, like Despenser and Elmham? Why was there no real trial at Westminster before a full jury of their peers? Why such haste?"

The earl's temper flared. "You think that would have guaranteed justice? That's what happened with Richard Arundel. He was tried before members of Parliament—a whole lot of them: Lords, Commons, even the Lord Bishops. And found guilty by all. And sentenced. You found that singularly lacking in justice, too, I recall."

"As did you."

"Perhaps..." the older man conceded. "But the truth is, even a trial at Westminster would've provided no surety that justice would ensue. What happened to Arundel proves that."

"That's just it," Harry objected. "It wouldn't have had to be like Arundel's trial: Rigged, Bushey primed to say what Richard wanted, though not necessarily what his Commons wanted; Bolingbroke and probably Gaunt schooled to perjure themselves as well. It could've been done right, with genuine representatives of the Commons and the Lords—not just tokens—to speak for themselves, and nary a proxy for the bishops, either, so it would've been very clear what the reverend fathers thought, and no chance for them to wriggle out of it later by saying their proxy misunderstood them. Trials can be fair. Justice can prevail."

"You think justice did not prevail today?"

"Aye. It did not."

"By God, Harry, I was one of the judges. Do you think me incapable of justice?"

"No. I think that today you were incapable of it, being too caught up with Henry. Perhaps you realized it and proceeded anyway. Perhaps you failed to recognize your own blindness and went blindly ahead. But wittingly or not, you perjured yourself, participating in such a mockery. You perjured yourself ... and justice."

"You call me a liar!" the earl's voice became a shout. "You dare call me a liar!"

"Not exactly. I say only that you helped give the lie to justice."

"And what *is* justice in this case? You were not here this morning. Pity. Had you been, you would've heard half of Bristol, clamoring for the heads of these three. Those folk knew guilt when they saw it. Had we not found these men guilty, executing them forthwith, I think we might indeed have been guilty of injustice. However, it seems, 'twasn't good enough for my firebrand son!"

Harry said nothing.

"You fool!" His father scowled. "Do you truly think that had there been a different trial, a `fair' trial as you put it, a trial in London if you will, the result would've been different?"

"Perhaps 'twould have," Harry answered. "At the very least, they might not have died. But regardless of that, everything could've been above reproach. All England would've known the trial was just. Now questions will always remain. Do you want that on your head?"

"And you, who are no trained jurist and never served in Commons or Privy Council, you know what justice is. You alone recognize it."

"No. Yet I do know what is *not* justice. What happened today was not."

Furious, Earl Henry lurched forward, as if to toss his son from the room.

Intercepting the move, Harry wrapped his stronger hands around his father's, directing the older man to a chair. "Please, Father, let's not come to fisticuffs."

They confronted each other, the father seated, arms crossed over his chest, eyeing his son caustically; the son standing, arms crossed as well, saddened and tired but defiant.

Harry broke the silence. "Do you not see what happened today? 'Tis of a piece, part of a series of things touching on my friend Bolingbroke. Look at the *res gestae*." He chose the jurist's term deliberately and enumerated Bolingbroke's role in plots and counterplots over a dozen years.

"Does it not give you pause?" he concluded. "Bolingbroke is capable of much good. But he has an unsettling habit of denouncing old comrades—who rather tend to end up dead. I'm not saying he necessarily has evil designs. I suspect he simply panics, turning on men without cause. Or perhaps he assures himself there *is* cause, however flimsy. And to prove that even former friends can't escape the consequences of their conduct, he moves fast, too fast, heedless of justice. Probably he isn't even aware of all he does. Yet if he has unlimited power as high steward, as he will unless reined in, God forbid what could come of it! Richard will not be in any position to restrain him. Nor is he fit to do so. Think on that!"

But his father seemed numb and discouraged, and another long silence prevailed.

Finally, Harry started to depart.

"Where are you going?" Though he spoke suddenly, the earl's voice was soft with curiosity now.

"To bathe, I hope!"

"Can you not wash here and send a squire to fetch you something to wear?" Earl Henry regarded Harry in paternal sternness. "I almost forgot. Your presence is bidden here tonight. Bolingbroke's planned a fine feast. With all that happened, there was no time for it earlier."

"Or no appetite for it either, with all that happened earlier!"

The earl ignored the comment and Harry again turned away. "Convey my regrets."

"You must be there," his father emphasized. "Many of the highest lords from the south and west will be there; bishops, also. And Archbishop Arundel, and Edmund of York, and Ralph Neville and the rest, all the leading men of the realm."

"I'd rather not see Bolingbroke and Neville tonight. I'm in no mood for pleasantries. And I refuse to dissemble."

"Goddamn it, Harry! To hell with your insufferable sense of righteousness! This is important—to me, and, whether you believe it or not, to you, too. Would you spurn a chance to dine with the best men in England?"

"No, Father." Harry was already halfway out the door. "I intend to dine with the best men in England: My troops."

Chapter VII
Wednesday, 30 July 1399 - Outside Bristol

The mule nickered eagerly when Agnes went to fetch him. Saddlebags crammed with honey and rolls taken from the oven before dawn, she—like the mule, Mungo—usually enjoyed her weekly excursion, exchanging her goods for the pickles and cheeses of a hamlet several miles away. This day, though, her mood mirrored the skies, wavering between darkest overcast and dull grey, with little hint of sunshine.

News of the executions had spread. "To be expected, with a man like Bushey, close to the king," she had told herself. "Best put it from m' mind." And she had tried. But gloomy awareness continued to seep into her consciousness, along with questions of why she was spared when one so powerful fell. A lowly widow bearing a hidden message, she had been stopped, taken to the younger Lord Percy, and lived. Bushey, a Speaker of the House of Commons, had awaited Bolingbroke, greeted him deferentially and perished.

Who could explain the ways of the world? Only God, perhaps, but He wasn't commenting.

Passing a stone cross, she knelt by the road, conflicted by gratitude for her own escape, regret at Bushey's death, and weary uncertainty. Unable to find the energy to pray for Bushey in a personal way, she relied on rote Latin, familiar even to unlettered farmwives: "*Memento, memento, Domini.* Lord remember him." Beyond that, she could pray no further. Let her work be prayer enough.

She patted the mule's neck." Let's be on."

Since she had left Hotspur, her activities had been frantic. After laboring over dough and kitchen, she had returned to the camp as promised, bearing bread, oatcakes, and fruit pies, 'for Sir Harry.' Conducted to his lines, she had found him absent, in town somewhere. But Hardyng, fresh from their exertions in the field, had warmly welcomed her (and her pies, in particular) and tried to pay her generously. Mumbling something about a small favor returned for a large one given, Agnes had refused money and disappeared again.

Today she proceeded to the village and disposed of her goods efficiently. Declining to linger for the usual post-market gossip, she headed the mule homeward again. The first few miles passed uneventfully, but then a smokey pall appeared on the horizon and the mule shuddered. "That's nothing, Mungo," she predicted. He quieted at the sound of her voice, and it took several twists in the road before she realized the pall's vicinity. "Holy Mary, let it not be." There was naught in that location except their mill homestead.

Kicking Mungo into a canter, she was seized by an apprehension fiercer than when she'd been accosted by Hotspur's guards. To lose her life as an old woman to whom death was commonplace was fearful enough. To lose her home, livelihood and the only family she knew was far more frightening.

Fear hammered at her, to be replaced by revulsion as she passed through her gate, torn from its hinges. Built of stone and timber, the mill smouldered, roof gone and blackened upper floors hanging as the wheel creaked in futility. The pond had prevented the fire from spreading in one direction, but looking the other way, through the smoke rising from debris, Agnes could see the burnt house of her in-laws, while more wisps rose from the site of her own cottage, beyond.

Her eyes brimmed with tears from both smoke and horror as she rode closer, covering her mouth with a hand to quell her stomach. "My kin, where are they?" Like the mill, the barn, chicken coop, shed, and even the privy had been destroyed. Nor were any of the animals around.

Dread becoming shock, she explored further. Among brambles bordering the paddock, she found her dead brother-in-law, mouth agape, shoulders awash in blood, neck cut through so deeply his head was nearly severed. A reddened pitchfork was cast aside at his feet while the lifeless sow lay behind him, her throat slit as well. A few paces away Agnes found the corpses of two strangers, men in garb bearing a greyhound and swan, pockmarked with scarlet pitchfork holes.

Dismounting, she forced herself to study everything in some detachment, to discern what had happened, though she wasn't sure why such thoroughness mattered. Most of it wasn't difficult: Her brother-in-law had died defending his pig and farm, felling two of his attackers before others had grabbed him from behind, pulled him into the brambles, and cut his throat, along with the pig's.

Yet why kill the pig, but steal the other animals? It made no sense.

Agnes led the jittery mule on and in the kitchen-garden found her sister-in-law dead on her back amid pea tendrils, her round face and long braids turned sideways, her throat, too, a mess of blood, with her legs spread open and skirt pulled up around her waist.

Swaying, Agnes dropped the reins, stumbled to a mulberry bush, and emptied her stomach, tears running down her face. She shook and then lay flat, incapable of moving at all.

No one came to help. But no one came to inflict further harm, either.

Finally, self-preservation overcame despair. All was quiet now, but she remained in danger; best to leave, immediately. There was nothing left anyway.

Taking time only to find the bucket, intact at the bottom of the well, she rinsed her mouth and face, walked several yards more to confirm that her house, likewise, was gone, and remounted Mungo. Yet where could she go? Not Bristol; danger lurked there, too, if her kinfolk's murderers had been among the mob crying for Bushey's execution. Nor was returning to the market hamlet wise. It also could be aflame. Or its residents, fearful of what misfortune she might bring down upon them, could bar entry. Besides, there wasn't enough time before nightfall for another journey. Her sole option seemed to be to hide in the woods. But that could be perilous, too.

Then inspiration struck. "That Lord Percy. He seemed kind; he would know what to do."

She urged Mungo into a fast trot, but he needed little encouragement and soon brought her to the perimeter of the Lancastrian camp. There, uncertainty stabbed again. After what had happened to Bushey, what had happened at the mill, and what had nearly happened at the hands of Hotspur's men, the army represented danger, too. She had made up her mind, though, and now mostly worried about not reaching Lord Harry before she collapsed.

"Holy Mother, thank you," she exhaled as sentries saw her and hurried her forward to Harry's lines, where he stowed personal gear while Hardyng supervised wagon-loading. Clearly, their forces were pulling out.

One glance at her was enough to tell Harry something was amiss. But when she managed only the plaintive "My Lord—ohhh—Sir Harry," before crumpling against a wagon, he knew that something truly grievous must have occurred.

Hunched, face averted, she began a fractured discourse, only partly intelligible. Finally, she raised her head to say something about requesting mercy or help. But she choked instead, eyes widening at the awareness that she was about to faint. Hands scrabbling at the wagon, she pitched forward.

Harry stepped closer to break her fall and found himself steadying her in his arms, like a son comforting a newly widowed mother.

Discovering that she was not going to collapse after all, she abandoned efforts to be strong and sobbed against his shoulder.

"'Tis all right," he said quietly, over her downcast head. "You're safe. Rest a little. Then tell me."

Nodding mutely, she wept for another minute or two before pulling away, suddenly aware she might be embarrassing him.

But if he was embarrassed, he didn't let on and instead put an arm around her and led her to a group of benches, beckoning Hardyng to follow: "Bring your pen and writing tablet, and a cup of wine."

As her composure returned, Agnes began her story again, more coherently, in sentences laced with anguish, while Hardyng recorded everything.

"These dead robbers," Harry asked at last, as she sipped the wine. "Could you tell who they were? Whence they came?"

Agnes shook her head. "But they had soldiers' badges, greyhound and swan."

Harry cursed.

Finally, with as many details as possible gleaned from her, Hardyng put his pen aside and Harry plied Agnes with less official queries. "What will you do next? And what can I give you to help?"

"First, I must go back, to bury my dead, afore—" her voice caught again. "—afore they rot. And what can you give me? Can you give me house, My Lord? Raise the dead to life? Give an old woman her livelihood again? Never. I have nothing. I am nothing. I will be nothing." She buried her face in her palms.

Locking his hands behind him, Harry strode off a distance. "Damnation!" A stream of swearing followed in English, French, and Northumbrian dialect. "For the love of the Lord: What do I do now?" he wondered. "I'm responsible for her. Not by law, but still… She trusts me. There's no one else for her, and no home, kin, occupation or means of working it, as she says. Damnation!"

Somberly, he came back.

"Aye, Mistress Agnes, I can give you a house, or tent, rather. I can't restore your dead, but I can give you other company, a whole army. I can give you livelihood, even. You'd best come with me until you find other protection. Doubtless," he added, "we'll chance across some nunnery, one that will take you in, as they oft do with widow-women. Fret not, I'll pay your dower. Until then, howe'er, you'd best come with us, if you'll have us. And take up whatever labor you wish."

She regarded him with tear-glazed eyes.

He went on. "God knows, there's plenty to do. The cellarers and sutlers are always crying for another set of hands. The priests need assistance with beggars and the injured among our own men. Then there's food. I, for one, need a cook. Usually, I just eat whatever my squires find, or what my men roast in campfires. My horses dine better of a night."

Flashes of life flickered on her dazed face. But she remained silent, for long moments.

He broke in, a trifle impatiently. "Well, Mistress?"

She nodded. "Yea," she found her voice, in a whisper. "You are my lord now."

Excusing himself, Harry pulled Hardyng aside. "Take her to the priests. They know more about charity and will know her wants better than I. Doubtless, she'll need clothes and everything else. Best someone see to it now, afore we leave town. I want her properly accoutered. She'll make herself useful, too, so long as she's with us, for she's too proud to do otherwise. Besides," he chuckled, "she's hardly the first woman to follow this army, and of much better repute than some.

"And bring Ian Kynge back with you," he directed. "I want him to ride out to this mill with you. As chaplain, he can bury her dead, with fitting prayers. Take a couple of men and be well-armed. See if you can identify these dead marauders. You'd better bury them, too, but strip them of any spoils first. Take their clothes if you can. I'd like to see if they are in Lancastrian livery."

Hardyng grimaced, mumbling something about gore, or lice, or both.

"All right," Harry relented. "Leave the clothes if they're too bloody, or full of pests. I'd rather not have you spreading vermin about, anyway. But check to make sure these two really were in livery of swans, or greyhounds." Glancing over at packhorses departing, he considered further. "When you're done with that, you and Kynge sniff around Bolingbroke's troops. Find out how much of a desertion problem he's got, whether his levies are missing any likely culprits."

Hardyng darted away.

"Thanks, John!" his commander thought in time to add.

Harry resumed his duties, pondering further. There was no way of knowing if the murderers had been in league with the pitch-forked robbers or another set entirely, opportunists finishing what others had begun. Anyone might have been responsible: neighbors with trumped-up grievances, cut-purses from Bristol, or, aye, maybe some of Henry's soldiers, run amok. Still, one thing was clear: Even when obtaining provisions, soldiers weren't supposed to purloin goods, and they certainly weren't allowed to kill or rape anyone. Indeed, such offenses were subject to swift court martial and execution. Sighing, he resolved to find his copy of the military code of conduct, The Statutes and Ordinances To Be Kept in Time of War, and have it read to his troops—and explained, explicitly.

He couldn't be responsible for other men's men. But he could do his damnedest to ensure his own behaved.

Chapter VIII
August 1399 - Carmarthen Castle, Wales

Thomas Percy slipped into the hall and found himself alone. Again. Unfriendly and cold, the room was thick with darkness, no sconces lit and only long-dead ashes in the hearths. Not even the dust stirred.

"Christ...."

He re-read the brief summons: *"Richard, by the grace of God King of England, etc., etc., bids the presence of Thomas Percy, Admiral and Earl, etc., in the great hall for urgent counsel."*

"So where is he?"

According to the old soldier who had brought the note, Richard had penned it in the chapel. Perhaps even now the king lingered there on his knees, Thomas thought, annoyance abating. After all, what man had more need of God's mercy, or protection, these days?

Rumors of the executions at Bristol had leapt the sea to Ireland, though for too long Richard had refused to believe them. Thomas and others, less skeptical, had urged a response. Finally, after delays due to weather, logistics, and his own hesitancy, Richard and a small force had sailed, landing at Milford Haven before pushing on to Pembroke and Carmarthen. There he had dithered again, calling Thomas "Uncle" and moping about the castle like a moody boy, pinning his hopes on his old friend Lord Salisbury, who supposedly hid in the hills of northern Wales with an army.

"Merde!"

Balling the note, Thomas threw it in a fireplace and eyed a bench beneath a small window. If he had to wait, it might as well be within the slim splash of light in the otherwise depressing place.

"*Eeeeyaggggg!*" A blood-curdling shriek disoriented him, as a ghostly figure in monastic garb catapulted over the bench.

The admiral pulled his knife with his right hand while his left shot out, stopping the apparition in mid-lunge. It tumbled but recovered in a neat somersault. Sitting cross-legged on the floor, head thrown back, smirking, it revealed itself as Richard, King of England.

"For God's sake! You damn near got yourself stabbed. Must you always jest?"

"No, Uncle. But why should I not jest now?"

Richard flopped onto the bench, stomach-first and then flipped over, regarding his seneschal with a cynical smile. "What else is left me?" The smooth lids closed on eyes alternately registering self-pity, hysteria, and calculation. "What else?"

"Your kingdom, by God." Thomas glowered. "If you would still have it."

"My kingdom. If I would have it. I think, dear Uncle, it would not have me!" Richard's laugh was acidic. "Or maybe it would have me dead, like Bushey, Wiltshire, and Green." He pursed his lips, lined of late with moustache and beard, smiling eerily. "Dead, like Bushey. Kings have died, too. Many. Murdered." His voice was calm, his eyes erratic. "Some cut down by axe, some by poison, some in battle. Some perhaps dead by their own hand. Some..."

"Enough." Thomas Percy's exasperation echoed. "You are not they. You are still king. And unless you chose to no longer be king, king you shall remain. I'll help you, though we're at a real disadvantage.

"'Disadvantage' hardly describes it," Thomas grumped to himself.

"We've no easy days ahead," he warned aloud. "We'll have to try brokering an agreement with Bolingbroke. Failing that, we may have to fight, though I don't recommend it. And once we've settled things,

I'll help you make amends. For make amends you must, to all your realm."

Richard sniffed in exaggerated surprise. "Fight? Ah yes, my proud admiral would fight, if reluctantly. Fight with what? Some of our troops remain in Eire. Others were to leave right after us. They've presumably landed by now; yet they haven't rejoined us. Cowards! So what does that leave us? A thousand men? Half that? Salisbury, perhaps? Or only you and I?"

Rhythmically kicking his heels against his bench, he went on. "I need not ask, 'against whom will you fight?' We know already. Against your noble kith and kin and the rest of that mob." His eyes fixed on Thomas. "They say your beloved nephew leads legions in Bolingbroke's army. Your great Harry Hotspur. I should've had his head when I had the chance. That's the 'amending' I wish I'd done."

Thomas' tone was sharp. "Harry does what he believes is right. He acts for the good of the country and of you."

"Tut, tut, good Uncle," Richard clucked. "Be not angry. Some things I tell you truly I'll never change. 'Tis not proper. Otherwise, I shall make amends, enough for you and everyone else. But a king amends himself as he sees fit, not at the behest of a mindless rabble."

"It's not just rabble."

"Maybe not. But I shall amend myself only when I, King Richard, decide to." He glanced at his monk's robes, chuckling. "I'll begin now. I'll amend king into friar and leave these problems to you." Jumping up, he grabbed Thomas' arm. "No! I shall be an abbot, ride forth with a dozen men, like St. Francis. No, like Christ and his Twelve, for it's like Christ I'm persecuted." The king smiled a cajoling smile and pranced away, only to pause, his expression inscrutable as his smile dissolved.

It sounded like he intended to retire to a monastery, Thomas thought. Yet… "You say you'll go. Then what? Speak plainly."

"No, Uncle." Richard suddenly stepped back toward Thomas. "But I promise you'll know all, tomorrow." He embraced Thomas. "Farewell, Uncle. Fret not." Skipping off, he disappeared down a stairway.

Thomas wanted to kick the walls. "He sought me for 'urgent counsel'? Well, by God, I'll have urgent counsel in the morn. And he'll give me better answers, or I'll beat them out of him myself."

In his tower that night, Thomas rubbed tired eyes, reviewing his list. There were one hundred men in the king's personal entourage. Thomas could summon another one hundred and fifty from his Worcester estates. And in late afternoon seven Cheshiremen, gentry all, had arrived, each with eighty armed followers. But that still gave him only eight hundred and seventeen men, total. Otherwise, the situation looked awful, as even Richard seemed to be realizing. "For too long he refused to see the truth, heeded vanity, not wisdom."

"Mark my words," Richard had insisted, leaving Ireland, "thousands will rally to me. Then I'll clap Bolingbroke in iron, and deal with him—as I did with Richard Arundel—and Old Man Northumberland, his son Harry, and that ballock's tit of an archbishop, Arundel, too. Once those fine heads decay over Tower Bridge, the rest of the realm will come to its senses!"

But thousands had not rallied to him. Nor were they likely to.

"Hell." Thomas stared at his meager troop roster again. He loathed the idea of having to fight. Their numbers were too few. "And there's the other..." he sighed. The opposing army included Hotspur and Earl Henry, his sole sibling. He could still see his brother, opulent as any monarch, confounding rivals as he swept through the hall at his first wedding, a seventeen-year-old claiming a rich widow several years his senior. Or the two of them as boys, joking surreptitiously at Mass, playing with their hounds at Alnwick, swimming the river below the castle.

Memories of his brother's son cut even more sharply: His own hands holding the infant Harry—not pink and plump like most babies but long and white, all huge, alert eyes and limbs that never stopped pummeling, until he tried to snuggle into Thomas' arms... The child, dispatched to Thomas' tutelage, greeting him with a self-conscious smile... An adolescent Harry, defeated in mock combat but begging Thomas to continue until he had improved, then by candlelight poring over some ancient Roman military text... Harry as a young man, emerging pale and thin from captivity in Scotland, tearing on horseback across the moors, laughing into the wind, reveling in a freedom never so prized. Harry, for whom Thomas would have fought against all odds, for whom Thomas would have died...

How could he oppose Harry in battle?

"To save Richard, I might have to kill Harry. And to protect Harry, I might have to abjure my oath and let Richard die." It came down to that: Nephew versus king, love for Harry versus affection for Richard, emotion versus honor, family devotion versus feudal duty. Ultimately, Thomas concluded, he'd have to opt for duty. But he knew, too, that if he faced Harry on some terrible field, he could do but two things: Escort Richard to safety behind the lines and enter battle himself unarmed, hoping only to be captured or killed immediately and spared further torment.

Better it never come to that.

No, they'd have to reach an interim agreement with Bolingbroke. Then they could all return to London, convene Parliament, mediate their differences, and create a new council to hold the king in check. Thomas had no qualms about installing Bolingbroke as high steward as part of all this. In many ways Bolingbroke was the perfect counterweight to Richard. They might even start to like each other again, or at least co-exist and cooperate.

"There really is no other way," Thomas told himself for the hundredth time. "Richard is going to have to placate Bolingbroke and the whole damn country. Or he'll end up like Bushey. And so will I."

Thomas never had been among the advisors most responsible for royal depredations, but that was of scarce comfort. "I thought I could serve Richard best, and serve England, by remaining at his side all this time, acting as the voice of reason, being the conscience he so often lacks. All I did was delude myself, God forgive me. I made myself more important than I am, flattered myself that sooner or later he'd have to come to his senses and heed me. Now it *is* later. Now it is too late. And still he doesn't heed me."

So far, no formal overture (or ultimatum) had arrived from Henry, but Thomas saw little gain in waiting for one: Let Richard claim the advantage and moral high ground by making the first move.

In the morning, if the king still refused to listen, Thomas would ride to Bolingbroke. They'd wasted too much time already. He was not about to let Richard waste any more.

———

After a troubled sleep, Thomas rose at dawn and wandered around the corner to the L-shaped garderobe. Moving through the antechamber, past the wash pitchers and sill inset with a carved sink, he veered into the L's lower tip and stopped short. There, atop the closed lid of the commode, lay the gold coronet Richard used when he didn't need a heavier ceremonial crown. Under the coronet was a parchment in Richard's loopy handwriting:

Beloved Uncle,

Know that I have left for the good of all. I hereby take leave of my offices of rule, until such time as I can return in a manner befitting a King. Until then, this is my final order to you: Dismiss the rest of my force here, disband my household, and send all away. Let no one stay. Further, Thomas, Earl of Worcester, you are forthwith relieved of all responsibilities as seneschal until such day as I order you reinstated. I act because you can no longer serve me as I deem best. Seek me not. Know only that I go with the humility of Francis, with my twelve, as Christ himself journeyed.

Until we meet again, I remain, Richard, King of England

Thomas swallowed hard. "The fool! This is the worst thing he could have done." Clutching the note and coronet, he raced toward Richard's chambers. Halfway there, his bladder reminded him why he'd approached the privy in the first place, and he went back, taking time afterward to wash in the sink and clean his teeth, as on a normal morning. Grabbing a furred robe from his room and leaving the coronet behind, he retraced his path to Richard's suite in less haste. Unless this was some elaborate stunt, the king was already long gone. God knew where.

As expected, he found no one in the king's quarters but the hoary soldier who had brought the previous day's summons. Shaking him awake, the Admiral managed to learn a little more. Richard had spent the evening overseeing the packing of a few clothes, a couple of small bags of jewels and coins, and a handful of personal and royal effects, including two ceremonial crowns. He'd also taken along three monastic habits from the chapel and left wearing another. Likewise, he'd ordered twenty horses saddled or packed and had quit the castle at midnight, accompanied by the twelve palace knights who made up his chamber guard, all clad like friars. They had departed in strict silence, under Richard's orders to awaken no one as they stole into the darkness.

The aged soldier didn't know their plans. Indeed, he'd gotten the impression no one but Richard knew. Letting him fall back into well-deserved sleep, Thomas made a quick but thorough search of the castle, verifying the old man's report. Except for their knives, it appeared the "monks" had ridden unarmed, swords and other weapons left behind with many belongings. Obviously, Richard was seeking to hide, not fight. For that much Thomas could be grateful. Richard had indeed transformed himself from a sovereign into a monkish fugitive who chose to vanish rather than confront difficult choices, leaving that chore to others, as usual. His action with the coronet had been typical, too. He hadn't quite shoved it down the privy shaft, to rest among human waste, but he'd come close. Which said exactly what he thought of his kingship these days.

"Hardly worth shit!"

Yet, the king had taken the more ornate crowns of state, suggesting he did not intend to permanently step aside. His note had been equally ambivalent, like Richard himself: part lucid, part cryptic, and mostly infuriating. The order about the royal household was definite enough, though, and Thomas ordered everyone to assemble before noon. Meanwhile, he closeted himself to compose his thoughts and find a bath and fresh clothes.

An hour later he was almost dressed when the door burst open before a disheveled chief constable of the realm: Edward Plantagenet, usually known as Aumale, an abbreviation of his title of Duke of Albemarle.

"Thomas! For God's sake, he's gone."

Head popping from a shirt pulled over grey locks, Thomas looked hard at Aumale and then dove into a tunic, momentarily shutting out his visitor. Aumale might have been cousin to Richard and Henry and son to Edmund of York, but right now he was an unwanted intrusion.

Aumale threw himself to the floor. "What are we supposed to do? Richard's gone. He told me naught. Oh, God," he whined softly, pulling himself up beside the bed and gripping its ornate footrail." Oh, God…"

"I know!" Thomas replied, testily. "And if it's any consolation, he told me naught, either. He left me orders, though." He motioned toward the bed. "Sit. Control yourself. I'll tell you what happened."

He finished a few minutes later. "So Richard's left himself even more vulnerable, wherever he is. "But for the moment, that's his problem."

Aumale fidgeted, nervy as a frightened doe. Bloodshot eyes darting out from blond bangs, he sought reassurance. "What of us?" he whimpered again, angular face puffy and rough with stubble, making him look far older than his twenty-five years. "Where does this leave me? Even my father's with Bolingbroke now." A doughy hand pawed at the bedcovers.

"That's our problem," Thomas pronounced. "Richard has left us on our own. He commanded me to disband the household and troops here. I'm announcing it presently. And I've already sent search parties out, though they won't find much. He's gone," Thomas emphasized. "We must leave, too. You and I have a task, though: Dealing with the rest of his baggage here. You are, or were, his constable, and I his seneschal. You see to whatever of his belongings you and your squires can manage. Transport it yourselves to your own estates for safekeeping. Do it immediately. I'll take responsibility for the rest. I hope to have it on the road ere nightfall. We don't want anything falling to thieves."

Aumale gulped. "Christ … I need some ale."

"That's the last thing you need." Thomas smiled wearily. "But fortify yourself, if you must. Then be about your duty, the king's duty. And may God guide you."

Aumale staggered to his feet and reached the door. "I'll do as you say. 'S'truth. I know not what else to do. But let this be on Richard's head. He has abandoned us, his friends, even I who loved him. The devil take him!"

The door slammed.

Shaking his head, Thomas resumed his preparations for meeting with the household. It wouldn't be one of the happier occasions he'd addressed them.

In late morn they dutifully gathered in the great hall: a dozen household servants, several Cheshiremen, cooks, foot soldiers, archers and more, including the crown herald who had brought the summons to Berwick and then sought to leave Richard and join Harry. Well, his day neared.

Standing before a fireplace, Thomas welcomed them, thanking them for their prompt attention on a difficult day. "I would that I might be the bearer of good tidings," he went on. "But I cannot, as many of you doubtless know…"

Dismantling a royal household and garrison seemed to call for profound words or ceremony. But Thomas found himself too drained for that and chose brevity over brilliance.

Some of the group listened meekly; others sobbed; many looked confused, and several seemed angry.

"Thus," Thomas concluded, "he bid me to close down his royal household, send you to your homes. Everyone must go: servants, soldiers, everyone. Leave, this day. You are no longer in King Richard's employ, nor England's employ. Nor am I."

Many, of course, had nowhere else to go. They'd been with the royal household their whole lives, taking up posts previously held by parents and grandparents or beginning their tenure under Richard's predecessor, Edward III. Where the king went, they went. They were now homeless. At best, they might make their way to

London, seek posts with other noble households, and wait for Richard to return or matters to be sorted out. Other military and household officials had indentures, contracting them to specific terms of service at specific rates of pay. Yet the legality of their termination, as in so much of what he had done, was of little consequence to Richard.

The admiral sought to allay their fears as best he could. "I shall provide letters of reference to any who want them. I'd advise all of you to leave for your towns and homes immediately. If you have none, seek out friends or kinsmen for shelter. See me to collect pay ere you depart. And any who would go to Worcestershire, escorting King Richard's possessions for storage there, tell me. I'll need wagons, teamsters and guards and will welcome any help..."

Raising a hand in quick assent, the crown herald pushed to the fore. Thomas acknowledged the offer with a nod. Others followed.

"Beyond that, there is little I can tell you," he told the group. "We must depart. All. I'm sorry."

Then came the moment he'd been avoiding. Reaching behind to the mantel, he picked up the seneschal's rod, the thin, elegant wooden staff that Richard had given him years earlier. It went everywhere the seneschal and king traveled, signifying that the royal household was in residence and in order. Holding it aloft, Thomas brought it down harshly and broke it over his knee, tossing the parts into the cool hearth. "It is over. The royal household is dissolved. Go now, all."

With that, he raised a hand in farewell and walked quickly from the hall.

Hours later, though, when midnight again neared and he was almost alone in the castle, no one saw him pad back into the hall and retrieve the broken pieces of the staff from the fireplace. Holding them close, like something sacred, he wept softly into the emptiness.

***

A Road from Wales to England

At first, as the admiral squinted into the haze, the white humps looked like chalky boulders, lost from a mason's wagon. But when he and his ten-man party rode closer, he recognized them for what they were: men's bodies, stripped naked and bloating in the sun, their own shadows mingling with bloodstains in ugly patches beside them. Three were on the road, one kinked into a bizarre mimicry of life with legs twisted under arms. Two more lay in shrubs near the verge; three more lay farther on.

"Halt! Weapons ready." Thomas dismounted. "Wait here."

Sword in hand he moved cautiously forward. The first man's torso had been hacked through, entrails sagging on the dirt, reeking with decay. In the bearded face Thomas recognized the crown herald. Two companions sprawled next to him with severed throats. On the grass, one man had been speared through his back; the second there had been stabbed. Those beyond had arrows in them. A couple of the dead had been mutilated: Stuffed between their teeth in contorted mouths, their genitals dangled in a grotesque repudiation of manhood, desecration that was the hallmark of the most rabid anti-English separatists in Wales.

The warmth of sunlight on Thomas' back chilled when he realized the dead were all members of the household he had dismissed a day earlier. This crew had left in late afternoon, four on horseback and four driving wagons into which they had carefully packed gold ornaments and jewels, hidden under common bedding, with silver candlesticks and other finery stowed below grain sacks and bedding.

Here, the wagon tracks dug into the road and then veered off across meadows and vanished, alongside hoofprints. Clearly, whoever was to blame had made off with everything. Thomas cursed inwardly: "Goddamn swine!"

The brigands—Welsh or malcontents of whatever origins posing as Welsh—typically moved silently, springing from nowhere, mowing down travelers like English wheat beneath Welsh hail. They'd been troublesome for years, but of late their numbers and barbarity had increased, fed by a breakdown of authority along the Anglo-Welsh border, especially near Cheshire.

"Richard himself encouraged this," Thomas realized sadly. "All those favors he lavished upon Cheshire, making it a special principality, granting unheard-of pardons from justice to those who dwelt there. All he did was make it a haven for all the miscreants of England, fleeing jail or execution elsewhere, and they spilled over into Wales, too, swaggering through villages, some in Richard's own livery or the colors of his Cheshire guards, stealing with impunity."

Now the results of Richard's largesse lay at Thomas' feet, while his men traded frightened glances, starting at every birdcall.

"We'll hasten our pace." He remounted. "We'd best be close to Bolingbroke's lines by nightfall. These poor fellows," he gestured toward the corpses, "want for burial, but there's too little time and too much risk. And it does them little good for us to die, too."

His men nodded and they galloped on. Within another hour, however, they encountered new groups: Victims still alive, shambling down the road, like a scene from the *Inferno*, penned by that Italian scribe, Dante. Some nude, others mostly so, they propped each other up, moving slowly toward England, away from a Welsh hell.

"God help us," Thomas murmured as he saw them, stumbling and blind, numb to anything but survival. Like the dead retainers down the road, the refugees, several also from Richard's household, had been robbed. For some reason, though, they hadn't been killed. Not that some wouldn't soon be dead anyway, of shock, exhaustion, or wounds, if not succored. So Thomas and his company scrounged in their saddlebags, sharing clothing, food and money. Two of the most desperate were lifted onto spare horses and then Thomas' small force rode on.

But more misery found them, in the form of a second, nearly identical group, and then a third, overtaken in a ghastly regularity. The second and third bands included women (some as naked as the men), several with small children in hand. They represented all ranks and occupations: Squires, a couple of clerics, two knights, seamstresses, merchants, farm families, grooms. Although most were English, a good number were Welsh, kinsmen, spouses, servitors or friends and colleagues of the English, or merely folk who'd offered to help and been attacked, too.

By afternoon, except for the armor and minimal clothing covering their own nakedness, Thomas and his escort were as bereft as the rest—saddlebags empty, food gone, medicine pouches depleted in salving and binding the wounds of others. Walking, fatigued and aching, they bore the most seriously injured on their horses or their own backs.

An ascetic, semi-clad old priest had replaced Thomas in the saddle, and, trudging alongside Thomas felt a new blister open, washing his heel in pain. It joined several others already bloodying his soles, in boots designed more for riding than walking. Limping, he scolded himself for not following his nephew's long-held advice, for Harry never settled for boots he couldn't wear as comfortably on a thirty-mile march as a forty-mile ride. Too long removed from northern scouting and fighting, Thomas had forgotten the wisdom of such simple stubbornness. Now his body cried for revenge.

"Damned murderers!" Gritting his teeth, he pushed on.

Somehow, as the agonizing day proceeded, they avoided further marauders. Twice, hearing rustling, Thomas sent his men into the brush, but they only discovered foraging pigs and a few cows begging to be milked. The pigs bolted but the cows found satisfaction, relieving their own discomfort while easing the pangs of the hungry.

Mile followed distressful mile, but eventually the distance from Wales spread behind them. Still, every sweeping curve; every rocky, muddy furlong; every incline, made safety seem endlessly remote. Finally, with an abiding gratitude, though one they were too weary to express, they saw the campfires of Bolingbroke's army, beacons of salvation in the dusk. Crossing a low hill, they stumbled onward.

Suddenly the outer lines of the army eddied around them. Hands reached out to carry away the wounded and Thomas found himself blessed by the departing old priest as he himself was led toward a familiar tent.

"Uncle!"

The man who had once hugged a lonely, uncertain boy now found himself wrapped in the strength of that same boy's grown-up arms.

"I feared for you." Harry released his hold. "What ... how did you ..."

"I'll tell you all, in time. Now I would rest..."

Thomas entered the tent, Harry's arm supporting him. Noticing the sword propped against a post, he glanced up. "Do me one duty, Harry. You've always been able to find your way in the night. Do so, now. Take good men and extra torches and horses. Find our people. They're out there, down the road, walking, half-dead, naked, set upon by outlaws. We brought the weakest with us. God forgive us, we could not bring them all. Save them for us, for me...."

He eased onto the cot, blissfully closing his eyes.

When he looked up a few minutes later, Harry was gone.

So was the sword.

Chapter IX
August 1399 - Conway Castle, Wales

Richard II, by the grace of God, King of England and Wales, Lord of Ireland and all the rest, leaned against a gate. Peering through the bars, face as wan as the sunlight washing the walls, he surveyed the extent of his domain: Across the next greensward, through another gate to the towers beyond, on to the barbican where castle precincts joined town parapet, then out to the town's exterior defenses...

Or maybe not even that far.

His realm was reduced to this: A long, narrow fortress, perched above the thin strand that disgorged the River Conway and met an encroaching sea.

"This place is supposed to confound foes," he groused silently. "All it does is confine me!"

There were sixteen with him now: the household knights, plus Bishop Thomas Merks of Carlisle; John Montague, Earl of Salisbury, and two squires, down from the mountains that rose in forbidding arcs behind him. Now relaxing inside, Merks and Montague had joined him the previous night—rather tardily, in Richard's opinion. But at least they had come. And that, Richard realized, was notable for Merks, a man so enamored of London comfort that he rarely journeyed anywhere and then only visited his northern diocese to collect tithes due him. Trained in arms, the other newcomer, Salisbury, was known for penning French poetry and had the long dark hair and brooding eyes of a jongleur, albeit one clad in the richest garments Parisian tailors could supply. "Little need for such elegance here."

Richard was anticipating only another monotonous day when deliverance arrived, in an unusual form, the personage of the Earl of Northumberland, seeking parley on Bolingbroke's behalf. Would the king speak with him? The squire who brought the news awaited Richard's reply.

Richard's hand jerked upward. "Admit my good cousin."

Shortly afterward Richard joined Earl Henry, Salisbury, and Merks in a tower room, meek substitute for a royal audience hall.

Decorous enough, Earl Henry dropped to his knee to kiss Richard's hand, though Richard eyed him sharply. "Did you come alone? Or is your ever-faithful son waiting with his ever-brave troops outside, as if I were some reiving Scot?" Dismissively, he motioned the earl up.

"I am alone. Harry's training the levies that rode to the duke's assistance. England's army, My Liege, men your own commanders, save Harry in the north, never bothered to instruct." A flash of pride lit Earl Henry's face. "Ah, but they're looking grand now..."

Richard only glared again. "You bring messages?"

"Yes, My Liege, I come from Duke Henry, steward of England. He bids you welcome home from Eire. And he sends me to reach agreement. He says he hopes to be good friends with you. But he wants you to come to him in person." The earl paused. "And he would ask several graces of you."

"He hopes to be my friend? Better I take one of your Cheviot adders to my bosom!" Richard spoke with a hiss the poisonous northern snake would have envied.

"He regrets anything he has done that you consider an offense, Sire." Earl Henry was as courteous as ever. "He himself would kneel before you and be known as your loving cousin and friend." The earl fell to his own knees again, on Bolingbroke's behalf.

The king turned his back.

"What does he want?" Richard finally faced forward again.

"Three things." Rising, Earl Henry recited from memory: "First, he wishes to have his land, and all that pertains to him, including his high stewardship. But in this he would never have anything that is yours, because you are king. Second, he would that you meet him, ride to London, and convene Parliament, and make known your restoration of his rights. Third, he wants, before this same Parliament, to bring to trial those who have corrupted you and broken the laws of our land. Anyone found guilty of treason or other offenses, can be punished impartially."

"As he did with Bushey," Salisbury muttered from the side of the room.

Earl Henry said nothing. Richard blanched.

"Rest assured," Earl Henry answered. "He wants only for Parliament to resolve such matters, so we may make England great again."

Richard looked unconvinced. "Names he those he would bring to trial?"

Earl Henry frowned. "Naturally, arraignment must wait until we can assemble Parliament, as proper jury and court."

"Name them!"

"My Liege," Earl Henry admonished. "Surely this is not the time, nor the pla—"

"Name them. Are any in this room?"

"My Liege," Earl Henry began, softly, "there are several. I know not all. But they include My Lord the Earl of Salisbury, and His Excellency, the Bishop of Carlisle."

"God's teeth!" Salisbury stepped forward. "I accuse you of high treason, Northumberland. And slander. And I'll have my due from you in trial by combat!"

Merks slumped against the fireplace and crossed himself.

"Done!" Earl Henry retorted to Salisbury, "and gladly."

"Enough!" Richard stepped between them, shoving Salisbury backward. "This will serve no one."

Earl Henry tried to make amends. "I'm sorry, My Liege, and … My Lords," he bowed toward Merks and Salisbury. "I sought to alarm no one. As I said, arraignments must wait on London. And I wish for any man under suspicion to be free to clear himself before Parliament and his peers, as law provides.

"As to my message: Shall My Liege respond to Duke Henry?"

Richard started to answer, but his composure crumbled. "Oh God…." He covered his face with his hands, tears coursing through his fingers. "Oh God… St. Edward, our champion… Jesu Christu, Domini…"

Earl Henry looked at the floor as the sing-song of despair and fear continued. Merks coughed and, like Salisbury, said nothing. Finally, Richard wiped reddened eyes. "Leave us, Northumberland." His voice was a strained whisper. "I would talk to these lords alone."

The earl exited.

Richard had hardly begun to confer with Merks and Salisbury, however, before another astounding visitor showed up, a sea-dampened Archbishop Arundel, with a message identical to Earl Henry's. "Why has he sent two of you, separately, bearing the same terms?" Richard demanded, after hearing him out.

"Prudence, My Liege," Arundel answered. "For us to be believed, and to distress you not, Northumberland and I had to come alone and unarmed. But it risks much for an archbishop or earl, fetching good price as hostages, to travel alone and unarmed. There was no guarantee Northumberland would not be seized by your men, or taken by Welsh outlaws. Or that I would not. So, My Lord of Lancaster dispatched both of us: the earl by road, in case I failed; and I by sea, as surety should he be waylaid."

"Or, equally likely," Richard thought, "should you, My Lord Archbishop, twist Henry's terms to foil me, still hating me for your exile and brother's death. Or should Northumberland prove false to Henry and try to craft his own bargain with me... But it seems you both spoke true. You bear Northumberland out, and he you."

He studied the archbishop for a few moments and then sent him off to join Earl Henry. Alone with his counselors, Richard resumed the conversation. "Gentlemen: I think we must grant their wishes. Verily, if it be as the Earl of Northumberland and Archbishop Arundel reported, I think Bolingbroke and I might make a good peace. For now." He paused. "But I also tell you: Whatever peace I do make with him here, as soon as I can, I will behead him, as he deserves."

Both Merks and Salisbury nodded, although it was unclear whether they were agreeing to Bolingbroke's execution or to the fact they had little recourse but to defer to him.

"Let there be no doubt among you," Richard added. "There shall be no Parliament on these matters and no trials. I would not see my friends go to London to die."

Merks grasped at other possibilities. "Is there no other way?" He looked at Salisbury. "Did you not leave men in the hills?"

Salisbury nodded.

"So what of them?"

It was Richard who responded. "We don't know how many are left." Still, even as he spoke, an idea took shape, fed by something Arundel had mentioned. "Or mayhap," he continued, with the old calculating smile. "Arundel spoke of the Welsh. To be sure, the Welsh are oft brigands. But Welsh knives and knaves might still be ours, if they can be used against Bolingbroke." The thought expanded. "And the Cheshiremen, those who tried to join us at Carmarthen, they will fight for us. I'm sure of it."

"But Sire," Salisbury recalled. "You ordered your seneschal to send everyone home, the Cheshiremen, too."

"Why, so I did," Richard remembered, happily. "And by now the Cheshiremen will most certainly be home. But Cheshire is close to us. The better to rally them."

He pulled Merks and Salisbury near. "Send your squires away, with two or three chamber knights—immediately, ere Northumberland and Arundel know our true number. They must go to the mountains, find our men there, and rally Cheshire. As soon as they have strength, they can show our banners openly. Then the people will come back, repenting the great wrongs done me. And as for Bolingbroke and his ilk: I'll flay them alive!" he tittered, eyes darting. "Today, though, I shall ride to Bolingbroke to make peace—for today." He laughed again, in discordant shrieks.

Merks nudged Salisbury, speaking in low tones. "Lunacy."

"Or parlous gamble," Salisbury agreed, "and our only chance." He dipped his head to the king, as Richard's laughter trailed off. "So be it, Majesty. Recall these emissaries; agree to Bolingbroke's terms."

But Merks had one more caveat. And so Arundel and Northumberland found themselves in the chapel, swearing to the agreement by oath upon the sacred host. Then they dispersed: Arundel to return by ship and alert Bolingbroke; Earl Henry next, leaving Richard to collect his belongings and soon follow. And indeed, two hours later, with his remaining knights Richard rode off as promised, taking the road toward Rhuddlan, to rejoin Earl Henry and dine before the journey into England.

Fast upon its ancient rocks, Conway slumbered in silence again.

* * *

Rural Cheshire, England

Henry Bolingbroke stretched his nakedness on silken bedcovers and reached toward the nude woman resting at his side. Pulling her atop his legs, her full breasts dangling, he curved his hands over her buttocks. Hips pushed and his male stalk rose, stout and pulsing, finding its entry as she straddled him. Her hands fondling his chest as his petted hers, he closed his eyes as desire reached a most satisfying culmination. She shrieked, too, equally exuberant, and he lowered himself back against the bed. Still astride, she retreated down his legs and regarded him with shy interest.

Voluptuously plump, she had a pretty circle of a face peeking from long, black tendrils of hair. Her eyes, jet like her hair, were small and coy; her legs stocky and pink, ending in amazingly delicate—and clean—feet.

She said something in Welsh, which he didn't understand, but her smile was bright, and he touched each breast in turn, reassuring her in English. "Magnificent!"

She seemed to comprehend the sentiment, if not every word, for she was as ignorant of English as he was of Welsh. Boldly, she smiled and tweaked his beard before reaching to tweak the coarse hair at the other end of his anatomy as well. He yelped, more surprised than hurt, and swatted her naked backside. Giggling, she began running her hands over him, up and down, up and down, until he realized his excitement was beginning anew.

"Would that I could fill all my hours as easy!" he murmured as they resumed her witchery and his pleasure.

Afterward, the young woman lay down, facing the opposite end of the bed, rubbing his legs and kissing his feet. Relaxing against the pillows, he began comparing this latest conquest with his other triumphs of late. Just as he had taken her—and she had given herself freely—had he not claimed all of England? Did not England herself leap to do his bidding, even as this woman had?

Yea...

He didn't even know her name; she was a dalliance, to be forgotten when he left this pleasant manor. Until then, however, he would make the most of her intoxicating charms, just as he always tried to seize unforeseen opportunities.

She was licking her way up his thighs, and he was about to succumb to another urgent throbbing in his loins, when an equally urgent rapping on the door distracted his mind and body.

He said nothing. The rapping continued. "God's blood—what?"

"The Earl of Westmorland, My Lord," the guard outside shouted. "Shall I admit him?"

Bolingbroke threw a leg over the bed. "Fuck!"

This word the Welsh woman knew, and she looked up in pleased expectation. But he only laughed, touched a nipple with his fingertip, and kissed her mouth hard. "No. But stay." Wrapping himself in a robe, he threw the bedcovers over the woman's nudity as someone knocked sharply again.

Henry swung the door open, glowered at Ralph Neville, allowed him to enter, and slammed the door shut.

Seeing the woman, Ralph grinned. "My recommendation was well-received. I chanced across her yesterday and had her myself last night, delectably so. And once I knew she wouldn't put a dagger in a sleeping Englishman, I sent her to you."

In the bed, the woman yawned as she recognized him and burrowed deep under the covers.

Ralph shook back his mouse-brown hair, cut off abruptly around his ears and shaved halfway up the back, in the old Norman style. He was tall, a typical Neville, but tending toward overweight and intimidating in his bulkiness, unlike his lanky and lighter brother, Lord Furnival.

"Come to reclaim her?" Bolingbroke asked, annoyed that the woman's visit had not been spontaneous.

"No, she's yours. I found another, not as pretty as this, but with better English, the better to tell her my wants." Ralph grinned again. "Of course, this one's Welshness has certain advantages. She cannot make demands of you or understand what we say."

He helped himself to some of Henry's ale. "Which is well, since we must talk. And then you can while away the rest of the afternoon."

Claiming a chair, he went on. "We must act quickly. We risk losing support here. These border idiots have always liked Richard. We've got to rein in some of our men, or they could cost us dearly."

"How so?"

"They're behaving like vandals. There've been complaints even of murders. Today I had a dozen mayors, vicars, and local gentry—some who would otherwise back you—waiting for me, pissed as a swarm of angry hornets. Their folk are being robbed blind, they said. They want it stopped."

Bolingbroke waved absently. "It's always thus, in war or when armies march. And it may be Richard's men, as much as ours. I see no cause for alarm."

"It threatens your support," Ralph explained. "Even with my brother Thom. He has lands nearby, you know. He was going to call up his forces to join us. But he told me today that he'll likely keep them at home instead, to defend his people, if the pillaging continues."

"Are all our levies doing it?"

"No. A few are worst: your men, Henry, men from the house of Lancaster. It's been happening since Bristol. The killings, too. I hear my cousin Harry investigated one case there himself. He concluded that your men were to blame. My brother, Thom, has been talking to Harry, also. You know how Thom has always looked up to him." Ralph shrugged, almost apologetically. "Harry was already drilling the men, the better to keep them from trouble, he said, and instill pride in them as honorable soldiery. Now he's been from one end of our camp to the other, lecturing on the rules of war."

Henry groaned.

Ralph nodded. "He worships the code of chivalry and thinks all the rest of us should, too. I find it truly tiresome, myself. But I'm not Harry."

"Thank God!" Bolingbroke slapped Ralph's back. "One is more than enough!" He twitched his beard. "As to these rampaging men, though: Perhaps you're right. But who could control them? It's one levy today, another on the morrow, a third after that—my men, yours, any lord's. I'll be damned if I'll trouble myself over it. Still, I want no cause for provocation, either among folk here or the Welsh across the dike." He returned to the bed, stretched out next to the dozing woman, looked at her longingly for a moment, and studied the ceiling.

Neville finished more of Henry's ale and picked his teeth with a penknife.

Finally, Bolingbroke arose, sighing. "God knows we all have enough on our hands. But I need a commander-in-chief, someone to lead the whole army: my men, your men, every lord's men; a strong man, able to handle many needs at once, and with the proper stature as well. Skilled in fighting and leading men in battle. Intelligent, too."

Neville's interest piqued.

"But I think I know just the man..." Henry cast a sidelong look at Neville, holding it, and the latter turned pink, grinning.

"I would be honored to be this commander," Ralph replied. "True, you've already made me acting marshal of England. But a capable man, as you say, is capable of much. And it must be someone with proper nobility."

"To be sure." Bolingbroke smiled. "That's why I intend to ask your northern cousin. Not you. I have other important work for you."

Neville deflated. "The Earl of Northumberland? You've already made him interim constable, sent him to find Richard. But if you wish him to be commander…"

"Not your senior Northumbrian cousin," Bolingbroke added, enjoying Neville's discomfort. "The other Lord Percy. Harry."

"Hotspur?" Neville gaped. "He's only a knight—no earl, much less a duke. Hardly a high nobleman."

Bolingbroke paused, reconsidering. It was true: Kings ranked first, followed by dukes, earls, barons, and then, on the lowest rung, knights. Whatever he might become on his father's death, Harry was still only a knight—and not even one ambitious enough to have wrested a higher rank for himself from Arundel's downfall two years earlier, as Ralph and he himself had. He scratched his moustache thoughtfully.

"Besides," Neville pressed his point. "Harry disagrees with what we did to Bushey and his ilk at Bristol. Who knows what else he thinks? Weren't you just complaining about him, too?"

"I was. But who's better placed to command our army? Who's a better fighter? Who's more respected, on the field or off? No one. And he needs no title as high lord. All of England regards him as the greatest knight in the realm. Many consider him the best in any land, anywhere. What more could I ask?

"Besides, it will serve him right," Bolingbroke emphasized, thumping knotted fingers against Neville's chest. "He wants law and order among our troops? He wants us to follow the rules of war? He wants us to honor his damned code of chivalry? Fine. Let him be commander. Let him govern the camp. Let him see all is done correctly." He smiled, red-gold head nodding and eyes closing into amber crescents, like those of a contented fox.

Neville pondered. "It may have merit." He spoke slowly, tested the proposal again, and then beamed. "Yea, I see it: Let Harry worry about some rule of war. Let's concern ourselves with rule of England!"

They exchanged knowing glances.

* * *

Saturday, 16 August 1399 - Flint Castle, Wales

The music reached Flint Castle first, drums and horns and the bittersweet trill of those pipes favored by Northumbrians and Scots. Next, the troops appeared: regiments orderly, steeds prancing, weapons ready. Mirroring sky and sea, their armor shone, their lines a streak of silver-blue along the coastal road. At the fore, the commander's pennant snapped in the breeze, lions and fish marching steadily closer, to halt beyond the castle walls.

From his bench atop the rounded keep, Richard watched them come: His army, his horses, his lances.

Except they weren't.

They now belonged to Henry Bolingbroke, Duke of Lancaster and High Steward of England, as he styled himself. High steward of England...

Well, that much Richard was willing to concede. Even more, he might give up—if he chose. But it had to be *his* choice.

Below, they began to fill the flats that shadowed Flint on two sides and separated the castle from the hamlet beyond. He stood on the parapet as they drew up row by row and rank by rank, scarcely a man or horse out of place. "Never have they moved so well, or looked so magnificent," he realized, both proud and frightened. "And Percy junior commands them... Damn him."

Even now, though, if he had to pick between Percies to condemn, he would rather have had the senior in his clutches. The humiliation of the trip from Conway gnawed. He and his companions had ridden peaceably toward Rhuddlan as intended. Short of the castle, they had rounded a curve and confronted an armed force, with Earl Henry in front, sword unsheathed.

"Treachery!" Richard had cried to his friends. "Ride hard, back to Conway. Save yourselves!" But another force had slipped from the hills behind, surrounding them, cutting off hope.

"Treason!" Richard had protested. "You betray us."

"No, My Liege, I save you," Earl Henry had answered. "These hills are thick with bandits. Had I not brought guards, then, yea, I most certainly would have betrayed you, allowing you to risk death or capture as a hostage. I had fortune's favor to make it alone this morn, leaving my men behind here to patrol. But you and I would be idiots to think we could ride all the way to Cheshire without protection."

With little alternative, Richard had acquiesced, seething inside. The worst of it was that Earl Henry was both so deceptive–arriving at Conway alone, misleading everyone–and undeniably correct: Traveling unescorted would have been foolhardy.

So here Richard was, atop Flint, encircled. With a final glance over the walls, he retreated below. It was time for lunch, and he would not postpone it, no matter how magnificently all those men aligned outside. Let them wait.

He was, after all, King of England.

―――

From his place ahead of the troops, though well back from the walls, Harry saw his uncle, Archbishop Arundel, and Aumale ride to the castle entrance and gain entry. Everything remained calm, and after a few minutes, he began wondering if he had grossly overreacted. The bulk of their army remained in Cheshire, but he'd brought several thousand along. Yet there was no sign of any force mustered on Richard's behalf. Only a couple of guards stood on the castle parapet, and lethargy seemed to cloak its every stone.

No movement at all occurred until a flourish trumpeted the arrival of Bolingbroke with the Earl Henry and several others. They, too, were promptly admitted.

The sun stretched lazily across the sky. On the Dee estuary, flanking the road, a rowboat bobbed. Inland, the twitter of birds blended with the occasional dog's bark and lumbering of a wagon through the town. Near serenity prevailed.

Nonetheless, for another half hour, Harry remained in stony attentiveness, eyes either on the castle or sweeping the circumference around him. Finally, he retrieved his copy of Vegetius' *Epitome of Military Science* from his saddlebag and began reading: *"On recruitment ... every recruit should in summer learn the art of swimming, for rivers are not always crossed by bridges, and armies both when advancing and retreating are frequently forced to swim... ."*

"That's one thing I've not drilled them in," he muttered, looking toward the shore. "I wonder..." His gaze returned to his well-worn book. Like other military men he was fond of Vegetius, a Roman who had lived one thousand years earlier but come much in vogue of late. Finishing another page, he surveyed the castle once more, saw its lassitude unchanged, and nudged Valdus down the lines, ordering the men to stand at ease.

Back in place, he dismounted and summoned Hardyng. "See if you can get into the castle. Politely: I don't want to have to rush the drawbridge to save your hide. Go afoot. Leave your sword and shield but take your writing tablet. See what's going on in there. Take notes, if you can."

The squire strung a leather-bound case over his shoulder and sauntered off as if he had no care in the world. Reaching the castle without hindrance, he disappeared around the side.

In far less time than Harry anticipated, he was back.

"'Tis all over!" Hardyng crowed. "The king is coming out, with Bolingbroke. Your uncle got me in," he added, guessing Harry's next question. "When I went 'round the back, a servant recognized our badge and thought I belonged with Lord Thomas. So I heard all!

"They conferred but briefly, Richard and Bolingbroke. Richard had come down, just as I caught up to them. He'd made Bolingbroke wait until he finished eating and talked to Archbishop Arundel."

He thumbed through parchment sheets on his tablet. "First, Bolingbroke bowed and took off his cap, and so Richard took off his hood, too, and said, 'My Fair Cousin, I welcome you right well.' It all looked a bit silly to me, like they were overdoing their courtesies. Probably they wanted to kill each other. But, anyway, then Bolingbroke said this: 'I have come back sooner than you sent for me, My Lord, and have good reasons. Everyone says that you have for twenty-two years governed them—all of us—very badly. And they are not content. But, if it pleases you, My Liege, I will help you govern better.' Then he bowed again.

"And then Richard looked kind of sick. But he said: 'If it pleases you, it pleases me.' Then they shook hands and smiled at everyone. Bolingbroke called for horses to be readied, and soon they will leave."

"Naught else happened?" Harry was surprised. "No fits from Richard? Or accusations from Bolingbroke? Nary a word from anyone else?"

Hardyng shook his head. "No. Perchance the meatiest talk occurred earlier. I heard the archbishop met with Richard for a long time, telling him no harm would befall and that we seek only to improve his rule. Mayhap that satisfied him."

"It should. 'Tis the truth. But thank God there's no need for arms." Harry remounted and began to turn Valdus.

"One more thing, Harry," Hardyng added. "Bolingbroke bids you to begin moving the men out only after he and the king depart. He wants to take Richard over to Chester as quickly as possible and not be encumbered by all these." He cocked a finger toward the lines.

"Even so," Harry agreed.

A few moments later, a small party exited the castle gate and headed east. Harry identified Bolingbroke, his uncle and others. Slumped in their midst was Richard, King of England. They rode rapidly, and after the last dust had settled, Harry ordered the army to follow.

By evening, they were all back at Chester: Bolingbroke with Richard and other high lords in the castle, Harry scuffing his boots in campfire grit, ready for a few rounds of ale with his lieutenants.

Chapter X
August 1399 - Rural Cheshire

The ragged line stretched across the road. Men stood at the front, a half-dozen with swords or maces, a few with spears or bows, the rest with knives, axes, pitchforks, cudgels, and whatever else they could find. Behind them came boys and women with staves, hatchets, scythes, scissors, and even long-handled skillets. Perhaps one hundred and fifty in all, they wore the drab black, russets and greens of commoners, nary a knight or reeve among them. Standing steadfast, they fingered their weapons with work-stained hands, proud and defiant, lifetimes of survival behind many.

Trotting down the road from the opposite direction, Harry approached with two hundred knights, men-at-arms, and mounted archers, responding to reports of a possible mob on the move. Henry, Richard, and the bulk of the army had already left for London, and in their wake the worst thing to occur had been a nocturnal attack on Henry's personal baggage train. But rumors flew that Richard had secretly summoned a host from Wales.

Closing the distance, Harry got a good look ahead–and abruptly halted.

"Oh My God."

Withdrawing his hand from his sword hilt, he turned to Knayton. "I'm going forward to speak to them. Do nothing."

"Unless they try to seize you or cut you down."

Harry smiled, pulling off his gauntlets. "If I'm overcome by old wives or farmers, I deserve my fate. Besides, I'm justice here now, and they're my liegemen and responsibility. But help me get this helmet off and take my shield. I hope to learn their purpose quickly," he added. "Cover me, but without undue show of arms."

Bareheaded, mail cowl loose around his neck, sword in its scabbard, he walked on. For the first few yards, he said nothing, but then paused. "Hold your weapons. I come in peace."

After several moments' silence, someone cried out: "Let him come, lads."

So he kept going until a figure pushed to the fore, and a spear whistled through the air. Harry felt its downdraft as he ducked; it skewered the ground at his heels. Shouts erupted from the crowd, with a simultaneous furor from Knayton and their soldiers. Biting back anger, Harry spun around to address the latter.

"Hold your fire. No harm done. Remain as you are."

Confusion continued among the civilians.

Stooping, Harry picked up the spear and strode on. The first ranks of the crowd parted in mute uneasiness as he plunged into their midst to tap the shoulder of a middle-aged farmer. Extending the spear, handle first, he smiled wryly. "I think you dropped this."

Slowly, the man took it. The crowd fell back as if expecting to be mowed down by Harry's companions. But he gave no such order and left his sword sheathed on his hip.

"Who's your leader this fine morn?"

A stocky, tonsured friar in the robes of a Franciscan jostled forward. "I'll speak for them. These are my parishioners. I am Robin Bordhewer, vicar of this parish."

"And this is my brother, Odom." The friar placed an arm around the spear-wielding farmer. "He once was under-reeve and man-at-arms to King Richard but took a bad fall from a horse. It riled the humours in his brain and he suffers fits of near-craziness at times.

Mostly, though, he's fine. He helped gather these folk. And I came along to offer whatever ministry I could."

"What's your intent?"

"We march to Chester." The friar seemed conciliatory but cautious. "More than that, I will say only to King Richard. Or, if he be gone, to the justice of Chester. Now, sir, if you would kindly stand aside, we can be on our way."

"The king left, yestere'en, with Henry Bolingbroke, Duke of Lancaster," Harry informed him.

"Then I will go to the justice." The friar took a step ahead. "We'll use our weapons only if thieves accost us, so please tell your men to let us pass. And we can be off to Chester."

"No need."

"I'll be the judge of that." The friar prepared to elbow his way onward.

"Peace, good Father." Harry placed a hand on the cleric's shoulder. "I only meant you need not go to Chester to see the justice. I am the justice—ad hoc, but still the justice. Sir Harry Percy."

"And your writ?"

"From Duke Henry, issued as high steward of England, afore he left Chester. 'Tis my charge now to uphold the laws of England here, equally and impartially amongst all."

"A rare miracle!" someone shouted.

"Aye. But, God willing, 'twill be so."

"Amen to that," Friar Robin agreed. He borrowed a pitchfork, stuck its tines down in the dirt, and leaned on it as if at his pulpit.

"We wanted to speak with you," he said as his parishioners clustered around. "We want assurances that those who favor the king will be treated fairly. We intend no harm, but we're affrighted. We heard what happened elsewhere: Men slain at Bristol, houses burned, churches looted, livestock driven off. We want to live in peace, as the loyal sons of King Richard that we are. We seek respect."

"My respect you have," Harry replied, "as long as you continue to earn it, as I trust you'll respect me. To begin with, though: Do you know anything about an ox cart—laden with grain, horse tack, and the like—taken from the cavalcade of the Duke of Lancaster?"

A low murmur rumbled through the crowd. Friar Robin turned, conducted a whispered consultation with a few others, and faced Harry again.

"There are," he said delicately, "four such oxen on my church green, not far hence—a large wagon, too. I spied the beasts and the rest of them in someone's yard. He'd never had anything so fine, and when I enquired, he admitted all. As penance in confession, I bade him fetch the lot of it to the church till I could address it properly." The friar swallowed. "He and his accomplices agreed. They're not evil lads, only given to temptation sometimes. They realized they couldn't use or sell it without suspicion. And we all feared reprisals. It was something I hoped to discuss with the justice. I wanted guarantees no one would be harmed if everything was returned."

Harry rubbed his forehead. "You say the oxen and other goods are close to hand? Can you bring them now?"

The friar nodded, turning to confer further with his congregants. A minute later, Odom and four men slipped across the fields.

"What of our possessions?" a woman asked. "Will you take them as penalty?"

"If the duke's property and beasts are returned whole, the matter is closed," Harry said. "But I expect no more trouble, for next time, I will come down hard on offenders and those who shelter them."

They nodded.

"Now, what else would you have of me?"

An old goatherd shouted. "Tell us of your battles in the North. And is it true you eat Scotsmen for breakfast?"

"Nay!" Harry feigned outrage, speaking in his deepest northern brogue. "'Tis a grievous falsehood. I only eat them for dinner!"

They laughed easily with him, and he was telling tales of the Borders when Odom and his companions returned with the oxen, pulling a wagon piled with gear, including horse blankets emblazoned with Bolingbroke's crest.

"I am grateful," Harry added, "and I'll not forget."

Bowing solemnly, Friar Robin addressed his flock. "Good people. 'Tis nigh unto noon. Our gardens need weeding, our fields fill with hay, our shops look for their owners, our bread is unbaked. Let us be about our tasks and leave the mustering of armed hosts to Sir Harry until he calls for us."

They began to turn back, scythes and axes held at their sides, oxen and wagon left on the road.

Harry's hand rested on the friar's arm. "Thank you. I will follow Duke Henry to London shortly. But I will doubtless return after Michaelmas, ere I leave Cheshire to the keeping of a permanent lord justice. Should cause arise meanwhile, send to me."

The friar shook hands warmly, and then Odom reached for Harry's hand as well. "My Lord, I am your man. Call on me, at will."

"I shall," Harry smiled. "And keep working with that spear. Looks like you could stand a little more practice!"

He grabbed the halters of the lead oxen and led the wagon back to Knayton. "Bolingbroke's missing belongings. See everything is inventoried; then send it on to London."

Knayton nodded and then, a bit annoyed, asked: "Is that what took so long?"

"In part. It seemed best to not involve anyone else in our parleys."

"Well enou..." Knayton responded. "But I was worried. And sore tempted to run that damned fool spearman straight through!"

"So was I," Harry admitted. "But now I'm just hungry."

Chester Castle

Harry and Knayton were finishing an impromptu lunch with his chaplain, Ian Kynge, and other aides when a clamor arose from the bailey. Instinctively, their eyes sought their weapons piled against a wall.

Kynge rose, glanced through a narrow window and hastened for the stairs. "Seems the watch has captured a couple of men. I'll calm things down."

Harry nodded but left the table and one of Agnes' fresh loaves, reluctantly trading a bread knife for his sword. Strapping it on, he peered outside.

A restless crowd milled below, among them the Northumbrians and Cheshiremen he'd combined into a new local watch. They were trying to protect two figures in dark monk's robes, cowering on the ground as other men lunged at them with knives or spears. Alongside the watch was a third man in the garb of the white canons, holding his pectoral cross high and attempting to dissuade the mob from violence.

From the corner of his eye, as he abandoned the window, Harry saw someone snake a rope, knotted with a noose, over an archway in the wall, tying the end to a hitching ring in taut readiness. The pack surged toward it, pushing the watchmen, the peacemaking canon, and two captives onward. The two looked oddly familiar, and Harry suddenly realized they were not monks at all but lieutenants of Richard's once-powerful guard.

Charging down the stairs, he met his chaplain, ascending. "You'd best come quick..." Kynge spoke in gasps as they rushed to the yard. "Some of the town ... mean ... to kill them..."

"Get Knayton and the rest," Harry ordered, but his companions were already barreling down the steps after him.

Sword in hand, he ran across the courtyard and cut the noose. Plunging into the mob, he cleared a perimeter at blade point around Richard's guardsmen. "Let no man move—or risk tasting steel." He pivoted slowly in their midst. "And anyone with arms, except the watch, drop them. Now!"

Knives and spears struck a metallic surrender as Knayton and his other aides quietly filled in behind.

"What's going on?" Harry asked.

A Northumbrian answered. "We found them," he gestured toward the pair, "on the road to Oswestry, in that shrine to St. Oswald. Took off like scared hares, they did, when we neared. These lads," he nodded toward local members of the watch, "recognized them as the king's men, but more scum than men, likely. We chased 'em to bring them back here, sort things out. This Father," he motioned toward the canon, "was praying at St. Oswald's. He got them to come along peaceful-like. But when we reached town, all these other folk came after us, fixing to make short work with the rope ... sayin' they had no use for Richard's churls, seein' as how they'd abused folks for years, bullyin' and lording it o'er all... We beat our way here."

One of the Chester watchmen continued. "And we found these on them." He untied a small leather sack. Out tumbled gold coins, jeweled pendants, three miniature silver reliquaries, and a shiny signet ring.

Harry sheathed his sword to pick up the ring. Brass... Studying it, especially the insignia cut into it, he spat and formed a bit of mud, tamping it with his boot. He tried the ring. There, stamped on the ground, was the personal seal of Richard, King of England. Except it wasn't quite Richard's seal, for a nearly unnoticeable wavy line at the top shouldn't have been there. Cleaning the ring face, Harry found the same tiny line incised. But only someone familiar with Richard's genuine seal would notice it or understand that Richard's ring was gold, not brass.

"Counterfeit!" Harry tossed it aside.

He towered over Richard's men. "Get up." They did, with as much dignity as they could manage, dusting themselves off. "Where did you get it, and the rest of this stuff?"

"From King Richard, when we tried to join him at Carmarthen, My Lord," one answered. "And he gave us the other things, too, bidding us go until he would send for us."

"He said we're free to use the ring howe'er we wanted," the second man commented. "He said it'd confuse Lord Bolingbroke, and many others, if letters under the signet suddenly appeared here, and there, and then someplace else. Perhaps," he speculated, "'twas not the only ring King Richard gave out."

"Doubtless not." Harry swore silently. Ingenious of Richard–and diabolically like him–to counterfeit his own signet ring, used for letters or writs when the great seal was inappropriate. Perhaps hundreds of documents, fraudulent, were surreptitiously flooding the country, to be used for illicit purposes or held in reserve to wreak future havoc. Equally inventive of Richard to put some tiny imperfection in the fake rings, so, if necessary, he could point to the flaw, impressed on some document, and disavow the whole thing as a forgery. Since forgery was a form of treason, it was even a way of eliminating unsuspecting minions, no longer needed for doing his dirty work, and easily discovered, found guilty, and executed.

Harry's stomach constricted in disgust.

Did these two know that? Or were they as stupid as they were greedy, hoping to use the ring for themselves, ignorant of the danger? Then again, could they be altogether innocent–thinking the ring real and that they somehow had been entrusted with some of Richard's most personal goods? No matter, for now. These were questions for a judicial court, not something for him to take up in the heat of the moment.

"Your names?"

"Sir Furman Waltheres," one replied, echoed by the other's "Sir Guilbert Gilespie."

Knights both, and royal servants, and certainly worthy of indictment under the law of treason.

Harry deliberated briefly before waving to two sergeants. "Lock them up 'til morn. Then prepare an escort of two or three of you. I'll assign a couple of knights to go along. Take them to London, to the Tower. They'll stand trial before Parliament, as is proper. And guard them well tonight. I want no illicit executions here." He replaced the ring and other items in the sack, throwing it to one of the sergeants. "Guard this, too."

They led their prisoners off. In the back of the crowd, the canon was starting toward the gate when Harry again noticed him. Small and slight, he wore his grey hair short but, despite his robe, untonsured.

"My God," Harry told himself, "there seems to be a surfeit of paters wandering Cheshire. First that friar on the road, now this one..."

"Good Father," he called out.

The canon bowed. "My compliments," Harry said. "I'm sorry your peaceful stop by St. Oswald's nearly came to violence. I'm grateful for your help. May we give you refreshment at our table?"

"No, My Lord, thank you. I've delayed enough." The canon's voice bore traces of a Welsh upbringing despite his impeccable English. "I was on my way to Wrexham. Now that all has ended well here, I must continue. By your leave."

"Of course."

The canon departed.

"As for you," Harry glared at the crowd, diminishing as men slunk away. "Know that I am lord here now and will uphold the law. Without exceptions. Reclaim your weapons and go. Be glad I don't charge you with attempted murder. And let us never see the likes of this day again."

They left far more quietly than they had come, and Harry's men barred the gate.

He pulled a few coins from his waist pouch and beckoned the watch. "Well done. You have spared us much mishap—all of you, from the town as well as from my own levies. Go now. Keep the taverns or shops busy. Surprise your sweethearts by coming home early. You are relieved of further duty this day."

They wandered off, amicably debating the merits of Cheshire versus Northumbrian ale.

"How about some ale or wine for us?" Knayton asked.

"You go," Harry sighed. "See if Richard or Bolingbroke left anything in the cellars. Enjoy it. But, alas, I've still got too many letters and petitions waiting. Looks as if no one has tended to governance here for years."

Later that afternoon Hardyng burst into Harry's quarters, exhausting anteroom and bedchamber before finding his lord on a porch overlooking a garden.

"Harry! Hey Harry ... My Lord." Hardyng momentarily subdued his excitement and remembered his manners. "See this."

"See what?" Harry looked up from a writing table laden with documents. "And where have you been lo' these many hours? I could've used you."

"The abbey. You told me to offer my services to Brother Gildas since he helped us with your orders that first evening. Remember? When you issued that writ, telling everyone that you'd govern equitably and that all should feel free to approach you, and–"

"Aye, I recall. And?"

"I've been with Brother Gildas in their library. He showed me their chronicles. Oh Harry, 'tis marvelous, what they have." Hardyng's eyes danced. "The history of all England and beyond! Book upon book, some written here, others penned elsewhere and exchanged with Chester. All about King Richard, and King Edward before him, and the second Edward, and the first, and his father—back to the Lionheart and the Conqueror, and earlier even. This, too, about you."

He shoved a vellum under Harry's hands. "Brother Gildas wrote that today. He says he's going to send copies to all the monasteries, to add to their chronicles just as he is adding it to his. And that was before we knew you'd quieted some other riot here, within these very walls."

Harry started to read. But before he could get beyond the first few words, Hardyng grabbed the sheet, as Knayton and others drifted in.

"It mentions King Richard's acquiescence to Henry," Hardyng explained, reading aloud: *"And what a wonder that the whole realm was pacified and stabilized in so little time. Except for some Cheshiremen, who raised an upheaval against Duke Henry, purloining the duke's transport. But through the uprightness of Harry Percy, their folly was checked."*

Cheers and applause broke out. Harry reddened, leaving his desk. "Enou!" In mock annoyance, he began pushing Knayton and the rest from the room. "Let monks dally o'er wild stories. You and I have work to do."

Grumbling good-naturedly, they retreated, except Hardyng. "What else needs to be done?"

Harry thought a moment. "Take down an order. I'm going to release the army, all the levies, including ours. Several of us will remain here, temporarily. The rest can go home."

Hardyng picked up a pen.

"And find Knayton again when we're finished," Harry continued. "He can lead our men back north—Agnes too, though I'll miss her cooking. She can keep the kitchen at Berwick, 'til something else turns up that suits her fancy."

"And where will *we* go, from here?" Hardyng wondered.

Harry smiled. "London!"

Chapter XI
Early September 1399 – London

Surrounded by Henry's entourage, a bedraggled Richard II arrived in London, where he found welcome sleep before reality punctured dreams of deliverance.

As he slumbered near dawn, a crowd raged from the Guild Hall to the Tower. Led by London's mayor, the mob chased the guards from the Tower walls and stormed the keep. Awakening to a nightmare, Richard fled to a heavy cabinet used to collect dirty bedding. Buried beneath unwashed sheets, his sweaty nightshirt enhancing the camouflage, he heard his pursuers rumble past.

Failing to locate him, they cornered lesser prey, a quartet of his palace knights, whom they dragged to the courtyard, pummeled into unconsciousness, and roped behind horses. The mayor hastily declared them guilty of crimes and sent them to the seafood market in Cheapside. Thrown onto the fishmongers' stone slabs, they were beheaded faster than cooks filleted a trout, their battered bodies trussed to gibbets and severed heads festooning the walls.

Closeted with Neville at his manor, Bolingbroke shared the news. Ralph trembled, color eroding from his lips: "My Lord, shall I send our guard to arrest this mayor and rabble? This is monstrous." (After all, unlike the Bristol executions, these came at the hands of a mob, without even the pretense of a trial.)

"Why?" Henry viewed Neville in mild surprise. "I ordered our men at the Tower to permit the citizens of London unhindered access to their king and his minions. Perhaps they were over-eager to see justice done. What of it? They've spared us the cost and time of a trial before the peers." He grinned. "On our journey here, Richard promised his friends there'd be no trials before Parliament for them. At least for these four, it seems he was right." He turned to a list before him. "Now, give me your ideas on entertainment and wines for our banquet. I've received word that my uncle Edmund of York, the Earl of Northumberland, Archbishop Arundel, and others are scarce two hours away. I wish to welcome them lavishly."

Bowl haircut wagging assent, Neville wondered aloud: "Does Harry ride with them?" And if so, he asked himself, would Hotspur protest the latest executions, as he had objected to those at Bristol?

"I've heard nothing of his approach," Henry replied. "And my spies are instructed to warn me as he nears the city. He intended to bide in Chester long enough to settle affairs there. I doubt we'll see him soon."

Neville smiled, relieved. One discontent per day was plenty.

———

Mid-September 1399 - Fairgrounds, London

Harry ran his hands over the chestnut's withers and examined her teeth with delicate quickness. Her ears dipped forward as she rewarded his gentleness with a lick. He was kneeling to check her hooves when robes rustled on her other side. Looking under her girth, Harry saw a round face peering back, pale eyes owlish behind thick lenses.

It was the white canon.

"Good morrow, Father! We seem to have picked the same horseflesh." Harry straightened. "You were at Chester that day."

"Yea, My Lord." The priest stood, too. "Your squires said to seek you here. Grand weather for a horse fair it is." He extended a hand below the mare's nostrils, patting her shoulder with the other. "And what a grand animal this is."

The mare sniffed his palm and rewarded him, too, with velvety nuzzling. Laughing in simple delight, the priest turned back toward Harry. "I'm Adam Usk."

Harry mentally sifted the name.

"I'm sorry I didn't introduce myself in Chester," Adam went on. "But I was bound for a chapter meeting at Wrexham. And you seemed to have matters in hand."

"What brought you there? Are you of the Cheshire clergy?"

Adam shook his head. "I'm Archbishop Arundel's man. I've long known him and rejoined him when he returned to England. After Richard's capitulation, I stayed behind to pay our courtesies to the clergy on the Welsh marches. The archbishop thought it prudent that he himself ride on with the other high lords."

Harry nodded. "Pleased to make your acquaintance. Yet I feel I've heard your name before. Can't recollect why, though."

Adam smiled. "Would it were because I'm a rich bishop! Instead, you and I are nearly brothers—sons of a sort to the House of Mortimer: You by the contract Earl Edmund made with your father, wedding you to Edmund's daughter. And I treated by Edmund as kin."

Harry remembered hearing of a cleric, a mysterious adoptee several years younger than Edmund himself. There'd been talk of how Edmund, a lonely adolescent already an earl, had learned of this lowly lad of potential, rescuing him from destitution and raising him in the Mortimer household like a brother. Wags had even maintained that Adam *was* a Mortimer, begotten out-of-wedlock by Edmund's father. And perhaps Adam believed as much, too.

"When I'd mastered Latin and French and mathematics and anything else Edmund's tutors could teach me," Adam continued, "he sent me to Oxford and saw me ordained. He always said the family could use a well-read lawyer and priest."

Indeed, Harry concurred silently. The Mortimers, including his wife and brothers-in-law, had never been known for erudition. At least Edmund had tried to bring a sharp mind into family counsels; all the better that it belonged to someone he'd genuinely liked.

"But though I was e'er away, I heard of you and your marriage to Mistress Elizabeth," Adam added, "a beautiful lady." More than that he would not say, for he always had found Elizabeth Mortimer coldly polite at best, as if she rejected this commoner her father had welcomed so generously. "Lord Edmund died young—God rest his soul—and others in the family ne'er saw need for me, learned or not." Adam's expression deepened in sadness. "So I hardly saw them. And you and I never met."

"Little matter now," Harry said awkwardly. "I, too, never spent much time with my wife's family. She—they—had their own pursuits. My road oft seemed to lead elsewhere."

"And still does," Adam thought, realizing the marriage must be a union in legality only.

As if allowing his silence to confirm Adam's guess, Harry resumed surveying the mare. Then, with a smile, he offered a hand. "A fine mare, as you said. A fine day, too, to make a friend, near-brother or whatever ilk. How may I be of service?"

"It's a matter that touches me personally," Adam replied. "But no less you or any man who cares about England. Perhaps we might stroll along the river, and you'll let me buy you a cup of ale?"

"Of course!"

"But first: this mare. Wish to purchase her? If so, you'd best look to it before someone else comes along."

"Aye."

So they found the owner, and Harry paid him and arranged to have the horse delivered to his quarters in Aldersgate. Then he and Adam set off, saying little until they had wound through crowded lanes, bought mugs of ale from a riverside vendor, and paused at a secluded knoll. Below, the Thames meandered in languorous color, shimmering blue under the sky, mysterious green in the shadows, rippling amber behind passing boats.

Adam relaxed against a tree trunk, raising his mug. "To a pleasant afternoon."

"And your generosity."

"Welcome refreshment," Adam smiled. "I did spend a little time enquiring after you."

Harry raised a questioning brow.

"You have a reputation for honesty and intelligence, as well as valor," Adam began. "After what I saw at Chester, I believe it's well-deserved. You've doubtless heard that when a mob seized four of Richard's knights here, the outcome was less peaceful."

"Aye."

"Guilty or not, they deserved a fair trial," Adam said. "Fortunately, your uncle and the archbishop, upon arriving here, convinced Henry to place a stronger guard at the Tower. 'Twill serve to protect the king but also ensure that no one tries to free him or any of his followers already arrested, like those two you sent down from Cheshire. Thank God, Henry agreed. Yet it was too late for Richard's four knights." Adam shook his head.

"Aye. 'Twas murder, and Henry blatantly ignores it."

Adam looked around warily. "May I speak in confidence?"

Harry nodded.

Adam began slowly. "As I mentioned, I'm trained in law—canon as well as Common—and in the liberal arts. So Bolingbroke and Neville asked me to join a commission of lawyers and scholars. They said they wanted us to advise Henry on the next steps in governance. Our commission met this morn. And we were asked to review this." Adam took a document from his belt pouch. "Best read it yourself—and keep that copy. What they showed us I copied out twice."

Purportedly from a chronicle, the text, in Latin, held that Edward I had not been the first-born son of Henry III and had come to the throne wrongly, one-hundred-twenty-seven years earlier. The true heir, the chronicle stated, had been Edward's handicapped, supposedly older brother, Aedmund—the Crouchback—unfairly disfavored for his misshapen back. Tracing Aedmund Crouchback's line to the House of Lancaster, John of Gaunt and Henry Bolingbroke, the document argued that the House of Lancaster, not the line represented by Edward I and King Richard, was the legitimate royal family.

"This is fraudulent," Harry told Adam. "I am descended from Henry III, by Aedmund Crouchback. And crippled and infirm or not, Aedmund was a younger son. Everyone knows that. My grandfather knew it. He married into Crouchback's line. Do you think he would have ignored it had he been kin to the true heirs to the throne? Hardly. He had to content himself with Northumberland and whatever else our family already held. Which is enough for me." Harry looked grim. "You say this came from Bolingbroke, and my cousin Ralph?"

Adam nodded. "They termed it 'part of a chronicle'; bade us to mark it well. When they left, we discussed it. Not a man amongst us had ere heard such a tale before. And we are well-schooled. So we've sent for all the chronicles we can obtain, from abbeys and priories throughout the land, that we might seek corroboration."

He regarded Harry earnestly. "I think this will find no corroboration. I think Gaunt forged it when Edward III grew daft in old age or during the troubles when Richard was a boy. I think Gaunt kept it lest he ever want to seize the throne. But, thank God, he never did use it. And we all know he had opportunities. Perhaps conscience ruled him in the end."

Adam's voice dropped further. "I think Bolingbroke may not have such scruples. And I fear what that may mean. Yet, I fear for England even as much, if Richard continues as king." Once again, he glanced about uneasily. "Some say Richard has lost his senses. Those who have seen him say he babbles like the village idiot, calling upon Edward II `of blessed memory'; or talking to his little wife, as if she were there beside him, praying she entreat her father, Charles VI, to send the armies of France to save him." His eyes flooded with feeling. "Imagine what would happen if Charles sent an army to these shores. Every Englishman from boy to doddering elder would be in arms, afeared Richard meant to surrender everything. And even if the French were driven off quickly, think of the bloodshed still. And for what?" he shivered.

"So there is talk," Adam said, "that even if Bolingbroke's chronicle is false, it hardly matters; that perhaps we'd best cast off Richard now, before his madness or misrule ruins us all." Adam seemed to weigh everything carefully as he continued. "Mind you, even if Bolingbroke is compelled to back down, Richard could still bring French might against us in a war of retribution. If he somehow triumphed, then Bolingbroke, Archbishop Arundel, you and I, and anyone who's ever questioned Richard would likely hang, or die first under torture."

Harry choked, as if he could already feel the noose tightening around the throat that swilled ale on such a pleasant afternoon. "My God! Let me make sure I understand: You think Henry intends to seize the throne?"

Adam nodded.

"Yet Richard may've gone daft? Or, if not, may scheme to bring the might of France down on us, even if he keeps his throne? And that, or Bolingbroke's plotting to be king, is what awaits us?"

Nodding again, Adam speculated: "And even if Richard didn't seek Charles' aid..."

"...Charles could decide on his own to invade," Harry finished. "'Tis said that he and Richard are very close and that 'twas they who sought Richard's marriage to Charles' little girl. Some hold that's where the real love match lies—betwixt Richard and Charles themselves."

Adam's sandaled heel ground into the dirt. "So 'tis rumored. But if Richard no longer ruled, the French would have a much more difficult time; have to fight a stronger king and all those who, even if they have little affection for Henry, would rush to expel the French." He frowned. "So there, it appears, lie our choices."

"Hell!" Harry seemed both pensive and peevish. "Why have you come to me with this?"

"Because I believe you seek to do what is right. Without you, Richard couldn't have been brought in. Yet you're not of Bolingbroke's privy circle. Not knowing you, but knowing of you, I wondered at your thoughts, for my own lie far from resolved."

Harry said nothing but left his ale cup on the grass and strode down to a Thames oblivious of the woes of its homeland. All silver sleekness, a fish jumped, rippling the surface before disappearing again, and ducks waddled from the rushes, a drake watching from a rock as his mate proudly led her brood into the shallows. He suddenly felt very old and world-weary. After a few minutes, he returned to Adam. "'Tis a sorry pass England comes to. But there's still a third way: To reform Richard's governance, setting good, strong men around him to advise and make him rule correctly and with the counsel of Parliament, as many of us— including Henry, I thought—intended."

Adam looked interested, so Harry went on: "That's the only viable path, even if Richard acts crazy; even should he seek to bring French vengeance upon us. The French we can handle. And if Richard really joins his cause to theirs and is exiled, or killed in battle, so be it. 'Twill be his doing.

"Yet, it needn't be so," he concluded. "Things can be made aright if Richard is reminded of his proper place; if he defers to advice from the Great Council—the leading lords and prelates, collected; if he pays heed to Parliament; if the law is upheld."

"Many ifs," Adam murmured.

"Even so," Harry persisted. "What else can we do? Richard is king."

"So was Edward II once England's monarch," Adam reminded him. "But Edward II fell, and your great-grandfather helped topple him. Few would argue today that was not for the good of England."

Harry responded with a melancholy half-smile. "True. But as I have learned as judge in our Borders courts, even if there are precedents for guidance, cases and men are never totally alike. Ultimately, you can only take precedent so far; then you must decide each case itself, and trust in God, the law, and your own wits, and pray you've done what is right."

He swore in Northumbrian dialect and Adam echoed him with an equally piquant curse in Welsh.

"What will you do next?" Harry asked as they began retracing their steps.

"Visit Richard to witness his state with my own eyes. You could help me," Adam proposed. "Not by coming. Many know of your last audience with Richard; how you rode hard for your life. Better your presence not annoy him or lead others to think you're there because you want revenge."

"Aye."

"But I'd like Ian Kynge to go along," Adam continued. "I know him from the old days in London. He's a fine priest and would make a good bishop. Give him leave to accompany me. Verily, I should like him to join me when our commission next meets. I could make use of his abilities."

"Aye, if he agrees."

They reached the ale-monger and deposited their empty tankards. Harry turned toward Aldersgate.

"I'll send to you soon," Adam promised. "And may God give us wisdom."

———

Startled by the darkness, Ian Kynge and Adam entered Richard's chamber in the Tower. Whitewashed, with cream-colored floor tile, two windows, and wall sconces, the room should have been bright enough. But under Richard's residency or Bolingbroke's custody, it had sunk into blackness, lit only by a meager candle on the floor. Before it, cross-legged, head in his hands, sat Richard, King of England.

He looked up, saying nothing.

A servant, or jailer, had admitted Adam and Ian, but they had been announced by no heralds. Nor had they been made to wait by any of the lackeys who had long encrusted Richard's throne.

Rocking back and forth, Richard stared ahead. Adam and Ian sank to their knees and lurched across the floor, afraid to raise their heads higher than the king's. As they neared, Adam reached out to take Richard's hand for the customary kiss of fealty. But Richard drew away, inching backward on his haunches into a corner, to regard them with dazed eyes. His fingers played over the crown on his honey-colored locks, one moment acting as if he meant to take it off, the next as if he were cramming it harder onto his scalp. Finally, he fluttered both hands into his lap before raising the right again, inviting Adam and Ian to come closer.

"Join me on this cold ground, my throne now," he directed. "'Dust you are, oh man; unto dust willst you return.' They say Charlemagne declared that a king's corpse is as dead as any man's, it's just that his burial shroud is grander. Verily!" Richard's voice crescendoed, trailing off into cynical laughter.

"Come!"

Adam and Ian approached on their knees. But they stopped when Richard glared at them again and broke into another cold laugh. He was still tittering when a door opened, and servants in Lancastrian livery entered. One found a chair, while two others set up a trestle table, covered it with a cloth, and placed Richard's supper upon it. A fourth lit the wall sconces. Then, they all departed as soundlessly as they had arrived.

The king seated himself at the table, tucked the napkin under his wavering chin, and picked up fork and knife. "Complete your embassy. And get up, damn you!"

"My Liege, we have no embassy," Adam explained. "We came as men of the cloth to see if we could do anything to help your body or soul."

Richard uncovered a dish but ignored it. "Help? Yea," he said in tones of unexpected clarity. "You could change this land. You see what a treacherous, unfaithful realm it is. Unnatural! How many kings has it killed or spurned? How many acts of malice have there been against me, its rightful liege?" He mumbled something as he speared a piece of beef. "Go! Think on it. I wish no guests."

Adam stepped forward as if to try to comfort Richard.

The king only stared again. *"Noli me tangere!"* Abruptly, he stood. Nearly knocking over his table, he charged at them with a serving fork, laughing caustically.

Hastily bowing, they exited. But before they even reached the stairs, they could hear his laughter turn to prolonged sobs.

"Noli me tangere!"

Touch me not.

"So be it," Adam concluded.

Saying little, he and Ian proceeded to St. Paul's, where Adam paused at the cloister gate. "I would pray, now."

"So ought I," Ian nodded. "But first, I'd like to write of what befell us. Then—God forgive me—I think I could praise the spirit in wine 'ere I make my way to a chapel."

Adam left him with a brotherly hug. "God is everywhere, as much in good company over wine as in the stillness of a cathedral. Go. I will seek you out again soon.

———

Tall and big-boned, a solid man though not a fat one, Kynge hunched over his desk. Unsure of the future of his observations, he still was determined to compile them. Perhaps someday they would prove useful to a chronicler. Pushing brown hair back from his forehead, grey eyes intent, plain farmer's face studious, he scratched his pen over the last page. Finally, folding the sheets into his breviary, he left his lodging, a cottage behind Harry's Aldersgate inn. A tavern-cum-hostelry for knights, merchants, and like travelers, it had been purchased years earlier by Baron Henry Percy and willed to his grandson, though Harry used it only on rare visits to London.

Entering through the tavern, Ian ascended stairs, proceeded through an ante-room, climbed another two flights and entered a vestibule. Knocking on a door, he gave his name, heard Harry say, "come in," and entered.

On a bed under an eave, Harry stretched, dropping a book.

Kynge placed it on a bedside table. "You re-read Master Chaucer."

"No," Harry corrected. "I read Master Chaucer. And I hear he's drafting a whole set of new tales about pilgrims and Canterbury. It's taken me this long, though, just to catch up with what he's already written."

"Well worth your time," Kynge recommended, throwing himself on the matching bed under the other eave. "Arrghh!" His fist pounded the pillow. "It's worse than we thought."

"What is?"

"Richard! Adam Usk and I've been to see him." He recounted their visit. "He acts like a lunatic, Harry. Perhaps he should be in the care of the monks at St. Bart's, and far from the throne."

"And too near us," Harry laughed, remembering that St. Bartholomew's Hospital, already two-hundred-seventy-five years old, was just down the lane from Aldersgate. "Think he really is crazy?"

Kynge shrugged. "He certainly seems strange. Yet many say he's always been odd. Certainly, now he's affrighted as well. But crazy? Perhaps only another madman would know."

Harry braced himself on an elbow. "I suspect 'tis partly mummery. Richard has always been given to fits. At times, he may actually be daft, temporarily, overcome by tantrums. But he plays to that, too, so that no one can tell exactly what he'll do. He's never gone completely mad afore, though. Nor is he mad now, I reckon. Perhaps 'tis only another of his games."

Kynge snorted. "Dangerous game: He gives evidence to those seeking to overthrow him."

Harry smiled. "It may be only craftiness. You know what Bolingbroke intends: To put Richard and his worst advisors on trial. And Parliament has been called—in Richard's name—to meet, the perfect venue."

He looked at Kynge. "What better defense could Richard have than to feign insanity? He doubtless assumes that Parliament and Henry would try to reprimand, or imprison, or even behead a king who does manifest wrongs. But who among them would condemn a king who's crazy? None. You know how it is with madmen: Oft they're hailed as seers and saints.

"No," he went on. "At worst, Richard might be sent off to recover his senses before facing charges. But that may be what he wants: To lie low and secretly obtain aid from France. I suppose we must permit him to do it—to think he can buy time." He fell back on his bed. "Twill buy a moment's peace for us all."

"While Bolingbroke as steward, and the council, and a few from the House of Commons, begin trying to set his course straight," Kynge suggested.

"Aye. I trust it wouldn't be long afore Richard could rule again himself. Presumably, he'd be chastened and smarter by then and rule justly, guided by council and Parliament.

"But enough of that." Harry got up and tried to dump Kynge from his mattress.

Ian groaned. "Where'd you have me go now?"

"Downstairs, for supper and the finest wine this inn can supply!"

September 1399 - Lambeth Palace, Southwark

On Adam's invitation, the three met some days later, in a private parlor in the Archbishop of Canterbury's palace, across the Thames. The dinner matched the incomparable quality of the cellars, newly restocked with the reds of the Medoc and Burgundy, the delicate golds of Germany, the tawny sweet wines of Portugal, and retsin-flavored imports from Byzantium. Had their agenda been less sobering, they might have spent a pleasantly inebriated evening drinking their way across Europe and through the archbishop's casks.

But it was not a typical night.

Nonetheless, an attentive host, proud of his quarters in the episcopal household, Adam declined to broach the weightiest matters until the meal was finished and the table bore only their wine flagons and a tray of sweets and nuts.

"You haven't been privy to our commission, Harry," he began, "so I wanted you to know, before word spills across London."

Harry nodded, smashing a walnut with the hilt of his knife.

"We received the last of the chronicles from monasteries," Adam said. "Like those we'd read earlier, not one contained anything like Bolingbroke's story about his House of Lancaster being the true line to the throne."

"'Twas faux, and badly crafted at that," Kynge commented.

"In the end," Adam added, "most of the group found this was troubling, but perhaps not the most important thing. Other concerns might matter more, they said. Many had been to see Richard and found his conduct alarming. Even so, I myself consider him fanciful, but not truly insane."

Kynge interrupted. "And those who've visited him most recently say he seemed as sound as ever."

"Thus," Adam resumed, "we spent much time deliberating today. Then we took a vote."

He leaned across the table toward Harry. "We voted to accept Bolingbroke's claim, whether his chronicle is true or not. I voted so. I'm not pleased at the way Bolingbroke has cozened his way to the crown. But I fear even more if Richard remains king. I'm not proud of my vote. But I'm not ashamed of it either."

Harry's eyes narrowed, holding Adam's gaze, saying nothing. Then he looked at Kynge. "Ian?"

"Being only scribe to Adam and the rest, I shared not in their vote," the younger priest replied. "But Adam sought my thoughts privately. And I had to agree: That we can no longer bear the risk of Richard."

"But this chronicle—fake!" Harry began. "And Henry's oath—that day, in Doncaster: He swore he wouldn't seek the throne himself. He lies. Lies. Not just to me or the others who witnessed his promise, but to God."

Ever the theologian and lawyer, Adam spoke in calm, measured tones. "An oath given in ignorance of what it really means, or of what may occur or be demanded later, is not necessarily as binding as one given with full knowledge. Probably at Doncaster, Henry believed what he swore. But matters change. Should his best judgment not change as well?"

Harry rose from the table and began pacing, his long legs and energy reducing the room to tight walls around them. "What of honesty? What of a man's word? Shall they change, too? No longer matter? Shall every promise or pact later be voided when it suddenly becomes inconvenient? And if so, what of our laws? Are they not a form of pact to which we commit ourselves, for the common good?"

"Others who were at Doncaster do not raise such objections," Adam replied. "They're willing to go along with Henry now."

"They must heed their own minds," Harry answered. "I don't like this. But I'm hardly an earl, nor canonist or lawyer." He strode back, placed powerful hands on the table, palms down. "I am a knight. A knight is bound to truth and honesty. His word—even without him swearing on a Bible—his word is his bond. Or should be.

"Like Henry, I am a Knight of the Garter. A singular honor, that." He seemed lost in distant thought. "Only a few can hold it simultaneously, chosen for special service to the realm. And, no matter how deserving another man may be, if there's no place for him, he must wait until an existing Knight of the Garter dies.

"We swear, as this Order of the Garter, to uphold all the virtues of knighthood even more than other knights. I promised that extra charge gladly. So, I assumed, did Henry." Harry's voice softened wistfully. "It's apparent his pledge meant naught."

The room hung in silence. Ian glanced at the door as if considering escape, torn between respect for

Adam and regard for Harry and everything he espoused.

Slowly, Harry sat down again.

Adam poured more wine. "On the commission, we acted as we thought we must. God have mercy on us if we were wrong." He clicked his cup against Harry's. "Let this not mar our friendship. Believe me, if we cherish England, never was it more crucial for everyone to work together, differing opinions or not."

Harry sadly clicked his cup in return.

"Truly, Harry," Adam assured him, "I welcome this no more than you. How is it we must suffer either the evils of a tyrant or the greed of a usurper? But at least the usurper seems capable and sane. And desiring the crown so much, he can more easily be curbed should he reach too far."

"Yea," Kynge echoed. "To prosper, Henry will have to defer to Parliament and rule well."

That, Harry had to concede, was something. "Even so, I like this not. I like it not at all."

"Nor I," Adam admitted. "Nor many of us, I venture. Sometimes, though, it's not ours to like or dislike. 'Tis only ours to accept and go forward."

Saturday, 20 September 1399

London seethed with rumours thick as oppressive fog.

Richard was crazy. No, already dead. No, just tired and willing, even thrilled, to relinquish his throne. No, seeking only a respite. The tale had as many wrinkles as the old men spreading it in alehouses. On one point, though, all agreed: Bolingbroke itched to become king and no doubt soon would.

In the Earl of Northumberland's London manse, Harry found himself renewing the debate he'd had with Adam and Ian, though he faced his father and uncle this time. Again, he brought up Bolingbroke's oath, eliciting a sigh from his uncle and a muttered epithet from his father.

"Perhaps Henry breaks whatever promise he swore at Doncaster and elsewhere," Thomas acknowledged. "But hasn't Richard broken his oath, too—everything he promised at his coronation and since: To govern well, and in accord with the law? Surely he has. I was there. I saw it and could do little to stop it." Regret and memory filled his eyes. "Thus, it seems, we have two broken oaths, two men guilty of that. It appears we must choose between them."

"And you'd blithely choose Bolingbroke, like Adam's commission did."

"No, lad," Thomas demurred. "Like you, I wish there were another way. I fear there's not. Too many men no longer agree with us; too many questions remain about Richard."

Leaning against the mantel, Harry persisted. "So we have no middle road? Richard's kingship cannot be reformed? He can't rule properly, with Henry as high steward and a decent council? Hell!" The inevitable pacing began. "Can't we still hope this king changes for the better? Must all be despair?"

The older Percies turned to each other; conferred at length in low tones.

Finally, Earl Henry addressed Harry. "I've many reservations about Richard. But—all right: I do still think it's possible to make him a better king. 'Twon't be easy, but it is possible." He smiled, surrendering. "For that, I shall I argue, to the extent that I can—but not forever."

"I, too, will present Richard's case as long as prudent," Thomas pledged. "Doubtless, I'll get the chance tomorrow."

"The senior barons of the Great Council, including your uncle and me, will meet," Earl Henry explained. "I'll raise your arguments, Harry. We'll see how we fare." He shook his head unhappily. "Yet, unlike you, maybe I've forgotten how to hope."

Chapter XII
Sunday, 21 September 1399 - London

When the barons met, the Percies held firm. Temporarily.

"Presenting Richard's cause was nigh unto impossible," Earl Henry informed Harry afterward. "Bolingbroke appeared, touting his supposed chronicle. When 'twas questioned, he simply took another tack."

Thomas elaborated. "He said he sought the crown `if not as its *most* direct heir—as my chronicle states and I believe—then as *a* direct heir.' He also asserted claims `by right of conquest, if a blessedly peaceful conquest' and by 'popular will.' He said we'd hear more about that 'popular will' when Parliament convenes. And after he left, the majority agreed his claims are valid, spurious chronicle notwithstanding."

"We urged them to discuss it further," Earl Henry added. "We failed. So, ultimately, we went along."

"Hell," Harry responded. "You capitulated!"

The Earl snorted. "Could we be so conceited as to declare our opinion better than everyone else's? Could we be sure we were still right, that you are right? No. Thus I chose to defer to the judgment of my peers. I shall continue to do so. I shan't risk making an ass of myself and enemies of them."

"So 'tis over?"

"Not quite. If Richard is deposed, the barons want it done legally, respectfully. We also know we're but a few considering something affecting the whole realm. We've demanded that the question be put before the full Lords and Commons."

"Then God help Parliament." Harry replied.

———

Monday, 29 September 1399 - Tower of London

Various priests, including the Archbishop of Canterbury; and lords, among them the two Percy earls and Ralph Neville; gathered at the drawbridge, assigned by the peers to deliver documents to Richard. After a short delay, they were admitted and proceeded to the keep, where they twisted up and down stairways before entering the presence of their monarch, soon to be their ex-monarch.

They found the chamber well-lit, far from the infernal darkness they expected after the reports from recent visitors.

Richard watched as they blinked at the candles and then approached. "Now I know why Bolingbroke's felons took such care with hearth and tapers," he informed them. "It suggests I'm well-treated. But I'm not well-treated, either here or by my subjects—subjects like you, My Lords." He focused on Thomas Percy. "Even you, my e'er-loyal seneschal. *Et tu Thomi*!" Bitter laughter veered into keening wail.

Thomas said nothing, and a senior jurist glided past him to thrust a list of impeachment charges into Richard's hands.

"Tut!" the king tossed it over his shoulder. "Where's Bolingbroke? I'll do naught till he appears."

Archbishop Arundel stepped forward. "On his way, My Lord."

"How very good of him!"

Richard retreated to the end of the chamber and eased himself to the floor. Flinging his cape around him, he pulled head and limbs within, like a burrowing animal.

"What the...?" Neville muttered. Thomas and Earl Henry looked at each other. Others swore.

"Patience," Archbishop Arundel recommended.

At length, Henry arrived in a whirl of cloth-of-gold.

Pleasantries with the delegation followed. Then Henry eyed the hump at the end of the room. "And where might my gracious cousin be?"

The hump moved.

"Here!" Throwing off his cape, Richard crossed the floor. "Say your piece."

Henry smiled, addressing the delegation. "I would confer with my cousin alone."

Richard hiccupped in scorn, but the archbishop nodded, and Henry steered Richard to the corner. They spoke softly, too faintly to be understood, though they seemed polite enough.

Before long, however, the muffled comments escalated into heated exchanges.

"Fucking bastard!" Henry shoved Richard.

"Damned usurper!" Richard elbowed Henry.

Eyes meeting, Archbishop Arundel and Earl Henry hurried to separate the two. They remained with them for several fraught minutes before leading them back to the group. Nodding vaguely to the delegation, both Richard and Henry seemed tautly controlled.

Arundel tapped a jurist, who gave Richard a resignation letter.

Richard read it silently. Finally, biting his lip, he accepted a pen and slashed his name across the parchment, glowering.

"My Lord," Ralph proposed. "Since you've signed your resignation, I suggest you surrender to your successor your signet and crown."

Fingers quivering, Henry reached out to take them.

Thomas Percy whispered to his brother. "Bolingbroke's damn near wetting his drawers in lust."

Henry's hands remained outstretched.

Richard ignored them. "So, Cousin..." He drawled out the last word. "Your colors show. But, I tell you, were you the last man in this kingdom, I would not choose you as my successor." He smiled slyly. "I hear there's talk of me appearing afore Parliament, to bless your usurpation. I shall never appear before

Parliament as your serf. But I'm also told some of you want to bring me to trial. Well, Cousin, should charges be leveled against me, I expect—no, demand—a fair trial, a chance to defend myself, before our peers, as law provides."

He sank to the floor once more and sat mutely before removing his signet. Bypassing Henry, Richard gave the ring to Archbishop Arundel. Slowly raising his fingers to his head, Richard removed the crown as well, placing it on the floor in front of him. "My Lords, I resign my crown only to God, who established the monarchy and chose me to reign. To God alone—no man—do I relinquish it."

With a low sob, he fled the room.

The delegation stood numbly. Arundel edged them toward the door. "Let's be gone."

Thomas Percy stole a backward glance at the crown.

It remained on the floor, Henry's to retrieve at will.

Tuesday, 30 September 1399

"Wh—the hell...Umph!" A groggy John Hardyng stirred. "Oh, Harry ... My Lord."

Leaning over the bed, Harry grinned into his squire's sleep-laden eyes. "Time to be up, sir. Duty calls." Crossing to a window, he opened the shutters.

"Duty?" Hardyng blinked suspiciously "At this hour? I polished your boots last night and made sure you had clean clothing." He viewed Harry's apparel disapprovingly. "You must not have found it. Let me look again and draw you a bath. Then you can change and let me rest."

"Worry not," Harry responded, still brazenly cheerful. "I'm scrubbed enou'. And I found my other clothes. I just prefer these." He glanced at the faded leggings and shirt he wore under a tunic, shiny with age—all clean, but the garb of a lowly farmer, not a

Knight of the Garter or son of a mighty earl. "Dress plainly, too. No arms but a knife. And don't shave or tarry. 'Tis already well past dawn. You just spent too many hours yestere'en, drinking up London!" As if proving his point, he strode to the other window and opened it as well, admitting a stream of sunshine.

Hardyng shot naked from the bed. "I'll be down, apace."

Grumbling, he washed, eschewed his razor, and joined Harry and Kynge outdoors. Kynge, he noted, was clad in his oldest clerical robe, frayed at the hem and patched around the hood. He also sported a day's growth of beard. Only Harry was not bewhiskered. "An error," the latter admitted. "I only remembered not to after I'd shaved half my face."

"Pity you didn't leave the rest anyway," Kynge jested. "Even covering up half would have been an improvement."

Harry grabbed him, and they briefly tussled like schoolboys. "A fine way to greet a friend of a morn," Harry teased. "But we didn't come out here to fight amongst ourselves."

In fact, he told them, they were going to Westminster Hall because he wanted to witness the day's events—not as Sir Harry Percy, Knight of the Garter, Warden of the March, and Justice of Chester, but a simple, unobtrusive man.

"You weren't summoned?" Hardyng asked.

"I'm hardly a member of the House of Commons. Nor an earl like my father and uncle or Ralph in the House of Lords."

"Your own standing would've assured access, at least to observe," Kynge suggested.

"Aye. But I prefer this way."

"There was plenty of talk in the taverns last night," Hardyng chirped. "Bolingbroke's heralds bruited it about: how Richard gave up the rule gladly, praising Henry!"

"My uncle had a far different account," Harry cautioned.

They were soon elbow-to-elbow with what seemed half the populace of England. Pausing near the plaza at St. Martin le Grand, they bought sweet buns from the Augustinian canonesses of St. Mary's-in-Clerkenwell, who had joined other vendors in pursuing promising trade. Harry was telling a nun to keep his change when Kynge nudged him.

"Over there," Ian gestured with a half-eaten bun. Across the way, where the Church of St. Michael le Querne looked toward the Cheapside cross, 20 riders in Lancastrian livery turned their horses. Drawing abreast, they charged the square, swinging clubs and whips.

Like other pedestrians, Harry and his companions scrambled for cover against buildings. Arms around a shaking nun and child, he could only watch, stunned, as Bolingbroke's men crashed into the vendors, trampling pastries, crafts, clothware, merchants, and customers alike.

"Let all know Lancaster rules the streets now," one laughed. "We'll say when folk can gather!" They galloped down a lane.

As the crying child raced off and the nun ran toward the remnants of her cart, Harry's fists clenched. "They'll pay for that, if e'er I meet them again!"

Hardyng caught his shoulder. "Should we go back and arm? Chase them down?"

Harry shook his head. "Too few of us, even if in armor and mounted, unless we could gather enough men. But by then, they'd be long gone. And 'tis the job of the town fathers to keep the peace, not us. Still…" He left the threat unfinished.

Kynge had sprung forward to care for the wounded, and Harry and Hardyng assisted in bearing the more seriously injured to the churches and helping the nuns and merchants salvage what goods were left. When they finally resumed their steps toward

Westminster, their earlier light-heartedness had vanished. Their concern increased street by street as they encountered fewer random crowds and more packs of men. At least one in three seemed to be in Lancastrian garb, while many of the rest sported Henry's colors on hats or belts. Nearly all carried weapons or makeshift versions: cudgels, knives, hatchets, cleavers, even stockings weighted with rocks.

Harry and his aides came into the expansive Westminster palace yard, where crowds bobbed around another set of merchant booths, several rows wide. "Little wonder Bolingbroke's men cleared the stalls elsewhere," Harry thought. "Either Henry or the abbot of Westminster—or both—must be getting a fat piece of every coin exchanged."

The space between the booths and Westminster Hall teemed with more armed, rough-looking men.

Gamely, Harry pushed ahead.

"Back!" A swaggering pikeman loomed. "Louts ain't admitted, only such Lords and Commons as Duke Henry hisself wants. So go, pig, and take these swine with you." A stream of spit spewed toward Hardyng and Kynge.

"Who says?" Harry retorted.

"Me!" His challenger swung the pike.

Diving, Harry seized him around the waist, tossing him against his fellows. Hardyng managed to grab the pike while Harry tugged a sword away from one of the man's allies. Within moments, the rest tried to close in, but Hardyng's pike and the long blade in Harry's hand discouraged them.

"Let any who dares say that again!" Harry invited. There were no takers, but at the same time Kynge was whispering against the back of his neck.

"For God's sake, we can't fight the whole mob!"

"Can't we?" Harry replied, though he knew Ian was right. He cleared a wider circle and smiled when Kynge scooped up a fallen axe. An opposing axe jabbed at him, but the chaplain deflected it, and Harry smiled again.

"Let's see if we can at least get to the doors of the hall. 'Twill be victory enou'!"

Step by step, they advanced. Two men raised thick staffs against him, but Harry dove low again and cut at their legs. They jumped aside. His party proceeded another several yards, their adversaries swatting ineffectively, unable to close in. Still, Harry knew his advantage couldn't last.

Someone swiped Ian on the neck. Blood speckling his gown, the priest charged, using the blunt side of his axe to fell his attacker.

Harry's trio progressed another several feet, though the thud of hooves warned of Lancastrian reinforcements. Lunging ahead, Harry wounded two more ruffians. But the tip of a pike reached his chest, tearing his clothing and pricking his skin. That was enough to propel him farther. A moment later, flipping the sword to his left hand, he used the right to pull his knife. A thin line of red oozed from a man who had tried to tackle him. The sword kept a few more assailants at bay; then, suddenly, they were clear of assailants and pressing against Westminster Hall. Mysteriously, the doors swung open, and they stumbled inside.

"What in hell?" An irate voice greeted them.

Harry stepped forward.

"Who the hell do—" The voice trailed off. "Harry Percy..."

Harry looked into the amazed eyes of Peter Courtenay.

"My God, what was going on out there?" A few of Henry's followers spilled through the door, too, and Courtenay confronted them as well. "And what the hell were you doing? Didn't you know who he is? You nearly slew the son of the Earl of Northumberland—and a Knight of the Garter no less!" Frightened, they backed out, and the doors slammed shut.

Noticing blood on both Kynge and Harry, Courtenay pulled a couple of clean handkerchiefs from his surcoat. "Here. I trust you're not grievously cut?"

They shook their heads, and he seemed relieved, though he had eyed Harry's coarse apparel dubiously. "What sport does he play at?" Courtenay wondered, but decided it didn't matter; somehow, he rather liked this Hotspur.

"I'm sorry, Harry," he said. "We had no idea you wanted to come. Of course, you're welcome. Your squire and chaplain, too."

With a nod, he directed them within, but Harry didn't move.

"Tell me, Peter, how many others have you kept away?"

Courtenay looked unhappy. "We were told only to admit those personally approved by Henry—even if members of Parliament. 'Twas Henry's order. No one had challenged it till now."

As he spoke, raucous chanting began outside: "Bolingbroke! The throne for Bolingbroke!"

"A well-schooled choir," Harry noted. "If their song doesn't deter everyone, their manners certainly will."

"Perhaps it seems harsh. But Henry meant no ill. He only wanted everything to proceed"—Courtenay hesitated again—"unhindered." He tugged Harry's arm. "Why not join the other Knights of the Garter? Parliament's hardly begun. You're more than welcome."

Harry shook his head. "Find us a quieter doorway, and we'll be off."

Courtenay led them to a cellar tunnel that exited close to the river. Once more, he touched Harry's arm. "Sure you won't stay to witness the session?"

"No." Harry smiled grimly. "I've already seen enough."

Inside, the accusations against Richard mounted, dozens in all:

"... He has permitted his forces to rape, steal and murder with impunity, across the length and breadth of this realm... he has subverted the powers of Parliament, ceding its authority improperly to his own minions and forging its records to serve his ends... he has squandered the treasury and demanded ever-higher taxes... he has arrogated to himself the right to make all laws ... he has denied men their right to speak freely and commanded his sheriffs to jail any who dare question him... he has repeatedly violated the rights of a free people to trial before their peers..."

On and on, the recitation proceeded, punctuated by noisy assent. At the conclusion, only one man rose on Richard's behalf.

"My Lords, brother bishops, and distinguished men of the Commons," Bishop Merks began. "You seem certain to pass judgment on our king, to whom you have sworn fealty for more than twenty-two years, and inflict sentence of forfeiture, or worse. I bid you remember that in this land, there is no one, not even the most vile criminal, who is not at the very least brought before a court. Indeed, under law, he must be brought forth, in the flesh, for trial ere his guilt can be determined. Yet you intend to denounce King Richard when he is not even present to hear charges or make his defense. I bid you: Think well on what you do. Remember the law, ere you shame yourselves."

His audience squirmed.

"Whence Merks' backbone?" someone whispered. "It's always been pressed against fine cushions afore, not filled with steel."

Others tittered softly, and then silence prevailed.

Neville rose to fill the void. "The bishop is entitled to his opinion, however erroneous. But Richard is well aware of the claims against him. He received a copy yesterday. He removed his crown and signet and signed his resignation. There's no need for 'trial' or debate."

Neither he nor anyone else mentioned that Richard had also asserted his right to a trial.

Feet scuffed the floor nervously.

Archbishop Arundel motioned to Earl Henry. "I believe, my lords, it's time to call the question. We all know the Earl of Northumberland was disinclined, until recently, to remove Richard. Because he will, therefore, be the most impartial, let him preside over our poll."

It hardly took long, as all the lords, all the churchmen, all the representatives of towns and shires, methodically cast their votes on removing Richard—all "yeas" and nary a "nay," except from Merks.

"The result," Earl Henry concluded, "is nearly unanimous."

A bishop suggested that they consider candidates for the throne, and someone mentioned the eight-year-old Mortimer lord. By tradition, he was the most obvious royal heir, by virtue of descent from Lionel, an older son of Edward III, while Bolingbroke was born to a younger son, John of Gaunt. But Mortimer's name drew little response.

Mortimer might be the bud on the more senior stem, an abbot suggested, but he was, in fact, a great-great-grandson of Edward III, while Henry was only a grandson and thus actually closer to Edward chronologically. And they'd seen what happens when a boy takes the throne. 'Twas how Richard had begun. Let England be more prudent this time.

Moreover, others added, Henry was a man not only in full prime but full power. Had they not seen the agitators outside, threatening to break in, banging weapons against doors and rattling windows? Indeed, couldn't they clearly be heard, even now?

"Bolingbroke. Bolingbroke. The throne for Bolingbroke!"

Who then could argue for Mortimer?

Eyes turned toward the Percies, Mortimer's relatives-by-marriage. But they said nothing until prolonged attention compelled an answer. "It is not seemly for us to remonstrate on behalf of a kinsman," Earl Henry declared, obviously uncomfortable. "Others might say we were improperly biased. Thus, we remain impartial."

Nor did anyone else take up Mortimer's cause.

With little ado, it was over.

Henry arose, stated that he understood the throne to be vacant, and claimed it by right of descent and by having peacefully subdued the land through the grace of God and help of his friends.

As he spoke, the cries of his most vehement friends swelled anew outside.

"Bolingbroke, Bolingbroke! The throne for Bolingbroke!"

And so it became his.

―――

Friday, 10 October 1399

"Would you have me kill Dymock? For that's certainly what I'll have to do!" Harry's voice rose as he met with his father and uncle and now his wife, as well.

"If I attend his coronation farce, I must attend his banquet, since everyone shall parade from the abbey to the feast. The Knights of the Garter will go en mass, so I'd have to be amongst them. And you know what'll happen once everyone is seated for dinner."

"We'll finally get to eat," Thomas Percy quipped.

"Not immediately," Harry replied, unsmiling. "First, the great doors will open, and Thomas Dymock will ride into the hall on horseback. He'll announce he's the king's champion and that if anyone believes Henry is not and should not be king, then he—Dymock—challenges him to mortal combat. If I'm present, I'll hear his challenge. Honor will demand that I answer, for I do not, and cannot, believe Henry should be king. Of course, Dymock will take umbrage, and I'll have to slay him, or he'll slay me!" He surveyed his family. "Is that what you want? His blood, or mine, spilling on the tourney ground?"

His father swallowed a curse.

"Not that Henry would care about either Dymock or me! His path is already strewn with corpses!" Harry began counting.

"Richard Fitzalan, Earl of Arundel: You all remember him. Your sister was married to him, Lady," he reminded Elizabeth. "He was Henry's staunch friend a dozen years ago when they attempted to 'reform' Richard's regime. Rather familiar, is it not? Where is Arundel? Dead, beheaded after the noble Henry unfairly accused him!" He raised his hand with all five fingers extended, only to abruptly drop his thumb. "So, Arundel's gone.

"And who helped kill him? Why none other than John Bushey and Lord Wiltshire. Remember their names, for they will recur in this sorry tale. Or consider Thomas Woodstock, Duke of Gloucester, Henry's uncle, one more of the erstwhile Lords Appellant. Where's Gloucester? Dead like his partners, doubtless slain, in prison, probably by his jailer, Thomas Mowbray, on Richard's orders and likely with Henry's complicity."

Harry's forefinger closed tight on his hand.

"And Mowbray himself, another boon companion—where is he? Equally enshrouded and entombed this last month, dead overseas from his lingering malady, or so the news from Italy holds. How very opportune for Henry."

The middle finger fell.

Elizabeth tossed her long blond hair impatiently.

"Nor should you overlook Bushey and Wiltshire," Harry continued. "They helped Henry rid the realm of Arundel. Where're they now? High in Henry's counsel? No! Also dead, executed at a trial where he presided!" The last two fingers on his hand disappeared into his fist.

"And did I mention Henry Green, ill-fated sap, who was with Bushey and Wiltshire and got beheaded, too?" Raising his other hand, he dropped the thumb. "Or what of those palace knights slain here by the mayor and his henchmen with nary an objection from Henry?" The remaining four fingers fell. "How many more dead will he pile up to climb upon as he ascends the throne?"

The Earl of Northumberland opened his mouth to speak, but Elizabeth cut him off.

"You fool, Harry!" she hissed. "Think I care what Henry's done? I don't! I care about myself and my children! Yet you... You would slight Henry by shunning his coronation, lest you have to battle Dymock and make some silly point about your precious honor! You would go that far, disgrace us."

"Aye, I would, though far worse disgrace would it be for me to play the hypocrite, cheer Henry at his enthronement, toast him at his feast. That would make me a liar. Fool I may sometimes be. But as God is my witness, liar I hope never to be."

His father regarded him sternly. "You were personally invited to go to both the coronation and the feast. Do not affront such courtesies."

"So could I be bidden to go to hell! Should I accept that invitation, too?"

Earl Henry tried again. "There will be many at the coronation who, like you, wish things could've been otherwise. I'm among them. Yet, as I've told you, there comes a time when you must stop objecting and go along. And now, by God, is the time to go along. There's too much at stake otherwise: the well-being not just of England but of this family!"

Elizabeth picked up the argument. "Think of your children! Your son. My son. You might just as well disinherit him and Elissa, too. What chance will they have for advancement at the palace if you set yet another king against you? You may think little of such favors for yourself; you've made that clear for years. But dare you deny them to your children?"

Maternal ambition flamed in her face, alongside fierce resentment of Harry. Watching, Earl Henry berated himself for having secretly sent for her, hoping she could help sway his son. Never had he guessed the depth of the rift between them.

"I want what's best for my children, like any father," Harry retorted. "But to me, what's best is allowing them to grow up in a land that esteems honesty and justice, with men who stand up for what is right, like I'm trying to do. Standing up for what is right is far more important than standing next to a king as a courtier whose only goal is gain. No, I'll not go to Henry's coronation and feast. Never!"

He paced and then stopped, right leg up on a bench, arms crossed atop his knee. "Once he becomes king, I suppose I shall have to live with it. But I'll not condone his coronation by my presence."

Elizabeth cast him a withering look. Gathering her skirts, she sailed to the far end of the room, waited there to overcome her rage, then faced him one last time. "So be it, Harry. But unless you change your mind immediately I shall never again be seen with you." Her tone was cold and steady. "We have already been apart, but from now on you'll no longer be welcome at my house. I do not want to be under the same roof with you again, ever, even in separate quarters. And I want all to know that we go our own ways. Do you understand?"

He nodded, numbly. "I cannot change my mind."

Her splendid lips curled in contempt. "So your decision is made. And mine." She took a few steps before halting. "I prefer that the children remain with me. They will be yours to see at will. But I want no part in your visits."

To this, too, he mutely agreed.

She addressed her father-in-law. "You, Papa, and you, Uncle Thomas," she looked at Worcester, "of course, will be as welcome as ever. I have no differences with you. And if you would be so good, Papa, as to find me a residence in London? I wish to establish my own household here."

Earl Henry concurred with a wan smile. "I ... understand, daughter, and think it best."

Her face brightened.

"She covets the chance to shine at the palace," the earl reminded himself. "That's all she's ever wanted. Harry did little to make it possible. Without him, she hopes to find it with our help."

"And Papa," Elizabeth interrupted his reverie. "Since I share not in Harry's misgivings, I wish to attend the coronation and feast—if you find it acceptable?"

"I do!" The earl beamed. "Thomas and I will be busy with duties for the ceremony and, indeed, all day." He glanced at his son, who only stiffened; Harry had not known previously that his father and uncle had been assigned leading roles in the festivities. "But Athol can escort you," the earl said, referring to his eldest grandchild, Henry Athol Percy, newly come of age.

"Thank you!" Elizabeth curtsied and almost danced from the room.

"Well, son?" Earl Henry barked. "Satisfied?"

"What would you have me say?" Harry replied wearily. "I wish her well. We never should've been together at all." He raised a hand. "I mean no criticism of you, Father. I was a small boy, she a babe, when you made the match, thinking it a good one. But they don't oft work out that way, do they?" He thought of Gaunt, blundering through two sad political unions before wedding his sweetheart; of Edward III's numerous mistresses; of all those connubially unhappy Plantagenets; of his dead brother Rafe, who had never resided with his appointed wife and whose loveless and childless marriage had ended in annulment.

"How long, Harry, will you continue to oppose Henry's coronation?" Thomas Percy spoke up from the corner.

"Until the last moment possible, and to Henry himself, if he'll listen. And if I fail," Harry smiled grimly, "I'll retreat."

Sunday, 12 October 1399 - Westminster Palace

To Harry's amazement, Bolingbroke agreed to a meeting, albeit only on the eve of the coronation.

Gowned in ermine-trimmed amber velvet, Henry was ebullient, if pleasantly tired, as he welcomed his guests: the two senior Percies, Ralph Neville, and Harry. Outside, midnight blackness descended, for Henry had earlier been preoccupied with inaugurating his new Knights of the Bath, named not for the showers that had dampened London but for the elaborate ritual washing its members underwent. Created to outshine even Edward III's Order of the Garter, the Bath already brimmed with notables: three princes—Henry's children—along with Athol Percy and other young aristocrats, joined by judges and seasoned knights who needed no further dubbing but welcomed the celebrated status membership presumably brought.

Although he, too, had been asked to join, Harry had declined lest his acceptance be perceived as approval of Henry's coronation.

Henry didn't seem offended.

"Harry!" Bolingbroke grabbed his hands. "I'm delighted you came. I heard you've been wishing to speak to me, though I daresay I know why. You're not enthused about my plans for the morrow." He gestured toward chairs and table by the hearth. Only after his servants had brought cups of excellent wine did he turn back to Harry. "Am I correct?"

"Aye. And if I may speak bluntly?"

Henry nodded, and Harry went on, "You can't be king. Or even if you can, you shouldn't, even if accepted by Parliament—a Parliament intimidated by a violent and vociferous mob, pounding on its doors!"

Henry's moustache quivered.

Harry continued. "You came, you said, to renew this realm as high steward. You stood for reform, you said; and restoration of the rule of law." Disappointment shaded his voice. "I believed you."

"I did intend reform. I still intend it. All that's different is that instead of being high steward, advising the king, I shall be king myself." Henry smiled.

Harry shook his head. "At Doncaster, you promised to seek only your patrimony. You made a covenant with us and with God. Then you instead plotted to seize the throne and ousted Richard. This was no covenant or promise. This was fraud. You've broken your oath. Lied, even to God."

Henry smiled again, somewhat less broadly. "My fair cousin speaks eloquently. Yet I trust God censures me not. Of course, God is not Harry Percy. And you, My Lords," he bowed toward Ralph and the senior Percies, "I think do not object to my kingship or find conflict with my comments at Doncaster."

Ralph answered quickly. "Not the least."

"Nor do I object any longer," Earl Henry added as Thomas nodded.

Bolingbroke looked again at Harry. "Doncaster was months ago. Things can change. A man can change his mind, no matter how settled things seemed."

"Aye. So a man can change his mind. That's why you should change yours now and call off your coronation."

Henry boggled.

"Aye," Harry acknowledged. "I know how unexpected 'twould be, how firm these plans seem. Still, you, if anyone, could do it. Leave most of the ceremony unchanged. But have Richard crowned again, pledge to uphold everything he was supposed to uphold at his first coronation. Formally announce you're assuming your place as high steward. Then let the festivities continue, in Richard's name and yours."

Ralph Neville slapped the table. "Idiocy! My fool cousin forgets that Parliament dethroned Richard and replaced him with a more worthy man."

Momentarily lost, Harry shot his uncle a glance. When Thomas Percy offered no assistance, he plunged ahead alone, as quietly persistent as the rain outside. "Surely what a Parliament has done the same Parliament can undo," Harry said. "I'm hardly a parliamentarian, but that's common sense. Besides, that Parliament might not have been legitimate. Anyone opposing you, Henry, was barred from entering. I saw it myself. And Courtenay confirmed it."

Bolingbroke swore. "Goddamn Courtenay."

"What sort of precedent is that?" Harry asked. "What if you, as king, are someday at odds with Parliament, as every king these past hundred years has been? Do you want some rabble-rouser among the members stirring everyone up, denying access to your supporters, and tilting the proceedings against you? What if they decide you should be overthrown, like Richard? Then what will you do, having yourself shown how 'tis done?"

"I'll have their heads!" Bolingbroke growled. Yet, for the first time in weeks, he appeared uneasy, fidgeting in his chair. He turned to Neville. "What did that soothsayer tell me, Ralph, ere we went to announce the Knights of the Bath?"

"That doddering imbecile?" Ralph complained.

Rubbing one hand over the other in tormented abstraction, Henry almost whimpered. "What did he say? I would hear it again."

Ralph scowled. "He said if you became king, you might live long enough to die quietly in your bed, instead of with a knife in your back or your head on the block, but that you'd certainly die too young, scarcely living past two-score-and-five. And he said you'd die accursed, your soul dead long afore that, rotted by suspicion of those around you, fearing even your own kith and kin."

"...Fearing even my own kith and kin," Henry repeated dully. Now thirty-three, he looked far older. Were the prediction correct, he would live only another dozen years. He thought of his eldest, Hal, at age twelve already full of promise but often aloof toward his father. Could he trust Hal? And for how long? Shaken, Henry banished the thought, but other figures crowded his mind, too: his sisters' spouses and his Beaufort half-brothers or these Neville and Percy kinsmen, including Harry, his second cousin. "Even my own kith and kin..."

Riveting on some unseen object in front of him, his eyes widened. For long moments, he looked with a glassy vagueness from Neville to Earl Henry and Thomas Percy and then to Harry as if he did not recognize any of them.

"Yea..." It was a drawn-out moan. "So the friar warned. Said I must not take the throne; begged me not to, lest many perish."

"Who was this soothsayer?" Thomas Percy wondered.

"Some damned Franciscan," Ralph grumped. "Got in somehow and then started with this bilge. I had him escorted out; should've had him speared alive!"

"No-o-o-o..." Henry stared at the tabletop. "That would have doomed me, certes."

Harry saw an opening. "What if this soothsayer spoke truth? Odd as he may've been, I think he was right: You shouldn't be crowned. What if God used him to warn you?"

Henry shifted uneasily.

"Stranger things have happened," Harry said. "Christ himself must have seemed passing strange to Pilate and his friends. They even mocked Him as a fool. What if your friar was like Christ? What if he, too, spoke God's truth?"

Alarm flooded Henry's face as Harry went on: "Perjury is a sin. Fraud is a sin. And whether it be a half-pence or a throne stolen, stealing is a sin. Would you be crowned king as a public sinner?"

Neville tittered. "Wouldn't be the first time for an English king!"

They chuckled, but Bolingbroke leaned across the table, clasping Harry's hands.

"You may be right," he said hoarsely. "I must dwell on this. Perhaps, as you say, it's not too late to save myself, save my soul from everlasting perdition." He looked around the table again—at Neville, who seemed irked; at Thomas Percy, who seemed amazed but relieved; at Earl Henry, who seemed bewildered; at Harry, who only held his same, direct gaze.

"Yet... So many arrangements have been made," Henry realized. "So many men are depending on me. So many favors are already given, even to you, Harry, though you knew it not. Today, I signed letters patent naming you lord of the Isle of Anglesey, off the coast of Wales, with all the privileges accruing thereunder."

Harry shrugged. "I accept, with gratitude, if it's an appointment that could be made by a high steward of England."

Henry chewed his moustache. "It could, I suppose. But I signed it as king. Who else uses letters patent?"

Harry elaborated. "And if Richard resumes the rule and rescinds my appointment, so be it. I have responsibility enough, without Anglesey."

Henry sighed. "Would 'twere that simple. I've already named other men to far higher posts. I doubt they will back off so amiably!"

The Earl of Northumberland lowered his goblet. "You've made me high constable of England. If you relinquish the throne, gladly would I relinquish the post of constable."

Thomas Percy followed. "And I'll forgo honors as special steward of ceremony, and all the rest."

The lot fell to Neville, Henry's choice as marshal of England, a post comparable to that of constable. Ralph frowned, drank wine, cleared his throat. "I am with my kinsmen in this," he said at last, to their surprise. "If my lord uncles and cousin Harry are willing to give up their new titles, then so am I. I'll cede the marshalsea, My Lord, if you cede the rule."

His reply threw the decision back to Henry, who, not having anticipated Neville's response, faltered. Slowly, though, resolution replaced fear. "So Richard had best find himself a new marshal. And another constable, master of ceremonies, and lord of Anglesey, though as high steward I shall certainly recommend each of you." Although speaking to them all, Henry focused on Harry.

"You win, Harry. You and that damned friar unsettled me. I'll not risk an early death and my eternal soul for the crown. Not when," a vestige of his usual craftiness flashed, "not when I can accomplish as much as high steward to a weak, ruined king. I'll bide my time. Sooner or later, Richard will assuredly flee to France of his own accord. Then the throne will be vacant, incontestably, and I can claim it without any doubts by anyone, especially you."

Henry's old sense of self began returning. "What a martyr I shall seem, a monarch-elect who gives up the throne to a discredited predecessor and accepts the lesser place. What Caesar ever shared authority so willingly?" His mind leaped ahead. "The chroniclers will love it. Think of what history will say! And after such a sacrifice, even God could never condemn me, no matter what I might do as man or king. And king I shall yet be, I doubt it not."

He seemed so changeably blissful that even Neville was unnerved, thinking that "Henry almost acts like Richard. What if he is half-demented, too?"

Henry continued, flush with new ideas. "On the morrow, the bells of Westminster Abbey and all the churches were to ring in jubilation, the monks chanting the 'Te Deum.' I'll order them to ring a dirge instead to show how much I give up. The monks can chant the 'De Profundis,' a fitting reminder that England cries out to

Him from the depths. Then perhaps God will hear and help set things aright!" He glowed. "Yea. That should work rather well, don't you think, cousins?"

Three of them looked on blankly.

But Harry's face registered both delight and doubt as he remembered earlier conversations and an oath in a Yorkshire chapel. "I want to believe you. But—forgive me—I'm not certain I can. Not after Doncaster."

Bolingbroke's exasperation erupted. "Doncaster be damned!" Rising, he pulled a dagger from a voluminous sleeve, gritted his teeth, and slashed the base of his thumb. The incision welled up, vivid scarlet. "On crusade, I learned that foreign warriors sometimes cut themselves thus to seal a promise with another. And the other man can cut himself too if he wishes, so their blood flows together, and they are like brothers."

Harry sprang up as well, drawing his knife to gash across the bottom of his own thumb. Dripping blood, he thrust his hand toward Henry. "As you say. But know I'm ever willing to shed blood for truth."

Bolingbroke joined his wounded palm to Harry's. The mingled warmth of their blood seeped over their wrists and splattered on the floor.

"Sweet Jesu..." Ralph, sickened at the sight, slipped low in his seat. "They're both crazy."

Ignoring him, Harry and Bolingbroke held their position for another several seconds. "We're agreed," Henry nodded. "So be it."

Thomas and his brother passed the two younger men clean napkins, and they stanched the bleeding.

"Remarkable." Earl Henry blinked as if convincing himself the scene had been real. Summoning a servant, he sent for fresh wine and, when the jug arrived, personally served them all. "A toast, My Lords."

"To England!" Harry proposed.

Five goblets clinked together.

"To friendship and brotherhood," Bolingbroke replied, and cups and voices rose again.

"To us!" Ralph suggested.

"And to peace," Earl Henry concluded, "throughout this realm."

Monday, 13 October 1399 - Westminster Palace

Harry was scraping a borrowed razor across his stubbled chin when the din began: Bells, assaulting the morn, thundering from Westminster Abbey to churches on the edge of London, peal upon peal, glory in every note.

His razor halted mid-stroke.

Clearly, this was no prelude to a somber ceremony. And the change in tune only meant one thing: Henry intended to be crowned, after all.

Lather over half his face, Harry opened the window and peered at monks below. Forming a neat queue, they began singing the victorious strains of the 'Te Deum,' followed by psalms evoking David's triumphant Biblical kingship. Slowly, they moved out from the alley.

Hurriedly finishing his shave, Harry dressed and left his quarters, a small room in the suite allocated to his uncle as steward of ceremonies. He was almost at Thomas' threshold when his uncle emerged from a side chamber, nearly colliding with him.

"Harry!" Thomas looked tired, pulling Harry within.

"What's the meaning of this? He intends to be crowned after all?"

"Yea," Thomas confirmed. "A little while ago, I got his note, telling me I'd be presiding over his coronation anyway. 'No matter what erroneous conclusions some may have reached yester-eve,' it said." Thomas sighed. "I was up much of the night, revising the ceremony to make it a reaffirmation of Richard's kingship and introduction of Henry as high steward. Now I can throw all that on the midden unless he changes his mind yet again."

Harry started forward. "I'll damned well make him."

His uncle restrained him. "You can't. Nobody knows where he is—probably closeted behind a hundred lances. He's hiding, so you can't talk him out of it again."

Harry tried to brush past. "I'll find him anyway. And tell him exactly what his word is worth, blood brother or not."

Again, Thomas pulled him back. "No, son, 'twill serve no purpose and could get you killed. Don't force me to suffer the sorrow of your death. Let the blood you shed last night be all you lose over this. You can't fight the whole palace guard, much less the public will, if enough folk, however misled or even coerced, opt to have Henry despite his misdeeds."

Harry said nothing.

"Remember what you told me several days ago?" Thomas asked. "That you'd oppose his coronation as long as you could; that if failing, you'd go in peace? Well, you didn't fail, for a time. You won, for a time. But in weakness, Henry gave in to temptation anyway. Probably someone, maybe even Ralph, got to him early this morn. Or perhaps he only humored his own worst vices. Somehow, though, he succumbed. That's not your fault. Be proud of what you did and leave it at that."

Leaning against a wall, Harry felt more defeated than he had ever felt outside of battle.

"Whatever happens, don't deprive the realm of your service," Thomas added. "England needs you, regardless of who sits on the throne: He's only a fleeting mortal. But England endures, England is real, England is eternal, as eternal as any land can be. Accept Henry, answer to him, as we all must now. But never forget that what you really serve is England. England, Lad."

Sadly, Harry nodded.

Thomas slapped his back. "Good man! Now I'd best be about my duties. It's going to be a trying day."

Harry set off for Aldersgate amid clanging bells, chanting choirs and retainers of this lord or that bustling about. Step by step, he fought his way against the crowds, all headed in the opposite direction, to the coronation. It was like swimming upriver, like crossing the sea against an unyielding tide. Despite the multitudes, aching loneliness engulfed him.

At his doorway, he fitted his key to the lock with his right hand, pressing his left against the ponderous wood. The cut on his palm throbbed, deepening into an ugly red. Somehow, he resisted the urge to tear the scab away and shake loose any drops of Bolingbroke's blood that might have pooled inside with his own.

Passing through the inn, he entered the stable to greet his horses and bury his face in Valdus' warm, rough mane. Then he took his solace in a long, rambling ride, far from the disillusion and dissolution of London.

Chapter XIII
Wednesday, 22 October 1399 - Westminster Palace

The servant left the tray, bowing his way out.

Ralph Neville lifted a pie onto King Henry's plate and speared the crust of a second, releasing plumes of cinnamon-scented steam. "What're you going to do about Harry? It's all the gossip—how he avoided your coronation. Never mind that all the rest of our family were there: Me, my Percy uncles, cousin Athol..."

The juice of succulent apples slid down his throat and Ralph licked his lips appreciatively. After an energetic night of reunion with Joanie Beaufort, Henry's half-sister and Ralph's longtime if long-ignored inamorata, a private breakfast with Henry was delight atop delight.

Henry stabbed a wayward bite of pastry. "Our cousin Harry? A relative trifle!" He laughed at his pun. "He harms himself in the end. When the bards sing of that day, praising all who exalted themselves by honoring me, his name won't be there. Who'll want to talk of Harry Hotspur then?"

"Probably many," Ralph predicted silently, reaching out to another pie for comfort and scattering empty egg, fruit, and bacon dishes. "At least," he conceded aloud, "once you were crowned, he did render fealty and promise his usual loyal service to England."

"And I welcomed him. Two days ago, I reappointed him Warden of the March. His term under his last appointment by Richard hadn't ended, but I thought it prudent to put my own seal on it."

"He accepted?"

"Yea. The Scots raided upon expiration of the truce last month. There wasn't much damage; his lieutenants repelled them admirably. Still, I think Harry wants to be back North himself."

"Then perhaps we should be grateful to the Scots."

Henry smiled. "Moreover," he continued, "I've also named Harry permanent justice of Cheshire, sheriff of Flint, and justiciar of North Wales, along with lord of Anglesey."

Neville looked puzzled. "He's had little or no experience in Wales or the border marches there."

"That hardly matters," Henry replied. "He also had scant experience in France, when Richard sent him over to govern Aquitaine. You remember that."

"'Struth, I don't," Neville confessed.

Henry explained. "The town fathers and nobles, who'd long been our vassals, got into a fierce dispute with my father, the Duke of Aquitaine, the highest official there under Richard. I don't know what bothered them—but father always angered easily; I oft argued with him, too. Anyway, the Crown needed to dispatch a new governor and picked Harry. But when he sailed to Bordeaux, the town elders denied entry, objecting that he was too 'lowly', a mere knight, not a duke, or earl. They also feared he was only my father's fawning surrogate and insisted they would shun anyone who did not come in the name of King Richard himself, or of his son, if Richard had one—and of course, Richard didn't. Otherwise, they would continue to bar their gates."

Neville hooted. "Hah! Harry must've been furious, laid siege or torched the town—and countryside, too."

"No," Henry said. "Though he was humiliated—in front of his troops, no less—he restrained his wrath. Nor did he flee back to his ships and England. He simply camped outside the city walls and invited all and sundry to visit. Slowly, they accepted. Lower ranks first, then elders and nobles. Over time, he convinced them that he had come in the name of Richard, and no one else. Thus, they admitted him. And I subsequently heard that by the time they did, they were so impressed by him that they genuinely welcomed him, too."

"No!" Neville's jaw dropped.

"Yea! Nor was that all. A while later, during peace talks, the French and English kings decided to cut Aquitaine loose from direct royal control. They said this granted it more autonomy, but the folk in Aquitaine feared it would just leave them more vulnerable to fresh efforts by my father or some other peer to wrest control again. They'd have none of it; demanded that they remain directly under the English Crown, with 'their own Lord Harry' governing them. They got their way." The king still sounded a bit incredulous. "All went well after that, too. In fact, when Harry's term ultimately ended, his departure from Bordeaux seems to have been as lamented as his arrival had been!"

"Unbelievable." Neville pronounced. "Well, has he agreed to duty in Wales and Cheshire now?"

"Yea."

"Happily for us," Neville observed. "It's a weighty responsibility. That, plus the North, should keep Harry quite busy—and no thorn in our sides here. Indeed, it's brilliant! You've made it seem you've gone out of your way to reconcile him despite his opposition to your coronation. So, you win plaudits for yourself for being gracious and spare us his presence here."

Henry basked. "I'm contemplating yet another charge for Harry, as well."

"More?"

"I think I'll make him guardian of my son Hal. It's probably wise to send the boy away. He's scarcely spoken to me since I had him brought back from Ireland. Oh, he answers when addressed, respectfully enough. Yet he moons over Richard."

"Wasn't Richard his guardian, when you were exiled?"

"Just so. Richard had Hal taken to court, surety for my good behaviour abroad. But Hal genuinely liked him; calls him 'Dear Uncle Richard' even now. And Richard became quite fond of Hal. He told me—in one of the few polite things we've said to each other—how proud he is of the boy."

"Richard always treated youngsters well, much better than he treated their elders," Neville noted. "Think of all the times he ignored matters of state to tell his little wife and her friends a story or join in their games. 'Twas all innocent as far as I could see, too. No lechery, like you find in some men."

"Yea," Henry agreed. "Maybe he ne'er grew up, so he's so content around children. Anyway, when he went to Ireland, he took Hal and two other lads along, as pages. And he ensured they'd be safe there when he sailed back to England." He shook his head. "Hal wasn't pleased to later return and find Richard confined in the Tower. He worries about him. Sometimes, I doubt Hal thinks I should be king at all."

Neville frowned. "Yet you'd send him off with Harry—who let all and sundry know he thought you shouldn't be crowned?"

"Seems odd, perhaps. Harry opposed me as long as he could. But once I was crowned, he accepted the will of the land. Not a bad example for my son, eh?" Sighing, Henry stroked his beard. "Sometimes I feel cursed by what that loathsome friar said: That I'll come to mistrust my own kith and kin. I don't want to suspect Hal as he grows up. I'd rather have him away from court, not exposed to any traitors here who may be gathering about me even now." He shot Neville a grim glance—whether in warning or in uncertainty, Ralph couldn't tell—and stared at the wall. "Better Hal should be in the company of an honest man, even one who frequently tries my patience."

"Might be dangerous, though," Ralph commented. "Harry is oft in the thick of it in the North."

"That's why I'm restricting Hal to attendance on Harry in Cheshire and Wales. The boy is Prince of Wales now, old enough to take interest in his domain. Wales has been peaceful, save for that brigandry last summer. But I won't let Hal campaign with Harry on the Borders. If he goes north, he'll stay in Berwick."

"Then it sounds perfect," Ralph concluded.

Henry's ego inflated like the dome of the latest pie being borne in. "But other affairs await us," he added as the servant set the sizzling delicacy before him. "Hear what I intend for the morrow when the Great Council meets. By the way, I've ordered Harry to be there, too."

Neville stifled a groan.

Curious chicks and ducks pecking at his heels, Harry crossed the palace yard. Before long, he would be off to his new assignments and Henry had offered him the pick of four horses. Aware of the ephemeral nature of royal generosity, he wanted to make his selection early, lest Henry pledge the same mounts to others, and still others again, and leave the palace stalls quite empty. There was another reason to choose quickly, too. Henry had summoned him to an audience mid-morn.

He paused at the stable entrance, adjusting his eyes to the mixture of gloom and sunbeams. Somewhere, a barn cat meowed, and hooves thumped against wood. Inhaling the sweet scent of hay, he took a few steps forward. He was nearly under the loft, when—Thud! A bundle of straw landed at his heels. As he dodged sideways, another bale followed the first.

"Damnation! Who goes?"

There was no response, but he scurried up the ladder to the loft. No one was visible, though a dim shadow betrayed a presence behind hay rolls.

Diving, he cornered the culprit and lifted him off his feet. It was a boy, in elegant Lancastrian livery, with cropped light-brown hair, hazel eyes, and a hint of the blood of John of Gaunt.

"Oow!" the boy yelped as Harry's grip tightened. "Put me down! Do you not know who I am?"

"No. Nor much care, either." Impervious to the fists pounding his back, Harry carried his catch almost to the edge of the loft. "Say you're sorry! Or I could throw you off!"

"Never!"

"Well enough. 'Twas nice to make your acquaintance, and I regret it's been so short!" Harry swung the boy. The young voice spluttered into protests. Harry swung him harder.

"I say—unhand me! I never meant to hurt you. I threw the straw the moment you were going to move anyway."

Setting him down on the loft floor, Harry stood over him. "You're omniscient? And your aim is so well-timed you'd risk harming someone to prove it? Would that all men were so perfect."

The boy's face sank. "Sorry. I won't do it again."

Harry stepped aside.

Suddenly proud, the boy pulled himself up to every inch of his young height. "And even if I am Prince of Wales and heir to all England, I'll not arrest you for insubordination."

Harry whistled in mock amazement. "Prince of Wales, is it?"

The boy nodded solemnly.

"Oh, aye. And I'm the emperor of Byzantium. But were you the pope himself, I still would've chastised you." Harry had seen the boy once or twice, years earlier, and recognition dawned; 'twas Henry's oldest, Hal. "So, tell me, My Prince," he half-bowed, though he refused to kneel. "Why are you hiding, itching to knock the head off anyone who nears?"

Hal lounged against the hay, chewing a clover stem. "The royal tailors were after me; wanted me to spend the whole morn being measured for stupid things, like pointed shoes, and doublets too tight to breathe in and so short they hardly cover my privy parts, and velvet gowns, and shirts with those big, wide sleeves that almost drag on the ground." He looked outraged. "How can a man move in gowns like that? Or draw a sword in those sleeves?" Sighing, he studied Harry's apparel: boots, leggings and a short-sleeved tunic over a shirt with cuffs tied snugly at his wrists, allowing unhindered movement of arms and hands. "You don't wear such nonsense."

Harry laughed. "No. My father has long since given up trying to turn me into a stylish gentleman of the court. But when I was your age, I had to put up with some indignities, too."

"Who's your father?" the boy wondered, and when Harry told him, Hal's face lit up. "Then you must be Sir Harry, the one they call Hotspur!" He jumped up, pumping Harry's hand enthusiastically. "Long have I wanted to meet you." Looking around, he saw they were still alone. "Can you teach me to fight like you, as a knight? Handle my sword? Use a lance? We could go now, take a couple of horses to the meadows upriver. No one need know."

Harry laughed. "I'd be honored to teach you. But I can't help you abscond with yourself. Doubtless, we'd be seen. I'd be accused of kidnapping the Prince of Wales. And I think I like you. But I don't want to hang for you."

Hal looked disappointed, though he nodded. "I'm supposed to be a prince, but I feel more like a prisoner." He sank back into the hay. "After the tailors are done with me, I'm bidden to appear before my father. He's picked a guardian for me and won't tell me who. Said he had to confer with the man first, to make sure he agrees. Of course, the fellow will agree. It's probably some greedy friend of his who'll promise Father anything and try to win favor by using me." A pessimism beyond his years showed. "I'd lief run away than answer to some prick.

"Begging your pardon," he apologized for the foul term.

"Knights should watch their language," Harry advised. "But that's something else you'll learn, if your father chooses your guardian wisely. For now, though, you'd best meet with these tailors. I came out here to pick horses for my command in Wales. But I expect that can wait. I, too, must attend upon your father while you're being measured. If possible, I'll ask him to select a worthy guardian."

He smiled at the boy. "Then maybe you can help me choose the best horses for Wales. And, if your father consents, we can try them and take them out on a brisk gallop. But first, you must do your duty by the tailors. 'Tis not fair to make them wait, lad. Tailors first, then more pleasant pursuits!"

Hal sang out in gratitude. "Done!"

―――

Two hours later, eyes downcast, Hal stood before his father.

"You promise, on your fealty and as a dutiful son, that you'll treat this man politely and obey him?"

Morose, Hal nodded. Henry had told him little, only that he had appointed a guardian, a well-regarded knight who was also well-lettered, intelligent, and of impeccable lineage—a second cousin, in fact. Hal scarcely found that reassuring; the extended Lancaster-Beaufort family harbored more than a few self-serving schemers.

"Try not to look so miserable. You'd think I was sending you to the gallows, not introducing you to your guardian." Henry signaled his secretary, John Norbury: "Go fetch him."

Moments later, a door opened.

Hal looked up. "Lord Harry!" He threw himself at Hotspur in an exuberant hug.

Harry laughed and rubbed the boy's head. "So, we meet again." Extricating himself, he turned Hal back toward his father.

"Lord Harry was going to throw me off the hayloft because I dumped straw on him. But now he's going to take me riding."

Astonished, the King blinked, then beamed. "I guess you've spared me official introductions, and I'm very pleased that you're both pleased." He gestured toward vellum sheets, awaiting their signatures on his desk. "You can tell me about your morning later, Hal. Now we've formalities to discharge."

An hour later, Harry and Hal got their chance to select horses for Wales. Hal had indeed accepted his guardian—and Harry his latest responsibility.

Henry convened fifty-eight of them the next day: Hal; two archbishops; thirteen bishops; seven abbots; one duke, six earls; twenty-five barons and three knights, including Harry. Maps covered the floor and fear of war topped the agenda: French navies prowled the coast, perhaps preparing to avenge Richard, and the Scots rumbled near the border.

As an experienced commander, Harry had been asked to lead the military discussions. "First," he pointed to the maps, "if I might call attention to some oft-vulnerable spots in the North and Southeast."

They spent an hour on defense before taking up other, looming business: The fate of Richard of Bordeaux. Two days earlier, the Commons had asked that he be produced for trial, as the former king himself had requested. It was the Great Council's turn to react.

"I think he should be brought before Parliament and tried," Bishop John Trevor of St. Asaph's in Wales declared. "Perhaps when Parliament met a few weeks ago, it did not seem the right time to discuss it. But I bid you to discuss it now."

A few voices rang out in support before Henry intervened: "I too would prefer to bring him to trial, but not one inflamed by passions. Can we do that with the Scots and French breathing down our necks? We may be at war ere another fortnight ends."

"If we do try him," Edmund of York added, "everything should be fair and honorable, not cobbled together to meet an arbitrary schedule."

William Colchester, Abbot of Westminster, concurred. "I fear for his life if he is brought before his accusers so soon, whilst anger waxes hot. I would not have him treated like Richard Arundel. Let's wait for an entirely new Parliament, one that can meet in less haste and resentment."

Applause followed. So did dissent.

"Humphh!" the Earl of Warwick grumped. "To me, 'twould be far more tempting to deal with Richard as he did with Gloucester: Let him perish 'mysteriously' in prison. Though I myself would favor public execution; much more definitive. I urge the Council to consider it."

"Hear, hear." Lord Cobham seconded.

"No!" Henry snapped. "I'll not countenance open talk of his death. I propose internal exile. Let him live out his years that way."

"And a trial?" a baron asked.

"Not soon, not until we've overcome these foreign perils."

Others loudly backed Henry, recommending that Richard also be denied access to former servitors and friends.

"Compared to a hasty trial and execution, this seems imminently reasonable," Ralph Neville observed. "We also might settle on a fitting residence for him. Leeds Castle?"

"Perfect," the king pronounced.

"Let's vote," Archbishop Arundel suggested. "We might likewise sign a summary of our discussion to be permanently affixed to the rolls of Parliament."

"Even so," Henry agreed.

"And if you, My Lord," Arundel pointed to the Earl of Northumberland, "would be so good as to pose the question and then inform the Commons of our decision?"

Earl Henry stood. "Are all in agreement that Richard of Bordeaux should be kept in safe and comfortable lodging until such time as 'tis deemed proper to bring him to trial?"

He spoke to everyone, though his eyes searched the back row for his son. But Harry's expression was impassive. "All in agreement?"

"Yea!" The response reverberated off the walls.

"Opposed?"

No one spoke.

"Opposed?" Earl Henry repeated more loudly.

Once more, they were silent, even Harry.

"I will convey our decision to the Commons," Earl Henry announced.

They recessed to allow clerks time to prepare the Parliament roll.

Within an hour, they were back, trouping one by one to a table with a parchment, unrolled to a new section summarizing their discussion. Harry was to sign it after higher lords and prelates but, due to military seniority, ahead of six barons and other knights. Uneasily, he watched them come and go to the table. There had to be a better way. But what? He was at a loss, as he had been during his father's poll, neither able to oppose Richard's captivity nor endorse it.

Automatically, he flexed his palm, then tried again. It shook, like his fingers. Shook! The hand that had so expertly wielded a sword in battle failed him now. How could it—as if mocking his strength? After surviving imprisonment and hardship, how could he tremble over a document? Embarrassed, hoping no one noticed, he closed his eyes, steeling his nerves.

Finally, when his turn came, he calmly approached the table, picked up the quill, and wrote.

Sir Harry Percy

There it lay, the ink glistening wet, his signature as firm as ever. So quickly the deed was done and so easily his name joined the rest recorded there. Indelible.

Forever.

Chapter XIV
December 1399 - St. Alban's

Bishop Thomas Merks planned his holidays carefully. Penalized by the new king for defending the old, he was placed under house arrest at St. Alban's. But the monks there had welcomed him affectionately, treating him less as a prisoner than as the fellow Benedictine he was. By December, he had settled in. Nonetheless, he averred that if he were ever free, he'd hasten to his northern see to fend off sacrilegious Scots or greedy Lancastrians seeking to supplant him. No potential successors had come forth, but everyone knew 'twas only a matter of time. He had never been the choice of clergy or faithful, landing in Carlisle when Richard and Pope Benedict IX colluded to overturn the clergy's episcopal election of a respected priest, William Strickland, and deposit Merks there instead.

Proud of the ancient tradition of electing their own leaders, their abbots, the Benedictines didn't condone the way Merks got Carlisle. But they also understood his desire to keep it once acquired. Some even assumed his arrest had shown him what really mattered: his flock. They were wrong, of course, but Merks wasn't about to enlighten them. Rather, he clung to routine. Then, one night, as the monks gathered for Matins, he lingered behind, unseen, until he could climb an outer wall. Squires from Lord Salisbury awaited him on the other side, and he was off. No one missed him in church, as occasional lapses by a guest were ignored. Likewise, when he didn't appear for breakfast, and his monastic cell was found vacant, no one thought anything but the obvious. "Godspeed," they prayed. Nor did they feel compelled to inform the king. Just as they hadn't questioned royal motives in dumping Merks into their midst, they wouldn't tattle on him when he left. If Bishop Merks hurried north to Carlisle, 'twas his business.

In fact, he rode south to London, where Abbot Colchester eagerly admitted him to Westminster.

"Originally, I took no sides," Colchester explained. "I had the abbey accommodate Parliament, as is customary. I accepted our share of money from the merchants in the yard. And we hosted the coronation, as requested."

"Yet you shelter me."

"Yea, brother. The more I see of this new king, the more I fear he's worse than the one we had. So, anyone who comes as Richard's friend, I greet as my friend, too."

Colchester soon found himself greeting friends regularly.

* * *

Wednesday, 17 December 1399 - Westminster Abbey

Christmas was a week away, although hardly anyone would have guessed. With meat frowned upon during Advent, the lay brothers who served as Colchester's chefs outdid themselves with alternatives: salmon poached in milk, herbed trout, and spiced crayfish with mushrooms. Alongside came an abundance of winter vegetables: dilled carrots, peas with onion, cabbage in wine, creamed kale and stewed parsnips; bread; spiced apple compote; poppyseed cakes, dried-cherry tarts, walnut confections, and custard with honey.

The board was groaning, like those gathered around it.

They were a high-ranking crowd, including Lord Salisbury, although four were less exalted than they'd been months earlier, for Henry had demoted them just as quickly as Richard had previously elevated them. Thus Edward 'Aumale' Plantagenet had been downgraded from Duke of Albemarle to Earl of Rutland; John Holland, Richard's half-brother and Henry's brother-in-law, was no longer Duke of Exeter but mere Earl of Huntington; his nephew, Thomas, erstwhile Duke of Surrey, had become Earl of Kent; and Thomas Despenser, briefly Earl of Gloucester, was again a lesser baron.

"And he replaced me," Roger Walden, ex-archbishop of Canterbury, complained.

"With Arundel, whom you had ousted earlier," Salisbury noted dryly.

All remained in Henry's good graces, however, and had been invited, with their entourages, to a tournament at Windsor over Epiphany, 6 January.

They plotted as they dined. They would arrive for the tourney as expected. Then they would seize the castle, admit their own armies, arrest Henry and reclaim the throne for Richard. If he did not die in the struggle, Henry would be tried for high treason and, certes, convicted and executed.

Or so the noblemen told Merks, Walden and Colchester.

Later, in the privacy of John Holland's room, a different stratagem took shape: Henry would be killed at Windsor. So would his children to prevent future Lancastrian threats. Doubtless, a number of tourney contestants would die as well, although perhaps some would join the earls rather than defend Henry. Then Richard could return.

"What if Henry flees?" Despenser wondered, pouring a cup of the abbey's prized ale.

"Think how many times he's already escaped," Aumale joined in. "I tell you, the man has nine lives. Like an accursed alley cat!"

John Holland smiled. "Even an alley cat can succumb to curdled cream."

Over the rim of a tankard, Salisbury eyed him with distaste. Through the years, Holland, too, had known many escapes, mostly from justice. The worst had been when Holland had sexually mutilated and murdered a friar accused of slandering Richard's royal family. "High birth and Richard's wont to hide scandals spared him," Salisbury recalled mentally. "But he was clearly implicated, and he denied naught. Then Holland jumped and killed the unarmed Stafford lordling and avoided the noose again."

"What if Henry is already dead when we seize the castle?" Holland continued. "What if he chances upon tainted meat or wine at dinner? What if it kills not just him but his sons and the garrison?"

"What do you mean?" Salisbury asked.

"Poison! Easy enough to put some in Henry's food and drink, especially over Christmas, when folk send him gifts: hams, cakes, ale."

Salisbury frowned. The others were intrigued.

"I can arrange it easily," Holland boasted. "As husband to his sister, it's natural for me to celebrate the holidays with him. I'll bring some of his favorite wine; Mosel, perhaps. He's terribly fond of that, especially the expensive vintages. I'll give him three casks for personal use. I'll send a fourth to the garrison. And the one for the garrison, and two of those for Henry, will be poisoned. The other I'll leave alone, and order that it be used first. That way, by the time his servants tap the second, they'll have accepted it as nothing but very good wine."

They looked skeptical.

"It's quite effective, this poison," Holland assured them. "I learned of it from Italian dukes when I went abroad after slaying young Stafford. It's tasteless and horribly lethal, though not right away."

"Huh?" Aumale gaped.

"Too incriminating if a man keels over the instant he drinks," Holland snapped. "Mixed with wine, it takes a couple of hours to kill. But then it does kill very nicely."

Salisbury almost asked how Holland could be so certain—and then realized he really didn't want to know. Still, he looked uncomfortable.

"God's blood, man," Holland exclaimed. "Have no thoughts of mercy. Did Henry have any for Bushey, Wiltshire, or Arundel, or those judges and knights who went to the block when he and that pack tried to seize the rule years ago?"

Thomas of Kent supported his uncle. "It'll save lives. If Henry's already dead, we won't need to fight the lords around him."

The notion of sparing lives, especially of noblemen, was appealing. They therefore agreed: Henry would be poisoned. Richard would be restored. And they would strike at Epiphany.

* * *

Sunday, 4 January 1400 - Windsor Castle

At Henry's invitation and Hal's insistence, Harry joined the king, Ralph Neville, and Joanie Beaufort in the royal apartments. It had already been dark for hours, and he felt pleasantly relaxed as Hal led him back to their chessboard, abandoned at the summons to eat.

"Your turn," Hal reminded him, and Harry moved a piece, then smiled as Hal, as usual, took forever studying a response.

As he waited, Harry went back over the dinner conversation. "What of Richard?" Bishop Beaufort, one of Henry's half-brothers, had asked. "Could you not bring him before a judicial court since France and Scotland haven't attacked? The Commons have been pressing for it again, and some bishops, too."

Henry had replied cautiously. "The Scots refuse to accept my overlordship. The French cannot be trusted, either. The time isn't right for Richard's trial."

"Just kill him quietly, like some suggested in October," John Beaufort, another sibling, had recommended.

"No!" Henry had retorted. "I transferred him from Leeds to Pontefract, a stronger fortress, and less comfortable. That's as far as I'll go. He's in no danger as long as he doesn't incite insurrection. And there's no sign of that!" He had glanced down the hall, seen nothing but kinsmen and friends, and returned to his meat.

"So Richard's safe," Harry concluded. "And I know the Scots are considering a new truce, maybe by spring. Perhaps then we can try Richard."

"Your turn, My Lord," Hal informed him, confident the implications of his move had gone unnoticed, and he would next nab one of Harry's knights.

Having anticipated the possibility, Harry deftly countered it and leaned back, still a little surprised to have spent so many hours in Henry's personal quarters.

A widower, the king liked to have his siblings around him. Of family members present at dinner, only the Beaufort brothers were now absent, off with the bishop of Rochester somewhere. Ralph and Joanie lounged against each other, her plump face blissful. Henry sat in a corner chair, strumming a lute. Finishing an instrumental, he segued into an Italian song. He had a fine voice, and they all clapped appreciatively. After another tune or two, he offered refreshments.

"Let's have some of that wine my brother-in-law provided. I saved it, so you didn't get a chance to try it at dinner. We still have two barrels left." The king smiled coyly. "I admit that Ralph, Bishop Beaufort, Holland, and I finished off one cask ourselves before Holland left to collect his team for the tourney. Quite excellent it was. John Holland has exquisite taste."

"And lots of money!" Hal piped up as Henry summoned a valet, who brought back a carafe and goblets: gold for the King, silver with gold trim for the prince, and embossed silver for the rest. They toasted each other, and Henry sampled the wine, letting it roll around his mouth before swallowing. "Like nectar for the gods." With another sip, he reluctantly set it aside. He had drunk heartily earlier and knew his limits. This he would savor slowly. He returned to the lute.

Too young for all but the weakest wine, Hal ignored his goblet. But Harry had drunk mostly water at dinner, filling his cup with from the pitcher provided to each diner before adding a splash of wine from the matching jug. Ready for real wine now, he took a deep draught of Mosel.

Reaching for his goblet while pinching Joanie's broad backside, Ralph swore. His goblet teetered on the settee arm and fell to the floor. "Hell!"

Henry brought a chord to a screeching finish, shrugging. "No matter, Ralph, there's plenty more."

Ralph disentwined himself from Joanie. "Save it. I prefer your Burgundy, anyway." Opening a cupboard, he filled a fresh cup from the decanter of red wine kept there.

"Joanie and I are thinking of getting married," he informed Henry as he sat down again.

"I thought you already were. What about those brats you've already brought into the world?"

Neville grinned with a hint of embarrassment. "There wasn't a ceremony afore. We had the banns read, as the church wants. But naught else happened after that, and, in fact, we were oft apart, even though we had long since plighted our tryst privily and started a family. And I admit," he blushed, "that I thrust my spear elsewhere for quite a while."

Joanie squeezed Ralph's hand. "Now we're together again. Forever! So, we think it's time to be properly wed, with all the rituals, even if we're already married to the extent most folk are."

Overhearing, Harry smiled. Like most couples able to choose their own mates—and many were not—

Neville and Joanie had become married in the traditional way: Having an exclusive relationship, which included sex; pledging themselves to each other, and being recognized by the community as a pair. They'd approached a chaplain, who, in a notice read at Mass, had announced their intended life together. "And that was that," Harry thought. With the ecclesial fathers still dickering over whether the sacrament required a nuptial ceremony, many unions, even among high nobles, were not celebrated with weddings. Ralph's first wedlock had begun quietly as a boy in an arranged match that had left him a young widower more burdened with fatherhood than grief. The second time, he and Joanie had been adults, freely choosing one another. Now, however belatedly, they wanted a wedding.

Across the room, Henry chuckled. "Well, if you never had a real ceremony earlier, 'tis a marvelous idea! We can use Westminster, perhaps in June, when the weather is good."

Joanie gulped nervously.

Ralph broke in. "We were thinking of something sooner. You see, Joanie is with child again."

Reddening, Joanie finished her drink and reached for the carafe of Holland's wine, refilling her cup.

Henry laughed. "All right, By God! You shall have whatever you wish! And maybe you can name this one after me." He called to his son. "Hal, come and congratulate your Uncle Ralph and Aunt Joanie."

Hal surreptitiously made a face to Harry but left the chessboard to dutifully embrace the prospective parents.

"Forget your game," Henry directed. "You'll be in the ceremony. You might as well help plan it now."

"You can bear the rings!" Joanie cooed.

Hal fidgeted. "By your leave, Father, and my Lord Uncle and Lady Aunt. I think I'd like go to bed." *Anything* to get out of listening to them discuss a wedding, his role in it, and their likely insistence on dressing him in some silly outfit for the occasion.

"If you must... Go." The king excused him. "And don't forget to say goodnight to Lord Harry."

Hal crossed the carpet and made his farewell.

Understanding the sudden departure, Harry handed Hal the princely goblet. "You might want it if you can't sleep. Let me mix the wine with water, so 'tis not so strong."

Hal gave it back, whispering. "You drink it. I don't want it. But don't let Father think I wasted something so fine." He ran off to his room, adjoining Harry's.

Harry took his leave as well, scooping up Hal's goblet on his way out. No sense letting a good German vintage go unappreciated!

———

Harry awoke with a start, his naked body drenched with sweat and the room spinning at wild angles against the light from the hearth. Simultaneously freezing and burning, he reached for the duvet, doubling over a few seconds later as pain ripped through him. Hand wrapped around the bedpost, he waited for it to subside and, when it did, realized he was about to vomit.

He stumbled into the garderobe, managing to fling himself to the floor at the commode before his stomach violently voided itself down the hole. Weakened and shaking, he remained on his knees, clinging to the commode, until he felt steadier. Then, groping his way to the wash stand at the front of the garderobe, he filled the basin from the ewer. After sponging himself from face to foot, he poured an extra cupful over his head. Cooler, feeling better, he was about to retrace his way to bed when another blinding wave of dizziness hit. Nearly blacking out, he grabbed the wash basin, carrying it to the floor with him. Lying on the cold stone, he retched and vomited again into the basin—and then once more—before falling back. Soon, though, his skin beaded with another hot-cold sweat, and the retching resumed until any food in his system was long gone, and he was losing blood as well as bile. Strength melting away, he lapsed into a troubled faint, only to choke awake again. Too disoriented to find the basin, he spewed blood and vomit all over himself and the floor. Eventually, his exhausted gut spent itself, and, head lolling on the tiles, he faded into unconsciousness.

First, Henry awoke ill, as the garrison simultaneously reported a strange, virulent malady, and then a robed Ralph Neville tore into the hallway, screaming that Joanie was dying.

Summoned from his bed, the royal physician ran to the King's chamber, where Henry recovered after throwing up. Joanie was much worse, and the physician feared the loss of her unborn child, even if she lived. Ralph was unharmed, however, and only that fact and the physician's careful questioning began providing answers, especially after Ralph remembered that he had spilled his goblet of Holland's wine and that Henry had drunk little. But Joanie had consumed two cups of Mosel while another barrel had gone to the garrison. And Hal, who had drunk nothing like Neville, was spared.

With a little cry, Hal sprang forward.

Beating on Harry's outer door, he got no response and tried the handle. Locked. Running back to his own room, he entered Harry's chamber through the door connecting the two. There, in the uneven firelight, he saw the long legs protruding from the garderobe. A second later, he stood over his guardian, comatose on the floor, the washbasin slopping over with reddened vomit and the man himself reeking of it.

"Lord Harry!" Hal knelt, repulsed by the smell and sight but even more worried. He searched for a pulse and found one, felt a latent warmth to the clammy skin, thought an eyelid flickered. In a few moments, he raced out again. Neville had returned to Joanie, and the physician was closeted with the king, so Hal sped up the tower stairs to the squires' lodging and awoke Hardyng, who roused Kynge. The three hurried back down. Hardyng refilled the wash pitchers with fresh water from the well and brought extra towels. Gently bathing Harry, they carried him to bed. Half-awakened, he murmured something about making sure Hal was all right, noticed the boy beside him, and drowsed off again. As they bundled blankets around him, the physician looked in, decided they were doing all they could, and hastened out to the garrison.

Hardyng mopped the garderobe floor before rejoining Ian and Hal. "What's wrong? I've been with Harry since I was twelve. I've never seen him sick like this."

Ralph entered from Hal's room. "The doctor thinks they've been poisoned—Joanie, too. It may've been Holland's wine, though he and Henry and I drank the very same wine two days ago." He was angry and confused. "I had the wine cellar servants confined but doubt they're responsible. Some murderous scoundrel snuck in."

Hal stared at the gold-trimmed goblet, standing empty on Harry's bedside table. His goblet. Mortified, he faced the others. "I gave mine to Lord Harry. I didn't want it. So he drank twice as much. What if I've killed him?" He choked on a sob.

Kynge placed a reassuring hand on the boy's shoulder. "Don't blame yourself. You didn't taint his drink, lad. And I don't think he'll die. He's rid himself of the poison now. He just needs to sleep, heal inside, and regain strength."

Neville looked down at his cousin with unexpected concern and seemed to find Kynge's words comforting as well. "Let me know if he takes a turn for the worse." He hurried back to Joanie.

Hal insisted on staying and was still there when heavy footfalls preceded pounding on the door.

In the bed, Harry stirred, though his eyes remained shut.

The knocking continued until Hardyng unlocked the door to admit Henry. Face set in an uncompromising scowl, the King wore chainmail, broadsword strapped on, coronet mounted to his mesh cowl. "Hal, come! The castle will soon be under siege. We ride to London." He looked somewhat wan but otherwise seemed fine.

Neville filled the doorway, and Henry addressed him as well. "I'm sorry to leave Joanie, and Harry, too. I've received a secret warning from Edmund of York. His son, Aumale, told him of a conspiracy to kill me and many of you. Aumale's pluck failed him, ere he could ride from his father's castle and rejoin the plotters. Salisbury was in on it, and both Hollands. Traitors!" His tone rose in disbelief. "Even John Holland, my sister's spouse, my own kith and kin."

He whirled. "Come, boy!"

Hal threw himself down beside Harry's bed. "No. I can't leave him. They meant to kill me. He drank the poison instead. I must help defend him, save Windsor."

Muttering angrily, Henry crossed the room.

Hal only dug in deeper until Harry's eyes struggled open, and he attempted to sit up. He turned toward Hal, voice hoarse. "Go, lad. Obey your father. These fellows are good protection," he nodded weakly at Kynge and Hardyng. "And doubtless, I look so terrible anyone breaking in will think me dead already."

He tried to punch Hal playfully. "Get you gone."

Eyes closing, he slumped onto the pillow, slack hand dropping to the bedcovers. Lifting it, Hal kissed it in fealty. Then he rose to accompany his father.

* * *

Mid-January 1400 - The Fen Country

John Holland rose from decaying rushes, peering through a crack in the wall. Grayness and cold were all that was out there, broken only by wispy white fog. Dampness filled his every bone. Yet the air outdoors was better than the stench of this shed. Sheep might once have sheltered here, but of late, it seemed to have harbored pigs—wild boars, probably. Now, the boars' loss was his gain. He probably resembled a pig himself anyway, clothes soiled, torn and slept in too many nights; matted hair green with marsh algae, beard so tangled it might have been braided. "May God damn them through eternity." He cursed his enemies. "And let Him start with that craven rat."

Aumale.

Fleeing the ancestral home after confessing to his father, Aumale had hurried to warn the conspirators that Henry knew of their plot. Then he had changed sides—yet again—and galloped straight to Henry, who had reached London.

In Windsor, Holland and his co-conspirators had discovered their royal prey had escaped and those left behind were too sick to pose threats. They raced after Henry.

Assembling an army, the king sent it after his pursuers. Realizing they were outnumbered, the earls detoured to regroup. But their ranks dwindled. Soon, only a few retainers were left for Salisbury, Thomas of Kent, and Merks. Worse off, John Holland found himself without a single servant. "Said they needn't suffer me anymore! Sucking sops!" He spoke to silence.

Leaving his comrades, he had headed east, hoping to sail for France. Now, he was bogged down—literally—in the swamps. Even his horse was gone, disappearing from a brothel in a pissant village where he had paused.

Wrapping arms over shoulders, he scratched fiercely. Either boars had larded his shed with fleas, or in that same whorehouse where he had lost his horse, he had picked up lice. He glowered. Misfortune had started with that damned poison. He should've doubled the dose.

"Here…ee."

The cries seemed so faint he mistook them for distant curlews. Then he heard yapping dogs.

Bird calls became shouts of men.

"'Struth, I seen the fattest boar e'er to waddle the land three days past."

"I spied him too, by that old sheep barn."

The baying increased.

Pupil pressed close to the crack again, Holland spotted at least a dozen men and twice as many hounds. He flattened himself into a corner against the slimy stone. He was doomed. One last time, he cursed his bad luck with the poison, wishing he'd saved some for himself.

* * *

Mid-January 1400

As his troops chased the insurgents, the king based himself in Oxford, commandeering the Carmelite priory's best quarters. There one afternoon, he eased himself into a chair worthy of a pope—or at least a king—sipping mead. "I hear Holland got his due," he told his secretary, Norbury.

"'True, Your Majesty. Hunters up east found him, dragged him to shire officials, who executed him."

"Too bad," Henry mused. "I'd lief had him hauled here so he could be humiliated before crowds, afore he died, maybe tortured, too. Yet, that makes one less traitor to put on trial. How many do we expect?"

Norbury counted mentally. "About eighty, transported here so you can preside over the proceedings. Most were captured with Salisbury and Thomas of Kent."

"Holed up in a house in Circencester, didn't they?"

"Exactly, My Liege. But town folk surrounded it and, after skirmishing, seized Salisbury, Thomas of Kent, and Merks."

The king finished his mead, and Norbury refilled the cup.

"They detained Salisbury and Kent initially, intending to send them to you, Sire. But one of the earls' retainers escaped and set the town afire. Once local men overcame the blaze, they immediately beheaded Kent and Salisbury, though not Merks; they considered him more innocent, apparently."

"Hmph! Anything from Cheshire?"

"Yea, My Lord, word that traitors there collaborated with Thomas of Kent. It's said they even stormed Chester Castle. But it's all vague."

Henry lowered his cup.

Norbury glanced into the mead jug. Empty. "Shall I fetch more?"

"Apace." Henry grinned.

Norbury scurried out. On his return, along with mead, he brought a messenger.

Henry barked at the latter. "You have news?"

"Yea, My King, or this, rather." The courier extended a thick sack tied with a cord. "With the compliments of Circencester."

Henry clawed at it, retrieving the mouldering heads of Salisbury and Thomas of Kent.

"Hah!" With guttural glee, he flung each at the Carmelites' pristine wall. Grey-brown dribbles stained the whitewash. "That's how to deal with traitors!"

Chapter XV
February 1400 - London

Richard, late King of England; later, lord of Bordeaux; and most lately, leading internal exile, was no more. Shrouded in velvet and linen, wrapped tightly with only his face visible, he lay in St. Paul's Cathedral. A halo of candles flickered at his head, and guards flanked his feet while monks on either side chanted his soul toward eternity. His former subjects streamed by endlessly, some mourning, a few unseemly merry, others merely curious, seeking to determine that he really was gone.

Only a few men anywhere knew exactly how he had died. And they weren't saying. Admittedly, in death, he looked serene, eyelids closed and pale cheek smooth, still regal if still too young to grace a bier.

Sic homines semper eunt et transit gloria mundi...

Nonetheless, many puzzled over the haste of his exit in the way of all flesh, his transit from the glories of this world to the next.

Even several Privy Council members wondered, their information limited to what had been divulged by one of Henry's confidential couriers, riding hard from Pontefract. "Richard is dead," the courier had reported, "of gross debilitation and shock at his plight and the failure of the uprising on his behalf. Whilst it might be sad to some, it should be perceived by the council as accruing to our liege, King Henry's, great advantage."

Taking that as a not-so-subtle warning to not ask how this great advantage had come about, the council busied itself with plans to bring the corpse to London to lie in state.

But as the cortege progressed through the countryside, so did rumors, including claims that Richard had been deliberately killed, denied adequate food and water, and confined in a frigid cell till he perished. Since the sources included several of Henry's retainers, too frightened to object before Richard's death but too troubled to remain entirely silent afterward, the allegation had widespread credibility.

The procession arrived in London as Harry prepared to return to Chester. Kynge was already en route to Wales, so only Hardyng joined Harry in paying final respects to Richard. They found the streets around the cathedral packed and a long queue in the nave. Inching toward the catafalque, they listened to the buzz around them.

Hardyng finally pulled Harry behind a pillar, whispering. "They're all saying the same thing."

"Aye, that Richard was murdered."

"But none blame Henry directly. 'Twas supposedly done by minions acting on their own."

"Hell. We know how royal authority works. Jailers would never attempt it on their own. Yet anything else is unthinkable."

Eventually reaching the bier, they paused in prayer, then hurried from the church. As they crossed the cloister, Harry turned things over in his mind. Treating Richard properly should have been to Henry's benefit, enhancing his reputation for benevolence while discouraging the erosion of esteem for kings, including deposed kings. Yet he remembered Henry's promise at Windsor: Richard would only be threatened if Henry were threatened. That same night, the coup had begun. Now Richard was dead.

"The body was almost entirely covered," Hardyng observed. "On Henry's command."

"Supposedly to deter folks from tearing off pieces of clothing, or even flesh, as relics," Harry said.

"Or did Henry and his lackeys want to hide mortal wounds or starvation?" Hardyng pressed.

"If they did, they tricked themselves. They hid any violence done to Richard but raised suspicion anyway."

Mingling with other travelers as they rode west the next morning, they heard a slightly different theory: That Richard had died from lack of food and water, but of his own volition, protesting his treatment by refusing to eat, only to weaken until his heart gave out.

"Richard might've been foolish enough for that. Nonetheless…" Doubt filled Harry's voice.

"Mayhap Henry was embarrassed Richard died in royal custody," Hardyng speculated. "So, he didn't want to say anything. Then, to counter allegations of murder, he had to say *something*, admit that Richard did starve—but by Richard's own choice. Still, what a sorry end for a king."

"Aye, even one who governed badly."

* * *

February 1400 - London

The sweat lay on Elizabeth Mortimer Percy's skin as easily as her body lay on Lord Thomas Camoys' bed. Snuggling into a pillow, she murmured joyfully as Camoys removed the combs from her head, unloosing her flowing tresses. Softly, he began a song:

> *There was a lady, of comeliness rare,*
> *the finest jewel found anywhere,*
> *Her hair was raiment of purest gold,*
> *her smile a pearl of grace untold…*

She giggled. "You never said you were a jongleur."

"I'm not." He kissed her. "I begged a court minstrel to write something worthy of you. Though no poet could ever do that."

"Worthy or not, I love you."

"No more than I love you."

Slipping naked into bed alongside her, he caressed her breasts and thighs.

"Ohhhhhhh, Tam." She used the nickname he shared only with closest friends. Arms reaching out, she pulled him atop her, parted her legs and felt him enter her with his usual, electrifying need.

"Ahh," he croaked, finally falling limp in her arms, where he dozed off as she contemplated her good fortune.

They had met several weeks earlier at a musicale organized by King Henry to entertain leading lords, including Elizabeth's father-in-law, and their guests. Given her idolization of the court, Earl Henry had invited her to accompany him.

And there, Elizabeth had chanced upon Camoys; chatted with Camoys; danced exclusively with Camoys—except for a reel with Earl Henry and a round with the King himself. No one, though, had dazzled her like Camoys, who had seemed equally drawn to her.

As evening drew nigh, King Henry excused himself but urged his guests to dance on if they wished. Preparing to likewise depart, Earl Henry sought to retrieve Elizabeth until Camoys politely intervened: "Please, let it be my honor to see the gracious lady home."

The earl had agreed.

And that had been the end of Elizabeth's life alone.

"I've been in love afore, but never like this!" she had confided, giddy and glowing after she and Camoys had consummated their bond a few days after meeting.

"In love with your husband."

"No. Never."

"Another, then?"

"A squire, when I was a young maiden. My guardians sent him off to die." Slowly, she had told him about Robbie.

"I'm sorry," he had kissed her cheeks. "But I shall make you forget him, make you happier than e'er you could have been."

So he had.

Not only did they share love, they shared an affinity for London and, especially, for the court, where Camoys had thrived for years, under first Richard and then Henry, drawing royal favor without triggering royal ire. He wasn't inclined to question things, he had explained. "Rulers live by their own rules. Why suppose otherwise—much less say otherwise and risk losing my fortune, if not my head?"

"You're wise, Tam," she had proclaimed.

"I must be. I found you."

Cuddling beside him now, she lost herself in dreams. Unlike those of her girlhood, these would last more than a summer. These would endure for life.

* * *

Late February 1400 - Chester Castle

By the time abbey bells sounded *nones*, the ninth hour, Petronilla Kingsley Clark had twisted her handkerchief into damp knots. It had started out white and starched, draped over her belt as she left for the castle. She had taken special care about it, just as she had tucked chestnut locks into a scarf bound up as a wimple and dressed in a freshly laundered green blouse and kirtle. But now, encouraged by nervous hands, her unruly hair had begun tumbling around her face, while the linen handkerchief looked as if it had been wrung out to dry. Again, she got up, balanced her ample weight upon booted feet, and looked at her brother-in-law, Raynard Kingsley, once a notary for Richard.

"How much longer can he be? Don't justices spend much of their day idle, with fine food and drink, servants at beck and call?" Her light-brown eyes flamed. "God knows Richard's justices hardly bestirred themselves! Yet, I hardly need to remind you. You knew what 'twas like to do their work for them, with little thanks for the doing. So what occupies this one?"

"Hush, Nilla. 'Twas my job as notary to assist those prior justices. But they're not here; it's the new man you seek, King Henry's man. Forget those from earlier."

"Humph. I think I'd best forget this one, too." She plumped down again. The new justice held regular open forums, allowing citizens to come to him with their complaints, petitions, or proposals. She had requested a more privy venue, though. An aide had brought the answer the previous day: The justice would see her at the castle. Now, her appointed time come and gone, she still dallied in his anteroom. "A plague on them all. What if this new fellow turns out to be no better than Massey?"

"The sheriff?"

"Yea. During that 6 January insurrection, all he did was hide, in this castle."

"Yea. Lamentable idiot."

"And lamentable idiot me to think tha—"

The outer door flew open, admitting a youthful-looking man she took for a squire, dark hair curling damply against his forehead, and his cape, which bore some nobleman's insignia, streaked by snow. He was racing through the room when Petronilla jumped up. "Sir! You there! We were expecting to meet with the justice. Could you not remind him?" Her shrill tone made her brother-in-law cringe. But the traveler seemed unperturbed as he paused, lean strong fingers toying with the handle of the inner door he had been about to open.

"He—that is, I—beg forgiveness, good mistress. You will be heard anon. Please excuse me." With a pleasant nod, he passed through the doorway.

A servant arrived shortly afterward, bearing a jug of ale and a plate of cheese.

"A worthy brew," Raynard said. "Kind of him to send it out."

A quarter-hour passed. Then the inner door swung open, and an even younger man greeted them, his freckled face and respectful manner reassuring. "I'm John Hardyng, scribe and squire to Lord Harry. He awaits your pleasure."

They followed, entering a stone-walled study, where the man they'd encountered earlier stood up from a writing table. Expecting him to lead them farther into the castle to the lord justice, Petronilla was amazed when Hardyng began introductions. "Mistress Petronilla Clark and Master Raynard Kingsley, My Lord." Hardyng nodded deferentially to the man behind the desk and turned back to them. "The Lord Harry Percy, Justice of Chester."

As Hardyng departed, Petronilla's cheeks burned. "Your Lordship; I had no idea. With pleas for your merciful pardon."

Harry waved off the apology with a grin. "No affront taken."

She noticed that in very little time, he had transformed himself. His hair was wetter than ever, and his face shone, too, though not from sleet. Obviously, he had shucked his dirty clothes, pitched a couple of buckets of hot water over his head and scrubbed before pulling on clean garments whose sole decoration was the miniature coat-of-arms embroidered on his tunic.

"My apologies." Seating himself again, he motioned them into chairs. "I thought my afternoon would be free, but there was a bad shipwreck yester'eve, off Flintshire, with casualties. As I am also sheriff of Flint and justiciar of North Wales, they sent for me." His smile disarmed them. "But you hardly came to discuss shipwrecks. Some other matter concerns you? Something that couldn't be delayed till my next public session, later this week?"

"It concerns that Epiphany rising against King Henry," Petronilla began. "I came to learn your intent regarding our local men, those accused of involvement. We heard what happened elsewhere."

"It seems many of the earls' lesser followers—middling squires, men-at-arms and the like—were taken to Oxford to await the king's justice," Raynard added.

"Then terrible things happened," Petronilla choked. "Yet many were probably nothing more than men doing their lords' bidding."

"Seems King Henry conducted hasty proceedings, at best," Raynard said. "Of the fourscore arrested, thirty were executed almost immediately—some tortured to death."

"Hell!" Harry swore silently. Recovering in Windsor from the poisoning, he had heard fractured accounts of this, along with the news that riots had rattled Chester, too—either as part of the disturbances or in unrelated mayhem taking advantage of the confusion.

"We ask you to spare us such ... such untoward trials here. Beyond the horror..." Petronilla crossed herself "...it would destroy this very town, and my fortunes and those of many an honest woman, if you hang the men here, as men were hanged at Oxford."

"Is your husband amongst them?"

"No. I've buried two husbands and married no third. But some folk say that my son, Jan Kingsley, was involved. Don't let him die, or the others, either."

Drops fell from her eyes as the bedraggled handkerchief finally found proper use.

Harry rubbed his chin. "Your son?"

Petronilla nodded.

"How old?"

"Five-and-twenty, Martinmas last."

He studied her. Probably fifteen years older than he, she appeared to be a shrewd merchant-woman, if fretful now. "Does he know you came?"

She shook her head as another thought entered his.

"Or anyone else? Were you bidden to come?"

She hesitated. "Some of the town fathers and guild leaders discussed our predicament. We—they—

suggested I seek your beneficence on behalf of us all and because of Jan."

"Kingsley," Harry repeated. "I've seen his name on land records. He enjoys an estimable share in the vicinity."

Petronilla nodded. "His bequest. I have a large house left to me by my second husband, Ivo Clark, the leather dealer. And I still earn decent coin as a glover. But my widow's portion comes from the farms my first husband left Jan and me. And I surrendered care of my own fields to Jan some time ago."

Harry understood the stakes: not just the fate of her son, but loss of her widow's sustenance, an important part of her income, should her son's lands be confiscated for treason and Jan imprisoned or executed, unable to work her fields. Beyond that, she worried about setbacks to her leather-goods business if the town's other merchants and farmers were hanged, broken financially, or forced to flee into Wales. The town could be ruined, sparking eternal hatred of King Henry—and his lord justice.

He had to move carefully.

"Mistress Clark, I'm afraid I'm not yet familiar with what happened here over Epiphany." Lifting a wide parchment from a shelf, Harry unrolled it across the desk. "This is the report from the preliminary inquest conducted by local magistrates before I returned. I only received it yesterday. Until I am thoroughly familiar with the case, I cannot comment. Moreover, I intend to dispense justice equally and impartially." His voice softened. "Of course, that means preserving the rights of the innocent, too."

"Then you will look kindly upon Chester and my son?"

He shrugged. "If your son and the others aren't culpable, they've naught to fear. Surely though, Mistress, you can't expect me to guarantee pardons or dismiss charges, ere I know what took place."

"Forgive me, My Lord." Her voice was strained. "Forget I said anything."

Raynard commented cautiously. "Let us revise our pleadings to ask only for your wise judgment, should you be called to render one, and for mercy toward any who need it."

Harry stood up. "That's all I can promise. And now, if you'll excuse me, I have much to do." He escorted them to the door, where he surprised Kingsley by reaching out to shake his hand. Flattering Petronilla by taking hers as well, he kissed it in gentlemanly deference.

"I will try," she assured him, "to trust in justice."

"If not in the justice—me," he thought with a wry smile as they left.

Returning to his desk, he began reading the preliminary report, groaning at the contorted Latin. Buried amid the verbiage, the important point seemed to be that numerous local men were suspected of sympathies for (or involvement in) the 6 January rioting. Many of the names belonged to prominent figures: a goldsmith, tailors, a physician, a mercer, other merchants, knights, yeoman farmers and gentry, not the sort usually embroiled in violence. Beyond that, the document revealed little; too many questions remained, among them young Kingsley's role in whatever had occurred.

He was going to have to investigate the whole thing himself, start to finish. Methodically, he began scribbling notes. It would be a long night—and, the way things were going, an even longer spring.

The Privy Council was out for blood, Cheshire blood, as became clear the following morning when Hardyng announced a courier bringing a message from king and council:

To the sheriffs and justices of the peace throughout the realm: Greetings. Know this regarding the uprisings of Epiphany It is the sense of the council that a general pardon be granted to all lieges of the king, except for the men of the shire of Chester.

Noting the last phrase, Harry swore silently and faced the courier. "Tell Our Gracious Majesty I will take any action warranted."

The messenger coughed. "Is that your only response, Sir? The king would learn exactly when and how you will bring these traitors to justice. As my liege and yours, the king, knows, there are scores of treasonous malefactors here. He expects many condemnations. Swiftly."

Harry's jaw set in grim composure as he pondered. "What would Henry have me do? Behead all the men of Cheshire? Who would that leave to govern or lead in battle if we're ever attacked?" Another thought struck. "So that's why she came when she did."

Petronilla's urgency now made even more sense: A couple of days from town, a Cheshireman riding east must have encountered this messenger headed west, discovered his mission, and high-tailed it back to Chester to warn town elders. Petronilla had been recruited to intervene, a woman, the easier to appeal to his chivalrous sympathies. Inwardly, he bowed to their cleverness.

Outwardly, he addressed the messenger. "Tell my lord sovereign that the assize court meets scarce a fortnight hence. This will be pursued then."

"You've nothing else to report?"

"Naught. Except that no genuine traitor shall escape justice."

———

Tuesday, 9 March 1400 - Chester Castle

In launching his investigation Harry summoned not one but three assize-court panels, judicial enquiry juries, to hear testimony and piece together what had happened. He then would have to determine what to do about it: Bring charges of high treason, initiate proceedings for lesser crimes, or conclude that no offenses at all had occurred and close the books.

To start, they all gathered in Chester Castle's great hall, with Harry in a suitably imposing chair behind the table on a dais, flanked by Hardyng and assize clerks. The jurors occupied pews to the sides while the public, including potential witnesses, filled benches on the stone floor. The fire burning in the massive fireplace and candles blazing from wall sconces provided a glow of warmth.

"Kindness itself, the fire, amidst the gloom," Harry heard an old woman whisper.

He explained the weighty matters at hand, thanked the jurors for serving, welcomed the public, especially any who could "shed light on the alleged occurrences over Epiphany," and promised to do his utmost to ensure justice. Then he dismissed the jurors to their own hearing rooms.

That was only the beginning. Throughout the day, and the next several, he moved from panel to panel—listening, taking notes, suggesting lines of inquiry, posing his own questions to witnesses:

"You could see this thievery firsthand?"

"Could you identify that man in armor you saw loosing arrows at the castle, demanding its surrender in the name of the former King, Richard?"

"Your cellar was looted?"

And so on, through a long list of witnesses that increased as the inquiry unfolded. After the first dozen individuals had failed to mention Jan Kingsley, Harry's curiosity got the better of him and he began asking directly: "Did you see young Kingsley, the Widow Clark's son, in this disturbance?"

"Yaah," an elderly candlemaker drawled. "Amongst the pack, to be sure. But once they's begun to steal and burn, Master Kingsley began t' cross 'em. Arguing he was, saying 'twasn't fittin'. And then I seed him runnin' ahead. Some's said he was runnin' so's to be first to rob the next shop. But he really was running to warn shopkeeps to be boltin' their shutters and guardin' their wares."

Several others corroborated the candlemaker's story, to Harry's satisfaction. At least on that score, Petronilla's worries were over.

Outlines of what had happened began to emerge, implicating Thomas of Kent, the now-dead earl. But Harry was uneasy. "What if the testimony is skewed?" he asked Hardyng. "I don't mean about Thomas of Kent, necessarily, but about some of these local men being in confederation with him. What if some of these folk summoned as witnesses…"

"… or coming forth on their own…"

"…Aye. What if some wrongly accuse others? There was unrest here last summer. What if various factions used the earls' plot as an excuse to carry on that feud—or older, unrelated ones, or neighbor-against-neighbor arguments?"

Hardyng frowned. "Possible, I suppose."

"Aye. We're going to have to do more, I'm going to suspend court temporarily."

Harry spent the next fortnight trudging through Chester himself, street after street, house after house, shop after shop. Then he set out on horseback through the countryside. At times, either Hardyng or Kynge accompanied him, but he sent them out separately as well, and the queries continued:

"Were you home over the 6th of January? Did anything unusual happen?"

"Are you sure 'twas this man, whose name you gave us, who stole your cow and burned your shed?"

On the investigation went, at manor and hovel, to knight and dame, laborer and apprentice, farmer and alewife.

"Where, exactly, did they break in? Through this window? May I climb over and examine the latches? Aye, I see 'tis too much to repair, till you have money to rebuild thoroughly...

"Is that, sergeant, where they struck you down when they tried to sunder the gate? Look here, John, see the hatchet and sword marks? Run your finger there, you can feel the depth of the thrust; 'tis a wonder no one was slain."

Frequently, he dragged himself and his aides back to the castle after dark, their minds and bodies exhausted because his inquiries were not.

"He revels in it," Kynge told Hardyng. "Hotspur on another hot-trod, as the Borderers would say. Only this time, his trail is a lot colder. But that doesn't deter Harry."

"Or mean there are any fewer ruined barns to climb through and splinter my shins on!"

The populace took note.

"Unheard of!" Petronilla observed at the market.

"Yea," a seamstress in the adjacent stall nodded. "No justice afore asked us for help. Or left his high bench to poke around, trying to figure things out for himself."

Eventually, convinced by the redundancy of the accounts and remaining physical evidence, he was satisfied: No particular local axes were being ground.

"That's almost worse, though—not for Cheshire, but for us," Hardyng commented.

"Aye," Harry replied. "Now there's no excuse for not proceeding.

After analyzing the material, his grand juries reported their findings. Each cited different groups of suspects; otherwise, they were closely identical. Written in Latin, although read aloud in English (however stilted) at Harry's session, they became a formal indictment:

The leaders came from Thomas, Earl of Kent, on the Monday preceding Epiphany, riding as far as Chester to diverse men of this same shire. And they informed these men that the said Earl of Kent and the Earl of Salisbury, in arms of war and accompanied by assorted others, had chased Henry, King of England, back to the city of London and the Tower there. Through this action, directed by the same earl, these leaders had been dispatched to this shire to ensure military readiness by all so that, with expediency, they could make a common purpose with everyone supporting the deliverance of Richard, the recent King of England. In this manner they proposed to gather near Shrewsbury on the following Wednesday. To this cause came these individuals...

Names followed, then the narrative resumed:

On that Saturday, by the hand and will of these same leaders, these aforenamed individuals within the shire of Chester arose in insurrection against the said Lord Henry, present King of England. Accordingly, with malevolent words, they ordered many ignorant men mustered and arrayed for battle. Furthermore, they themselves illegally levied a great many men as a force, with their confederates also consequently positioning themselves just outside the battlements, ready to later deliver the walls to King Richard and otherwise liberate the place. First, they entered the thoroughfare of the town and pressed upon Chester Castle itself, seeking talks with the castle's keepers, although such parlay was completely denied them.

Then they surged through the town and, likewise, through a wide portion of the surrounding district. Thus, under threat of death and without free will, numerous other men obeyed them. They captured the keys to the town, and by proclamations in the name and on the part of the aforesaid recent monarch, Richard, they disseminated orders that, any other affairs notwithstanding, all men in the town and shire capable of military defense, in as good a form and array as possible, should hasten and present and subject themselves to these leaders, under pain of otherwise losing life and limb and being hanged and drawn as traitors. Likewise, they claimed that other militarily capable men arose with them, persuading many here that Richard, the recent king of England, would be joining them.

After this they besieged Chester Castle, demanding it be relinquished to them in the name of Richard and that on behalf of the same Richard it be garrisoned.

But all was refused them. Next, in the presence of Bishop John of St. Asaph; John de Massy of Puddington, knight, the sheriff of Chester; and William Venables, the constable, who were staying in the castle to safeguard it, they commenced an assault—against this very castle.

So these leaders and other similar malefactors struck, in insurrection, in the above manner and form against the aforesaid Henry, King of England. Additionally, various robberies, extortions, oppressions and other transgressions they committed everywhere within the shire. Thus, they loosed destruction and depredations against the populace, in the town as well as the shire beyond.

In total, one hundred and twenty-five individuals, all men, were cited.

As the foremen continued reading, terse agreement, curses, and gasps came from the audience, some of whom, Harry guessed, must have been among those indicted. Finally, praising the jurors for their efforts and the public for its attentiveness, he arose. Now, he had to make sense of it all in terms of law. Meanwhile, the court stood adjourned.

March 1400 - Chester Castle

"What do you know about Glanville?" Harry caught Hardyng drowsing over a tome.

The squire shook himself awake like a terrier. "Not much. Your tutors never got that far with my schooling—not when I was listening, anyway." He brightened. "But let's see... He captured the king of Scotland at Alnwick in your family's backyard–except 'twas long before it was your family's backyard."

Harry laughed. "Aye, when Northumberland nearly became part of Scotland."

"Also, when he wasn't soldiering for Henry II, he wrote *A Treatise on the Law and Customs of England*." Hardyng uncurled from his corner. "The abbey's got a copy. Shall I borrow it? But I doubt 'twill help. It's more than two hundred years old, from before they differentiated between unwritten common law and law by statute." Slowly, he remembered more. "And before Parliament even existed to enact a statute on treason. But I'll fetch it if you wish."

Harry shook his head. "'You're right; it won't help much. Bracton, maybe? Though he probably couldn't offer much, either. Even he wrote more than one hundred years ago. Yet Bracton did hold that the law makes a king and that, thus, every king is beholden to law, and to God. I wonder..." Leaving his desk, he gazed out at another drizzly evening. "Maybe these local fellows believed Henry hadn't been made a king properly under law—I, too, had doubts—and they could reject him." He cast a questioning eye on Hardyng.

"You should be their lawyer, not the justice who must preside over their cases. You posit an excellent defense. But I wager the palace would never accept it."

"No. Henry wants their heads. On pikes. Posthaste." Returning to his chair, Harry picked up a hefty leather volume, opening it to a well-thumbed page with the Statute of Treasons of 1352:

"If a man conjectures or imagines the death of our lord the king... or oldest son and heir... makes war against our said lord king in his kingdom, or is an adherent of enemies to our lord the king, giving them aid or comfort in his kingdom or elsewhere ... these cases, specified above, it must be understood, are to be adjudged treason against our lord the king and his royal majesty... ."

Hardyng peered over Harry's shoulder. "It won't tell you anything we don't already know. By law, what those men did was high treason."

Harry's fist clenched and unclenched against the desk. "I reckon. They took up weapons and called for overthrowing Henry and restoring Richard, who was naught but a nobleman by then. Thus they surely 'imagined the death of the king.' They attacked the castle and officers of the peace. They coerced and threatened to kill others. They burned, stole, broke into, or otherwise destroyed the property of all and sundry."

"And conspired with Thomas of Kent et al," Hardyng added. "Thus, at least, indirectly, they abetted the attempt to poison Hal, royal heir. And kill you."

"Damned near succeeded, too." Harry's voice momentarily sharpened. "But perhaps because I nearly perished I'm loath to do anything that could send other men to their deaths."

"We've got to hold trials, or something, though," Hardyng argued. "They should be held accountable for what they did."

"Aye, but was it high treason?"

Hardyng pointed to the open page.

Harry slammed the book shut. "I realize what the letter of the law says. What of the spirit of the law, the spirit of justice? If we consider that, are they still guilty of high treason?" He got up and unlatched the wooden wardrobe, retrieving his oilskin cloak and brimmed hat. "I'm going for a walk."

Hardyng glanced out the window. "It's raining. Want me to come along?"

"No. One damned fool out in that is enough. I want to think, though. And out there I'm unlikely to be disturbed."

Harry stepped from the castle wall onto the adjacent city parapet and turned east toward the bridge over the River Dee. The rain tapered off, but dampness gripped his neck with cold fingers and oozed from the stones beside him. Grateful for his cloak, he curved around the wall.

"Halt!"

"Who goeth?"

He paused. "Sir Harry Percy."

Members of the town watch materialized from shadows. Lanterns shone in his face. "'The justice!"

A sergeant stared up at him. "My Lord! My men did not recognize you or know you were abroad this eve. I'm sorry. They should never—"

"No," Harry interrupted. "Had they not stopped me, it would've been alarming. Anyone wandering our walls in the dark should be challenged, or you and I fail our duty. So carry on."

With a polite refusal to join the off-duty men for a tankard in the guardroom, he continued; then paused at a battlement, watching fog skirring along the Dee, as unsettled as his thoughts.

"Can I spare Cheshiremen when others no more deeply implicated were brutally executed under Henry? Yet must men here die merely because those at Oxford did? Are they really traitors? A complicated question that, no matter what Hardyng thinks the law says."

The rioters had risen in the name of someone who had long been their king and who, as far as they knew, might re-appear and reign again. Several of them, as he had learned in his investigation, had ridden to Richard at Carmarthen the previous summer, only to arrive as he fled. They had ever been loyal and tried to remain loyal. At Epiphany, they'd been egged on by earls, some of the most prominent men in the realm, who had surely lied to them. Besides, Henry had usurped the throne and only possessed it for three months. Who could say unequivocally if he was the true king? There'd been royal rivals before, just as now two men professed to be pope. Back in the mid-1100s, the Empress Matilda and King Stephen had simultaneously claimed the crown, with folk aligning with one, then the other, depending on how powerful or legitimate either looked at a given moment. Later had come squabbles between Henry II and his estranged family, and between Richard the Lionheart and John. Were those earlier Englishmen all traitors for changing sides or, conversely, clinging to an old fealty when demands for a new one arose? Probably they were less treasonous than desperate. Was it so different now?

Somehow, he didn't think so. Lightning glimmered in the distance but did little to illumine his thoughts. He walked on. "There has to be a way…"

By the time he passed the Kaleyard Gate half an hour later, he thought he might have found it. He would press Henry for a general pardon for the whole shire, except the one hundred and twenty-five individuals cited in the grand jury indictment. Next, he would consider each of those case-by-case. On those found guilty, he'd impose penalties tempered by lenience toward any who confessed, saving the town the cost and turmoil of trials. He'd sentence them to financial restitution and physical toil repairing the damage. If they pledged good behavior, he'd parole them and try to get them permanent pardons. Any capable of military service would be given the chance to use their weapons to defend the realm instead of tearing it apart. The more he considered the plan, the more he liked it.

But would Henry?

* * *

Stricken with undiagnosed illness, King Henry suffered pangs of guilt for the hasty condemnations at Oxford. Lying in bed, he stayed the pending executions of twenty-two more men. Wracked with fresh pain some days later, he pardoned them entirely and reprieved fifteen others awaiting sentencing.

"So this from Sir Harry arrives at a propitious time for those Cheshiremen," Norbury told Bishop Beaufort one noon, waving a letter.

"Mayhap not," the bishop replied. "When I visited my sovereign brother yesterday, he was feeling better, starting to question his generosity to those he'd just spared. This morning he was in yet finer fettle—swearing he'd never be so hasty in magnanimity again. He'll doubtless ponder long over this Chester situation."

Norbury sighed. "Then it could drag on…"

"Precisely."

Indeed, Henry took weeks to make up his mind. Finally, he issued a general pardon for Cheshire, forgiving everyone except the one hundred and twenty-five men indicted by the assize. All but eight of these were ordered to pursue their cases and any pardons individually, as Harry had suggested. The last eight, the ringleaders, Henry considered too reprehensible for even minimal clemency.

In Cheshire, Harry regarded it as almost complete victory. All one hundred and seventeen lesser culprits duly pled guilty, agreeing to make restitution and reparation, and Harry promised to help them obtain permanent pardons from the Crown. In time, their pleas dribbled back, stamped 'approved' in ineradicable red.

Then the eight ringleaders agreed to identical terms, and Harry, paroling them, figured that if they behaved, he could probably get them fully pardoned, too. It just might take a while.

May 1400 - Chester Castle

Returning to the castle one afternoon, Harry stabled Redesraven. A loud whinny sounded from the usually vacant stall in the corner, and a big-boned, mostly bay-colored horse thrust its head over the door. Ears flicking forward, it bestowed a neigh of toothy laughter.

"Rags!" Harry recognized a welcome, if infrequent, visitor. Reaching out, he stroked the satin-smooth coat. A mischievous look in its eyes, the bay butted Harry's chest until he retrieved slices of dried apple from his belt purse, passing them along. "As much a beggar as ever," he observed as the horse crunched contentedly.

Thomas Percy's favorite mount, the bay was named for his motley coloring: chestnut-gold splashed with red, brown, white and black. "He looks," Thomas had once muttered, "like a pile a ragman left behind."

Remembering, Harry chuckled. "Yet your horse sense is wondrous, even if your looks are not. Where's your good master?" Rags could only answer with an affectionate lick, so Harry proceeded to the keep.

Indoors, approaching his personal parlor, he stopped short, listening.

"You know how he is." Hardyng spoke. "He likes to ride out without any guard or force, sometimes without even us."

"Harry does the same on the Borders, riding alone, being his own scout, checking the health of crops, the prosperity of villages, the state of defenses, and whatever else," Kynge added. "He says it's better than always relying on reports, that the advantages outweigh the dangers."

Thomas chuckled. "He's always done so."

"Anyway," Hardyng went on, "he may be out half the night. I swear, he drives himself like he's under the whip of some fanatical master—us too. But I'd follow him anywhere and could ask for no better lord or friend."

A clicking of goblets followed.

"A distraction now and then might serve him well," Hardyng remarked. "I know the lute and viol; Harry made sure I learned. And he likes them and the pipes. Yet I can never get him to sing."

Thomas laughed. "He says his voice *en song* is like a weasel ensnared."

"'Rot," Hardyng objected. "I've heard him. Sometimes, when he thinks no one is listening, he joins in chant with monks at Mass, or with our troops when we march, singing the old border ballads. Never otherwise, however."

Motionless outside the door, Harry took it all in.

"He leads a life as ascetic as any anchorite," Kynge observed. "Sometimes I pray he finds love. Now that Elizabeth has Camoys, 'tis even less reason for Harry to be alone."

Thomas Percy's voice came again. "How did he take the tidings? I understand his father wrote to him, explaining all.

Kynge answered. "In truth, Harry admitted he's relieved. He said now there's far less cause to fear that whatever he does will displease or hurt Elizabeth, that she's beyond him now, has found her man. Then he grew sad. The whole thing reminded him he has no love for himself. And he *should* have."

Before anyone could say anything else, Harry pretended to stumble over the threshold into the room. "Verily! I thought I detected gossip wafting about!"

They looked embarrassed as he bounded over to hug Thomas. "Greetings, Uncle. Had I known you were coming, I'd have been here."

Thomas brushed off the apology. "I knew we'd catch up sooner or later."

Harry turned toward Ian, pretending to chastise. "And what was it I heard from you? That I need a woman? Such a notion—from you, a man of the clergy. After all, I did enter into wedlock; no matter what happened—or didn't—afterward!"

Ian blushed. "Priests, too, can believe in love. As for your 'marriage': You know full well that if I were pope, I would long since have annulled many a supposed marriage, including yours."

Harry slapped his back. "I never knew you were such a heretic. You sound like a Lollard or Cathar, trying to abolish the sacraments."

Ian shook his head. "I preach no heresy. I want the sacraments to be what Christ intended: moments of grace that uplift and fill folk with God's joy. I abhor seeing them turned into travesties. There's penance: Forget genuine repentance. Men buy indulgences to supposedly speed entry to heaven. Or matrimony: More buying and selling—of sons and daughters. Away with such marriages, I say."

Hardyng puzzled. "But what of the Gospel? It says, 'What God hath joined together, let no man put asunder.'"

"Yea!" Kynge exclaimed. "'What *God* hath joined together, let no man put asunder. What God hath joined. God—not greedy men using their children for gain. God would only join those truly meant for each other, who truly love each other."

He looked solemn. "Lads and lasses holding hands and plighting their troth often have truer marriages than emperors wed with splendor. At least those voluntary marriages are founded on love." His voice rose. "Men and women are not meant to marry to increase a family's wealth, or military might, or rank at court. Nor should they wed simply to beget heirs to continue some exalted noble lineage and be united only in... uh ... intercou... uhh... copula–"

"Fucking!" Hardyng interjected, less delicately.

"Umhh...yea!" the chaplain resumed. "They're meant to know real love, lasting love, love that binds them, mind and body, heart and soul." He sounded almost reverential. "True love."

Silence fell.

Crossing the room, Harry poured a cup of Bordeaux. "True love," he echoed softly. "I daresay I'll never know what it is."

The pensiveness remained, briefly. Then he shrugged. "No matter. My horse loves me—yours too, Uncle, when I feed him apples. You three, I think, also love me, or at least like me and suffer my failings. And God loves me, I reckon."

He sank into a chair. "Enough prattle. What news from London, Uncle?"

Thomas groaned. "More than there's time for, now. That's partly why I came."

Kynge interrupted. "First, if I may have your honest opinion: Was Richard murdered?"

Frowning, Thomas sighed. But Harry's eyes seconded the question.

"I think he was," Thomas began. "Though I doubt anyone will ever be able to prove it."

"Did Henry order it?" Harry asked.

"I suspect he did. It would've been a spoken order, of course, naught in writing. But I've seen evidence suggesting it was no accident that Richard died when he did." Thomas paused. "In the confusion between Richard's dethronement and Henry's accession, no one could be certain of the condition of the Exchequer. Accordingly, a few weeks ago, Adam Usk and I were assigned to review its rolls. Along with considerable disorder, we found recent entries of great curiosity. One paid a messenger, going between London and Pontefract and back, in late January, on 'a matter of great urgency and secrecy, solely on the order of King Henry.'"

"Intriguing," Hardyng said.

"Truly," Thomas nodded. "Then Adam and I retrieved the minutes of the relevant council session. The council convened over several days; I was present only for part of it. Thus, Adam and I decided to check everything to see what might have been said in my absence about royal finances. We found little but discovered something else: It appears that, at one meeting of that February council, only a few select lords convened with Henry. The notes the clerks took in that meeting have disappeared. We could see where they began. At the end of one section, someone wrote: 'There follows a report pertinent to the death of Richard, recent king of England.' But that line was crossed out—obviously later—in ink of a different color. And underneath it, only halfway down a perfectly good piece of parchment, the sheet was cut off. In its place, someone had glued another sheet, minutes of discussion on unrelated, trivial matters."

Harry whistled.

"Yea," Thomas declared. "The record was tampered with. Whether on Henry's orders or on the part of some fretful clerk, who can say? Certainly, the clerks Adam and I questioned seemed to know nothing. What discussion of Richard's death could have been so troublesome that any record of it had to be excised? I have my suspicions." His head shook sadly. "That's why I think Henry may not be innocent in Richard's death. But if guilty, he did no worse than Richard. Richard, too, surreptitiously ordered the murder of others. Twice, I saw it happen—or thought I saw it happen. But I could never find clinching proof. So, I had to drop it; I fear we must with Henry."

Harry seemed to want to kick something, but nothing was available—not that it would've done any good. "Can this country find none but killers to be kings?"

Thomas smiled grimly. "Perhaps it's in their blood, all the way back to Henry II and Becket or John and his nephews."

"That same old Plantagenet blood flows through your veins and mine," Harry reminded him. "You're no murderer, nor am I." He paused briefly, then resumed. "Yet, as you mention, Uncle, these are only suspicions. We can't say anyone is guilty until it's proven. That's what our law holds, for kings as well as commoners. So be it."

He leaned back in his chair, dark lashes brushing his cheek as his eyes closed.

Hardyng approached, gently kicking the muddy boots. "Let me not disturb your nap, My Lord. But dinner will be ready in an hour. If you wish to wash and change before you preside at table," he sniffed the air, "and as you smell rather like 'horse,' I wager you should—you'd best bestir yourself. I've already heated water for a bath."

Harry laughed. "Now, who sounds like a fanatical whip-master? But off I go. I'll see you all anon."

―――

His uncle later found him atop a tower, awaiting the summons to dine. From a window below, Hardyng's lute and mellow tenor rose in a ballad. Leaning against the crenellation, Harry faced west, toward Wales, where the sunset spilled its amber-red abundance over the countryside. In time, he switched his gaze to the northeast, streaked with purple and black. Aware he was no longer alone, he glanced over his shoulder before turning back northeast as a first star began to twinkle.

"Composing poetry, Harry? You used to, you know, as a boy. Never let me see it though; used to take it out to the barns to read to the horses."

Harry remembered. "Aye. But all they could ever say was 'nay'! So I gave up. I was never very good anyway. Hardyng is far better. I leave rhyming and music to him."

"So they tell me. You might try it again, though, just for yourself. A few pastimes can be good for a man. You need not live out duty all day and all night, too." Thomas studied his nephew. "I worry you'll burn through like a shooting star extinguished afore its time. Nonetheless," he admitted, "you appear as hale and hearty, as ever. You enjoy your Cheshire command, I think. I've also heard good reports of your governance."

Harry shrugged. "God has favored us so far. And I have enjoyed my tenure. But I wouldn't wish to stay forever." His eyes turned northeast again, where more stars began to shine. "Perhaps I am a little lonely. I miss Northumberland. I want to go home a while, back to the Borders..." The sentence faded on a note of yearning.

Through the increasing dusk, he saw Thomas's tentative smile.

"That's one of the things I rode here to tell you," Thomas announced, "although I don't know whether it's good news or not. You'll soon get your chance to go North. In fact, no one will be needed there more than you."

Harry regarded him quizzically, and Thomas swallowed hard before finishing:

"Henry has decided to invade Scotland!"

Chapter XVI
Late June 1400 - Chester Castle

Royal plans to subjugate Scotland caused problems even before Hotspur left Cheshire. A letter from Thomas Percy in London brought the first portents:

Harry,
As you know, Henry commanded lords of the realm to assemble, with arrays, at Newcastle-upon-Tyne, 9 July. Be advised: He dispatched the order not through the usual officials but through palace favorites. Thus, the summons to Owain Glyn Dwr, of Glyndyfrdwy in Wales, was not given to you to transmit but to Reginald Grey of Ruthin.

"Hell." Harry's shoulders tensed. "Grey's a boor who alienates others. For Henry to do this, rely on him—especially after that recent scrap over Glyn Dwr's property. My uncle mentions that." Harry read silently and summarized. "Having gotten greedy, or greedier, Grey seized some of Glyn Dwr's land. They're neighbors. Glyn Dwr, well within his rights, objected. But he got nowhere, so he took the case all the way to the Privy Council—and lost."

"Henry pulled rank or something," Hardyng recalled.

"Aye. He directed the council to favor Grey, one of his most devoted—or rabid—courtiers."

"Arf, arf! Is that to say he's a son of a bitch?"

"Something like that! Anyway, my uncle writes more." Harry read aloud:

Obviously this manipulation of the Privy Council was blatantly unfair. Bishop John Trevor, of St. Asaph, warned that a gross miscarriage of justice was occurring and would likely spawn more evil. But Trevor spoke in vain. 'He's only another trifling Welshman,' some said. So they ruled in Grey's favor.

"Thus ended the lawsuit but not the grudge," Harry added.

"Grey returned to these parts gloating," Hardyng recalled.

"Aye, but not for long," Harry chuckled. "He was shunned by Welsh and English alike. So, he's been sulking. Which, as my uncle cautions, could mean trouble:"

By the time you receive this, Grey doubtless will have acted. Or not acted. He'll probably 'lose' Glyn Dwr's order and never deliver it or try some other chicanery. You might inform Glyn Dwr of what happened and use your good judgment as to any mollification.

Your devoted uncle

"Jesu!" Hardyng cursed. "We arrayed the levies we were supposed to raise and sent most off to Newcastle. We intended to leave with the remainder tomorrow. Now what'll you do?"

"Delay our departure; try to straighten this out; and contact Glyn Dwr. Maybe it's not too late."

Thursday, 1 July 1400 - Chester Castle

Glyn Dwr replied to Harry's alert with promptness, politeness, and no hint of his whereabouts:

My Lord: I appreciate your kindness in informing me. Lord Grey did not deliver my orders till the eve of the day I was expected to march to join the king. Thus there was no time to muster my men. I convey regrets for not joining this campaign. Under the circumstances, I have found it prudent to leave Glyndyfrdwy and enter seclusion for a time.

Owain Glyn Dwr

Another message arrived shortly afterward, bearing the royal seal:
To Sir Harry Percy, justiciar of North Wales, justice of Chester, etc.:

Owain Glyn Dwr has refused to attend upon Us as ordered with his men. You are hereby commanded to raise a like number of soldiers in replacement, without delay, reporting to Us in Newcastle as previously instructed.

From the King

"Damnation! Henry's dumped the whole mess on me!" Harry told Hardyng.
"Should I tell the others?"
"Aye. Also, the prince was somewhere in the yard. Send him in. I'll have to issue an order calling up more men—under my name but on his behalf also. He may as well know."

Hal ran into the study as Harry blotted his draft.
"Another call to arms?" The boy's eyes widened. "In my name, too? Let me see!" Wedging himself alongside Harry's desk, he read slowly, for the text was in Latin. Then he protested. "It's too mealy-mouthed!

You just say we need men to march in aid of the king against the Scots."

"So?"

"You should make it stronger, make the Scots sound horrid, monstrous—like the demons they are!" The prince's imagination waxed vivid. "Say what Father says, that they threaten to destroy the whole English race, every last one of us, and our English language, too!"

Harry shook his head. "Everyone knows the Scots stand little chance of that. They're fierce, but not that fierce. Would you have us look like milksops, fearful we could be so easily overrun? Besides, not all Scots are terrible."

"No?"

"No. Of course, we need to remind them to behave. Some raided the North when your father was being crowned last October. But that hardly means they're all devils. Best not to create demons where none exist."

"But our language ... they want to destroy our English language, like Father says!"

"Nay, Lad. The Scots, at least those in the Lowlands—the very ones who invade England—speak English, too. They talk just like I do."

Hal doubled over, giggling. "That's what I mean. They destroy English. They talk just like you!" He laughed with the glee of twelve-year-olds impressed with their own wit.

Slowly, Harry reddened. Aye... The burr, cadences and vocabulary of the North still colored his speech. He was too old to change. Nor did he want to. He said nothing until Hal's whoops subsided. "All right, Lad. What would you say?"

Re-reading the text, Hal demanded that it condemn the Scots, "in their pernicious evil, forever scheming and battling to destroy the people of England—and our language, too."

Harry pondered. Hal had a point. Prejudice against enemies could be good propaganda. And good propaganda wasn't a bad recruitment tool, one that in this case might prod Welsh to unite with English against a common, perceived foe. Yet what Hal wanted to say, in effect, accused the Scots of seeking the racial annihilation of England. That was a weighty charge, one Harry would never level on his own.

He regarded Hal. "You sure?"

"Yea. Put it in. It's what Father would say."

"Well, that's true enough," Harry thought.

Thus, Hal got his way, though Harry tempered the wording, calling up men to rally against the Scots, "who crave nothing less than to continuously wage war against the folk and language of this realm." He couldn't hide a trace of a grin as he finished. Too young, Hal missed the irony: A Northumbrian who spoke English in Borders dialect drafted an order, in Latin, urging men who spoke English with Welsh accents to confront Scotsmen who also spoke English—but ostensibly wanted to destroy the language!

By evening, the writ had been copied, in Welsh and English as well as Latin, proclaimed, and tacked on walls throughout the region. Before week's end, his ranks boasted five hundred more soldiers, including some of the Cheshiremen spared of treason charges that spring. With them, clearly bygones were bygones.

Making up for lost time, Harry's troops reached the North ahead of expectations. Nothing, he thought, could now keep the whole army from convincing the Scots to trade belligerence for peace.

He failed entirely to reckon on the king.

Henry was desperately short of revenue for invasions or much of anything else. Richard had left a treasury richer than many had assumed, given his extravagances. Yet, under Henry, it had drained away—like liquid gold through palace sewers. Disregarding pledges made at Doncaster and elsewhere, he imposed heavy taxes and pressured bishops and abbots for open-ended loans or aid, *pro viagis Regi versus*

Scotiam: "for the excursion of the King against Scotland."

The churchmen gave begrudgingly, if at all.

"I'll be damned if I'll let alms for the poor go to his treasury, so he can rattle swords over the border," one abbot groused.

"Peace, brother. Do whatever you can," Archbishop Arundel soothed. "Best not express your objections too loudly, though."

Nor did Henry seem able to manage supplies. En route to Newcastle, he had to appeal to fifteen cities for barley, wine, fodder, and other staples for his army, telling his ministers in London to "pawn the crown jewels, if needs must," to fund it all. Upon reaching Newcastle, he frittered away more days, money, and provisions. Meanwhile, he penned an urgent demand to the Scottish King, Robert III, instructing him to appear at Edinburgh on 28 August, to render homage. Dispatching heralds under truce flags, he had the writ read in towns across lower Scotland.

The Scots ignored both message and messengers.

Trying again, Henry issued "a request to all dukes, earls, and other magnates of Scotland to induce the king of Scots to do homage and fealty, and, if he will not assent, to do homage and fealty themselves." Then he consumed hours planning an elaborate homage ceremony.

"'Tis folly," Harry told Knayton and Hardyng in a break from sword practice on another uneventful day. "The Scots won't do a thing to 'induce' Robert to kiss Henry's ring."

"Or any other part of him!" Hardyng laughed. "What's next?"

"Doubtless, little."

"Whilst you pay our men with your own money since Henry doesn't have a farthing!" observed Knayton.

"Aye."

Eventually, Henry inched ahead. Entering Scotland, they skirted Edinburgh to reach Leith on the coast. Little sense of triumph prevailed, however, as supplies and money dwindled further.

Finally, weary of both the English and the stale repetitiveness of his nobles' anti-English jokes, King Robert sent emissaries. They listened politely to Henry, promised to consider his request, and galloped away.

"Considering a request is one thing," Harry noted. "Complying is another."

Yet, if the Scots refused to do homage, they also refused to fight, regarding Henry's army as a prickly English rose trailing errantly over the border, too piddly to cull and destined to wither, anyway. Nor did Henry have the means to force the Scots' hand. Ultimately. even he realized it, announcing he would return to London forthwith, escorted by a select retinue; the army could follow on its own. Glumly dining alone, he spent a final night at Leith, anxious only for dawn and his departure.

In a far better mood, Harry rode into Edinburgh on the invitation of Sir John Montgomery, an old Scottish friend. They had hardly started out as friends, though, had been just the opposite—until one chaotic Lammastide, when the world turned upside down.

* * *

Wednesday, 5 August 1388 - Otterburn, England

The Scots spread out in happy disarray.

They had spent the day under a broiling sun, investing the Otterburn peel tower at the crossroads and stream that gave the locale its name. When, by late afternoon, they had failed to make a dent in the bastion's thick walls, their leader, Earl Jamie Douglas, had called a halt. Bivouacking nearby, steamy armor replaced by lighter garb (or naught but their underwear—or less), they turned to cooking, eating, swigging ale, and bragging of past feats and future glories, especially those certain to come when they returned to the tower.

Already, they'd raided as far south as Durham and given the English a good dust-up at Newcastle. Although their attempted siege there failed, they had departed in high spirits, for among those left lying inert below the city wall had been England's famed Hotspur.

Counterattacking out Newcastle's main gate, Harry had plunged headlong into the would-be besiegers, searching for Douglas. Recognizing his rival, Douglas had galloped free of a pack of men and invited pursuit across the field. Harry had given it, pausing only to jam his pennant into the earth, defining his territory and intent. Douglas had swept in a wide circle, taunting, finger raised in an obscene gesture. Then he'd careened back, straight at Harry. Lances had joined, but with neither gaining advantage they had raced past one another and wheeled to meet again.

Thus, the duel had begun.

Abandoning their siege, the Scots had settled on the grass to watch while the English crowded city battlements above, equally spellbound. Several unproductive charges had ensued before Douglas altered his aim slightly, charged again, and dug his lance into Harry's side, which was protected by chainmail hauberk but not a breastplate-cuirass. A follow-up thrust with the lance's blunt end had hit Harry's helmet, tumbling him to the dirt. Plucking the English pennant from the ground, Douglas had sped off, sounding a merry retreat.

Unconscious and bleeding, Harry had been carried away by his brother Rafe and other anxious lieutenants. Along with the jagged tear from Douglas' lance, he had three cracked ribs. Nonetheless, after some sleep and the binding of his wounds, he'd pronounced himself fit enough to lead a chase. 'Twas

St. Oswald's feast, after all, an auspicious day for a Northumbrian army to take the field. Following a thirty-mile march in the same heat that left Douglas' men sweltering, the English had crept close to the Scottish camp.

———

Well into their cups, only belatedly did the Scots realize they were under attack by someone left for dead miles away. Caught without armor or weapons, they turned to fight in disorder.

Overrunning the baggage train, cooking fires, and reserve horses, Harry's force barreled into the main Scottish lines. They dispatched the foremost ranks effortlessly. But atop a hillock, others began re-arming, ironically, assisted by the destruction of their wagons, which had haphazardly strewn belongings, allowing men to equip themselves, even with gear not their own.

Hell broke loose 'neath the setting sun.

Speaking the same Borders English, the two sides mistook one another in the dusk and units in both fell back, re-assembled, and pushed onward, only to crumble again when their comrades, thinking them the enemy, hit their flanks. Smoke and close quarters hindered the archers and left little room for cavalry. Dismounted, Harry and his lieutenants fought on foot alongside their men.

So did the Scots.

In time, a rising moon aided visibility, and the English forced the Scots back toward their last flimsy shelter, the tents of Douglas and his aides.

One of Scotland's leading men, Douglas was the most powerful border laird, a tall bear of a man. But having taken too long to perceive the danger, he, too, had joined the fray in makeshift armor, including a borrowed helmet. Launching himself into the first Englishmen he encountered, he smashed energetically with his axe. Dropping it a few minutes later, after nearly severing a Northumbrian head, he switched to his equally intimidating broadsword until he could grabble at his feet for his weapon of choice. His beefy paw closed on the axe, and he raised it with a fierce cry. But the action had cost precious seconds, and as he spun back, spears stabbed his thigh and shoulder. Smarting with pain, he continued, axe emptying the space around him. Then, a cry came from nowhere.

"Esperance!"

Hotspur had cut his way through the Scottish ranks. Within moments, he confronted Douglas, who, already wounded by others, now turned on his new opponent with a vengeance.

The contest begun at Newcastle resumed.

Batting away an axe slash, Harry thrust hard with his sword, bringing the point up firmly against Douglas' chin. "Yield! I pledge your life and safety!"

"Never! You English cockscomb!" Too-small helmet bobbing atop his head, axe arcing, Douglas reeled backward but managed to dislodge Harry's sword.

Avoiding the axe, Harry pressed on. When another axe slash failed, he seized a tiny opening, again bringing his sword to Douglas' neck. Douglas removed it with a swipe, but the sword fell mere inches. Automatically, Harry leaned forward, weight falling on his sword arm. His blade dug into Douglas' chest. Douglas lurched but recovered as a trio of his vassals attempted to reach him. Deterred as much by Douglas' erratic attacks as Harry's, they found it wasn't easy.

Dripping blood, Douglas continued his berserk onslaught.

"Yield!" Harry urged anew as Douglas' blood spurted from multiple wounds. "Your life's secure, on my honor. Yield." Even in the tumult, the anguish in his voice rang out.

But Douglas only became more enraged, axe whirling, though he retreated slightly.

That left Douglas' three vassals free to concentrate on Harry, who overcame the first two, while the third, Sir John Montgomery, tried to reach Douglas.

Montgomery was too late. Within seconds, he saw Douglas stumble toward him, stop cold, convulse, and crumble, dying on the English soil he had sought to subdue.

Pivoting, Montgomery took up the fight against Harry. Although about a dozen years older, he had been spared vigorous efforts earlier, and his strength equaled that of his now-tiring foe. For long minutes, neither gave way. Then Harry began to weave on his feet. After more parrying, Montgomery forced him back. Staggering, Harry fell, sprawled on the ground, a scarlet stream trickling across his armor, drowning the Percy lion on his tabard.

Abruptly, Montgomery halted. "Holy St. Andrew!" He gasped at the blood, for Harry otherwise looked unscathed. Leaning over the outstretched legs, knife at Harry's throat, Montgomery sought surrender. Under the flickering skies, he could guess the torment in the alert eyes, watching through visor slits.

Harry turned his head toward the sword still clutched in his hand, weighing a final bid for escape, though it surely meant death.

"Don't be a fool, Lad," Montgomery admonished. "Yield! You're bleeding fearsome fast. Yield?" The question came in a kinder tone.

Hesitantly, Harry dropped the sword. "I yie... yield..."

"Then I, Sir John Montgomery, take you as prisoner and hostage, and pledge that you shall be kept safe, so help me God, as long as you promise never to attempt to flee. Agreed?"

"Aye. I am... Sssi..."

"Sir Harry Percy. I ken you well enou'," Montgomery barked, as Harry groped for his sword

again—not to threaten his captor with it but to present it.

"Ahhh hell!" Montgomery laid Harry's sword aside and sheathed his own. Bending, he stripped off his gloves and slipped his left arm behind Harry's back, extending his right arm. Raising his own arms, Harry helped Montgomery tug his gauntlets off. Silently, the two clasped hands, signifying a formal surrender but also lending Harry a strong hand of support.

Carefully, Montgomery raised him to a sitting position. "Here Lad, you look sore hurt. And you're bleeding. Lean on me." Mutely, Harry complied, until he felt his balance returning. Gently, Montgomery removed Harry's sword-belt, returning the sword to the scabbard, and lifted his captive's helmet, followed by his own. Heads bared, sweaty faces shining in the moonlight, they regarded each other in respect. Then Montgomery began peeling back Harry's tabard, chainmail, and undershirt, searching for wounds. "By all the saints of Scotland!" He shook his head. "How be it that a man can shed so much blood with nary a cut? Be you some miraculous relic, Lad? Bleeding like a sealed vial of holy blood?"

"No!" Harry laughed when he had least expected to. "Only a relic of banging lances yestere'en with him." He tipped his head toward the fallen Douglas. "My wound must've reopened."

Montgomery's fingers found the stiff bandage wrapping Harry's midriff and felt the lengthy, deep gash beneath, oozing steadily, warm and sticky to his touch. Harry gasped, tears dotting his lashes.

How, John Montgomery wondered, had Percy been able to fight at all—much less successfully, half the night—and after a long march? His admiration grew. Smoothing the bandage back in place, he applied pressure until the bleeding abated. "C'mon Lad..." Slowly, he rose. "We'd best get you to a physician."

Braced by his captor, Harry got up and they lumbered ahead. But after several steps he paused.

"What's wrong? Too weak to go farther?"

"No." The cheeks that had been devoid of color reddened. "It's just that ... I have to piss."

"Well, go ahead, but not all over my boots!" Montgomery pulled him behind a tree and discreetly turned around, allowing Harry to lean against him, back to back.

Mission accomplished, Harry propped on Montgomery's shoulder, they continued on to the lines of the wounded. There Montgomery left him to the chaplains and doctors, after sending a squire for clean clothes.

Slowly comprehending that their commander had been vanquished, the English began quitting the field, not so much surrendering as melting away to surrounding fields and forests. Douglas' fate, still unknown to all but a few, the Scots assumed they had won but also began drifting off. Some, Montgomery included, chased the escaping English. Others, exhausted, simply looked for an untrammeled piece of earth, stretching out in sleep. The slain from both nations lay where they had fallen, awaiting a common grave, to share a unity in death that had eluded them in life.

Numbly, Harry submitted to the care of an elderly priest. Stripping him naked and tossing the blood-soaked garments aside, the cleric skillfully cleansed his wound with whisky and packed it with a salve of yarrow, rue and bramble.

"Be not so downcast, son," the old man advised, bandaging him anew. "You may've lost the battle, but you've surely won the war. Look about. Even now, our good Scotsmen are leaving their spoils and pulling back, just like your English. So what did this gain us? Many dead for you, but too many for us as well." The priest helped him pull on fresh underbriefs, shirt,

tunic, and leggings, all Montgomery's and a reasonable fit, and blessed him before moving on.

Sick with mortification and fears for his men, including his brother, Rafe, Harry sank to the ground. From snatches of overheard conversations, he knew that Rafe had been seriously wounded and borne to a tent, where, Harry guessed, he was probably now dead. "He pulled me from the field at Newcastle. Yet I brought him out here to perish ... all these others, too."

Dawn traced ivory across the sky, but he scarcely noticed. Nor did he immediately heed the din slowly building around him. Eventually, though, a few realities penetrated: The Scots felt compelled to withdraw, for if the sun was about to greet them, so was another English army under the bishop of Durham, augmented by the men from his own ranks who had managed to flee Otterburn.

Another realization followed: Some of the Scots intended to kill the prisoners, in general, lest they hinder a retreat, and Harry Hotspur, first and foremost, to avenge Douglas. Dizzily getting to his feet, he reached for his sword and knife, only to despair: He'd surrendered them to Montgomery. Edging behind the dubious protection of several firs, he heard the yelling increase. Tramping feet smashed into the brush. For long seconds, he stood there, determined to fight with his bare hands if necessary.

"Get Percy! Kill him!"

More crashing sounded, followed by new, startled cries of pain.

Cautiously, he peered through the firs.

Earl George Dunbar, his counterpart as Scottish warden of the March, sat atop a magnificent steed, the horse's powerful haunches edging backward and Dunbar's boots lashing out at anyone within reach. The men fell back.

Scowling, Dunbar dismounted. Of medium height, with balding pate, unbearded cheeks, a trim physique, and enough wrinkles to make him look distinguished *but not doddering, he might have stepped from the niche of a Roman villa, a marble emperor come to life.*

"Silence!" Dunbar's green eyes were hard. "With Lord Jamie's death, I command now. What's the cause of this unseemly riot?"

The prisoners would only prevent a swift return to Scotland, two men asserted. English lives weren't worth the death of even one more Scotsman, three more maintained. The fewer Englishmen left in the world, the better, another claimed.

"Above all, kill Percy!" a seventh contended. "He murdered Douglas in cold blood, after Lord Jamie had surrendered. Then he robbed his body; left it there naked and cold!"

Harry stiffened, recognizing the voice of William Stewart. As a young knight of England, Stewart had renounced his allegiance to become a vassal of Clan Douglas. Later, before Harry's tenure as warden, Stewart had helped Scotland seize Teviotdale, then under English jurisdiction. Now a venerable Scottish magnate, he remained a wanted man in Northumberland. "Traitor!" Harry slammed one fist into the other, praying. "If I can kill just one of them, let it be him."

"Lord William's right," a baron yelled. "Kill Percy."

Vehement "ayes" followed.

Dunbar frowned, reconsidering. The prisoners, this Hotspur too, could be more trouble than they were worth, he told himself. And the Dunbars, in particular, might gain from eliminating him. Dunbar looked back at the mob. "Mayhap you're right."

Hoofbeats forced them to turn their heads.

"By all the saints of Scotland!" Montgomery galloped up with half a dozen knights. "What goes here?"

"We're about to spare ourselves a burden, put the axe to these English heads." Stewart swaggered forward.

"There are good arguments for slaying—" Dunbar began.

"Never!" Montgomery flung himself from his horse. "Killing any o' these men would be murder! 'Gainst the laws of nature itself!"

"Also the laws of war!" one of his companions echoed.

"'And the law of Scotland," a third added.

"'Twould violate our oaths as knights and our honor as men," a fourth warned. "Nor could we e'er again expect quarter from the English, should they capture any of us."

"Perhaps, but think of the gains—or are you too dense a fool, Montgomery?" Dunbar sneered. "Killing Percy would remove their warden and—"

"You hell-spawn sumph, Dunbar," Montgomery growled. "There's scarce a man in Scotland you haven't offended, strutting and bullying, tryin' to lord it over us. But I'll not let you get away with this." He threw a glove down in challenge and shoved his way through the pack. Clasping Harry's wrist, he led him into their midst. "Look this man in the face. And tell him—and me—why you want to slay him!"

Stewart repeated his accusation.

Montgomery bristled. "'Tis a lie! He slew Lord Jamie in fair combat. I saw it with my own eyes. After cutting him badly, Sir Harry bade him to surrender, holding back his own might. Lord Jamie refused. And he succumbed—from the cut Sir Harry gave him, to be sure, but from other wounds, too. Then Sir Harry and I fought and I captured him. And, by God, I'll have my ransom from him."

"A pox on your ransom," a middling laird protested. "Kill Percy, as a warning to England."

"Would you kill a man who's unarmed, and wounded too?" Montgomery asked hotly.

"Wounded?"

"Aye, not by me but from fighting with Lord Jamie at Newcastle. I had to hold him up just so he could piss.

I dragged him to the physicians myself. There, o'er yonder, he lay, too spent to do otherwise." Montgomery glowered at them. "Whoever robbed Lord Jamie's body, 'twasn't Sir Harry. I'll swear to that. And to kill him you'll have to kill me and any others who refuse to countenance your murderous ways!"

His companions advanced, swords unsheathed, circling Montgomery and Harry. One of Montgomery's squires broke through the ring with an additional sword, which Montgomery pressed into his captive's hand. "Here, Lad. Defend yourself, if this comes to fighting. Flee if you can. You'll be absolved of any ransom obligation."

Harry grasped the hilt with something akin to his usual vigor, standing as firmly as he could, shoulder-to-shoulder with Montgomery.

Dunbar groaned. "Put up your weapons," he directed the mob. "Let's begin the retreat before the Durham array gets here. Bring everyone, including our wounded—and the prisoners. But tie their hands and feet. Let them lie in the baggage wagons or across the saddle."

He stepped up to Harry. "And I'll take that sword."

Trembling slightly, Harry relinquished it.

Montgomery draped an arm around him, whispering. "Buck up, Lad. I won't let you be harmed."

Slowly, the throng dispersed.

Allowing Harry to mount a horse, Montgomery tied his wrists loosely in front. Likewise, with a slack rope that went from Harry's right foot to the left, across the saddle, only vaguely did he follow Dunbar's order to bind the prisoners' feet because, "I'll be damned if I'll dump an honorable man in a wagon, or toss him o'er a saddle like a sack o' grain!"

The Scots returned home.

Montgomery's rights notwithstanding, on their arrival in Edinburgh, Harry was declared a royal Scottish prisoner and tossed into a dank dungeon, with only Montgomery's Psalter for company. He languished for days before they moved him, in chains, to Dunbar's castle on the coast. Objecting strenuously to King Robert, Montgomery finally procured his captive's release into his own custody. He took Harry back with him to Ayrshire, where his castle of Eaglesham was comfortable and well-fortified but hardly huge. "Perhaps I'll use your ransom to do something grander," he said. "Add an outer wall, a better hall. I've been told Robert himself set your ransom at £4,600. A man could construct a big bothy with that!"

"And not be the first to trade a hostage for a house!" Harry chuckled.

Indeed, ransoms built fortresses as well as fortunes and taking hostages was a hallowed practice. It even saved lives since by sparing opponents in battle, knights could earn pretty sums later. Formal rules governed everything, too: Hostages had to disavow escape attempts or retaliation, and captors had to treat them well. Sometimes, warm friendships even developed between captor and captive. Usually, too, prisoners could obtain paroles, returning home to arrange their affairs in their absences or collect ransom money. And severely wounded men were often sent home to convalesce before assuming their roles as captives.

"So your brother Rafe's safe at Alnwick, paroled for healing," Montgomery informed Harry, two weeks after their arrival at Eaglesham.

"Thank God for that," Harry said, "and that you retrieved me. I hardly saw Dunbar at his castle at all and feared he'd still have me slain."

"It violates the code of chivalry to kill hostages," Montgomery pointed out.

"Aye, but he was ready enough at Otterburn. It's happened elsewhere, too."

"But why? 'Tis hard to get ransom from a corpse!"

As the weeks went by, though, Harry wondered if he might still end up a corpse in Ayrshire, not because Montgomery murdered him but because he died there in his dotage.

"Your king's dragging his feet about authorizing ransom. Won't let your father, Parliament or anyone else intervene," Montgomery observed months into Harry's stay. "And he's appointed that ass Mowbray as warden in your stead."

"Sweet Jesu," Harry shook his head. "Yet I suppose it makes sense in Richard's twisted scheme of things. Mowbray was one of those Lord's Appellants who rose against him a couple of years ago. Now Richard can use my post to lure Mowbray back into his royal web like a spider trapping a fly."

"Och!" Montgomery laughed. "Seems your fly only got his feet stuck in Borders muck. I heard in Edinburgh that he arrived on the Borders saying he'd never be stupid like you and get caught in a debacle like Otterburn. Our lairds in his neck o' the woods then tested him, went out raiding and pillaging with no hindrance."

"Hell!"

"The tale gets better. Mowbray made one pissant foray, only to scurry back inside his castle again without even seeing a Scot. The man's got the ballocks of a castrated goose. But he sent a message."

"To the Scots?"

"Aye. Wrote griping and moaning that as he'd too few men to fight, maybe we could forget about e'er raiding again and just go away!"

"No!"

"'Tis true! But I hear that he's since run back to London, finding the Borders a wee too inhospitable for his liking. Though our friends in London also say he got Richard to continue his warden's salary."

"No wonder there's been no money for my ransom."

"I reckon not. But don't fret, Lad. I'm a patient man."

Just how patient became apparent as the seasons rolled by. Meanwhile, the two became less captor and captive than men whose friendship spanned a border and near-fatal combat. In fact, so solicitous did Montgomery become that at times he fretted like a clucking hen, disconcerted that despite excellent food—the same he himself ate—Harry never regained weight lost when imprisoned in Edinburgh and Dunbar's castle. He had the run of Montgomery's domains but even summer sun couldn't coax color into his complexion. Perhaps, Montgomery mused, that's what depriving a man of independence did, even one held under the best conditions. For someone like Harry, freedom was life itself; taking it from him stole something from his very core.

Their amicable existence continued until one afternoon when Harry returned to the castle, a deer slung over his shoulders. Even more exuberant than usual, Montgomery waited at the gate.

"Glad tidings, Lad! And that deer you shot 'twill be 'specially welcome this eve. We'll make a right feast o' it. But you'll have to share the guest-of-honor honors with another." Montgomery winked. "That'd be one Donach MacLarty, the best castle architect in these parts."

The dead deer slid from Harry's shoulders. "You mean?"

"Aye! Your ransom's come."

"After nearly fifteen months."

"Aye. Seems your Parliament had been pestering Richard, and he finally acted. Better late than never, I say."

Harry left for Northumberland the next day. Reinstated as warden, he resumed his duties as if there had been no interruption—except for the long list of things to be fixed after Mowbray's disastrous tenure. Separated by one-hundred and thirty miles, he *and Montgomery saw one another infrequently. But they remained on good terms, and Harry always welcomed a reunion.*

* * *

Montgomery was lodged in a guesthouse within Edinburgh Castle, which crowned a steep precipice overlooking the town. Showing the sentries his safe-conduct pass, Harry was admitted and directed to the proper apartment. There, a squire answered his knock, though Montgomery was close behind.

"Good e'en' and welcome. 'Tis been too long since I've seen you, Lad."

A brawny man, straight and tough, Montgomery remained beardless but sported a wide mustache and grey-brown locks that fell just below his ears. He was dressed in a summer-weight surcoat, belted with a broad band of leather studded with brass and silver. Arm draped over Harry, he led the way to a parlor, partly paneled and cozy with a fireplace and leaded windows that caught the evening sun. The table contained two place settings; wine, cider and ale; and Scottish cheeses, including Montgomery's favorite, a berry-flavored Crowdie, and the creamy Cadoc that Harry had delectably discovered during his captivity.

Montgomery directed Harry to a chair. "I thought we'd have a quaff and wee bite together, ere we join my household in the hall. And I prepared something special." He pointed to one of the plates, lidded with a round cover. "What'll you drink? Wine?"

"Please." Harry waited for Montgomery to fill the goblets, hand him one, and seat himself. "To you, John," he toasted, "the best captor and one of the best friends a man could have."

"And to you, Harry, as honorable an *English* gentleman as any could be, and one whom I've always liked right well."

Harry wondered about the emphasis on his nationality but dismissed it, reaching for the cheese.

"After you." Montgomery tapped the covered dish and popped a piece of Crowdie into his mouth.

Harry swallowed a wedge of Cadoc. Lifting the lid over his plate, he looked up. Then he averted his eyes, face flooding with a scarlet embarrassment beyond anything Montgomery had seen at Otterburn. The plate contained nothing but a copy of Harry's call-to-arms in Cheshire. Neatly written in English, the text spilled across the page, inked in black, except for the phrase about the Scots. That stood out in crimson, like blood:

"...who crave nothing less than to continuously wage war against the folk and language of this realm."

"Oh God." Harry groaned, realizing what this was all about. "I'm sorry. Truly sorry, John. I should have known better... Hell, I did know better... What can I say?" He could scarcely raise his head.

Montgomery seemed equally distressed. "How could you, Lad? From you, of all men. 'Tis bad enough what your king's been trying to do up here. But for you to stoop to that, a call to hatred. Baiting men to belittle each other. Painting us as barbarians, frothing at the mouth to kill Englishmen..." His voice pitched emotionally. "Did you learn naught, all those months you dwellt with me? Did you not see how we live? That we be just like you—especially like you, a Borderer?"

Harry waited for the tirade to end.

"And to say we want to fight against the English language. Christ-sakes, Lad! What am I speaking to you in? Gaelic? No. Verily, you'd consider *that* a heathen tongue." He stared stonily at Harry.

"I... I'm sorry, John. I shouldn't have written it. 'Twas wrong..."

"Aye, to say the least!"

Harry groaned softly again. "How did you come by it?"

Montgomery smiled slyly. "Think we don't know what happens in England? And on those other borders of yours?"

"Spies."

"No. Farmers and wool merchants. A couple of my neighbors were in Chester, buying some o' those black Welsh sheep, to augment our flocks. They heard your call-to-arms proclaimed in English. One had the sense to copy it down."

"Oh God..." Harry buried his head in his hands. By now, it must be all over Scotland that the English warden of the March had maligned Scotsmen in order to raise Welshmen and Cheshiremen against them. How much trouble had he stirred with that careless bigotry, those few inflammatory words? And in light of Henry's arrogant demands for fealty, wouldn't the Scots strike back—not immediately, with the English army still in Scotland, but in due time? Of course...

He cursed softly. True, the Scots had started it all the previous year by raiding England. But his writ wouldn't help. Now, he'd have to work thrice as hard to keep things calm.

"I've been a fool, John, and wrong, damned wrong." He wasn't wearing his sword indoors, but he stood and pulled his knife, extending it to Montgomery hilt first.

"What's that for?" Montgomery slowly took it. "So I can slit your fine English throat? Well, I won't do it! I'm damned peeved at you, Lad, and sore disappointed. But I'm not that angry."

"Nor I that mad at myself," Harry answered with a faint laugh. "And if I were, I'd fall on my sword, outside, and not bleed like a stuck pig all over your table. No, I give you my knife so that I can surrender to you, again, like all those years ago, and ask your forgiveness."

Montgomery cast an appraising eye, but it simply confirmed what he already knew. So he put Harry's knife down and came around the table. "Forgiveness granted."

"Then I'm at your service in doing whatever you think best in mending fences—or, perhaps, tearing them down—along our borders."

Montgomery boxed him in jest and they embraced, pounding each other's back.

Returning to his seat, Harry picked up his knife, shredding the parchment into a pile on the plate. Cider jug in hand, he poured a copious amount over it.

Back in his own chair, Montgomery watched. "Now what're you doing?"

Harry picked up a spoon. "Preparing to eat my words."

With a roar, Montgomery jerked the plate from reach. "Not in this house! I won't have you puking all over King Robert's rugs." Turning to the fire, he tossed the soggy mush onto the flames, which flared and hissed eagerly. "'Struth, I thought about catching and killing a chough. I was going to put it on your plate, with your writ in its beak, and tell you to eat crow. But I decided 'twouldn't be fair to the poor beastie birdie."

They laughed again.

"I suppose," Harry mused, "that afore leaving Scotland, I'd best gather the leading Lowlands lairds, provide good food and drink, apologize for that writ, and seek their help in keeping the peace despite it—and everything else."

Montgomery grinned. "I rather thought you'd feel that way. I've arranged it. They're waiting in the hall."

Several hours later, Montgomery pounded his back again. "You did it. I'm right proud of you, Lad. You won not only their forgiveness but their continued respect."

"Aye. Doesn't mean they'll never raid England again." Harry accepted a cup of Montgomery's prize whisky. "But perhaps one incendiary arrow has been doused. For now, 'tis all I can ask."

* * *

August 1400 - Berwick Castle, England

Hal was petulant. "Why can't you come with me? You're supposed to be my guardian. Anyway, I don't want to go to Paris."

Harry knelt on the floor next to a trunk. Given Hal's unhappiness, he had excused the attendants who might have done the packing and were finishing the job themselves so that he could teach the prince not to rely on servants for simple tasks and to give them time together. "You know I can't go. We've talked about that. I need to stay in the North. After the ruckus we raised in Scotland, I must see to our defenses, especially with the royal army returned to London."

Hal was still glum. "But I don't want to go to France alone."

"You won't," Harry replied. "Archbishop Arundel and my uncle will join you down the coast. They're much better ambassadors than I. 'Tis time you met the French king, too. Once you're older, you may have to govern our Calais territory. It will help, especially after the business with King Richard, if you get to know Charles of France soon, and let him see what a fine person you are."

"And maybe," Harry added mentally, "convince him that not all of the House of Lancaster are notorious usurpers and that you could be a good match for his daughter, Isabel." Hal didn't know it, but in sending him on a courtesy visit, Henry hoped both to placate the French and increase the chances of marrying Hal to Isabel, Richard's child-bride and child-widow. "She's his old playmate from Richard's court," Harry remembered. "They were fond of each other. In a few years they could grow up to find that fondness had blossomed into love. And that would serve Henry, too."

As he knew, Henry would happily marry off his children without considering *amour* at all. But if he could pair Hal with someone the boy genuinely fancied, it would help solidify the link. Besides, Harry's thoughts continued, Charles suffered episodic descents into madness; he could die, retire, anytime, "and how opportune that'd be for Henry, aptly positioned to try claiming France himself or ruling it as regent for Hal and Isabel."

Hal knew nothing of this.

The prince tried again. "I can go to Paris later. You and I should get on with my training as a soldier and my other lessons."

"That'll wait," Harry assured him, though he took pride in the boy's interest. Indoors, he kept Hal occupied with Latin, French, arithmetic, and history. (Hal particularly enjoyed Bede's biographies of early kings, like Oswald.) Outdoors, he provided instruction in riding, swordplay, jousting, archery, and the other skills a knight required. In Chester and Wales, he also tutored Hal in basic governance, ensuring his presence at sessions of the Prince's Council, which Harry headed, and having him sit alongside as Harry dealt with petitions or presided over assemblies. Wherever they were, too, he taught Hal to make his own way on the land, through the mountains and across the moors: finding water for himself and his horse; catching and cleaning fish; foraging for the berries that sweetened an afternoon, or the leeks and herbs that flavored a fireside stew; reading the constellations by night and the tracks of animals, or other men, by day; attuning his ears to the slightest sound, lest snapping twig or frenzied bird cries warned of danger. After the ostentatious palace in London, Hal wandered through this new, simpler world with undisguised delight. It was hardly surprising that he would eschew a trip to Paris and the lavish French court.

But the choice was not his.

With a sigh, Harry crammed underclothes into the trunk and slammed it shut. Picking up a pair of scarlet shoes with long, curling toes (perfect, in Henry's estimation, for France,) he shuddered, tossing them into a half-filled smaller box. He was reaching into the wardrobe for another pair when someone knocked on the door.

"Come in," Harry called out, and two dusty men in Henry's livery entered, carrying an ornate coffer.

Harry glanced at the box, aware of what it contained. "Set it down."

One of the men placed it on a table, unlocked it, and opened the lid. There, on lush red velvet, lay a golden crown, glistening with diamonds, rubies, and all the luster of Richard II's days. Hal had not seen it since Ireland. He cringed. "That was King Richard's."

"So it was, My Prince," the senior messenger purred. "Henceforth, it's yours, from your sovereign father. I beg your lordship to try it on. Then, if it needs adjustment, we can have Berwick smiths tend to it ere you leave. And we can report back to the King, as commanded." He held it out.

Hal stretched a tentative hand and then snatched the crown, throwing it across the room. "I don't want it!" His voice trembled. "I'd rather have Richard back." With a muffled cry, he fled.

Harry replaced the crown in its container and extended an open palm for the key. The messenger surrendered it.

"Don't trouble yourselves. I'll deal with this," Harry informed the pair. "And it'd be best if you departed. Please accept my regrets at the unhappy reception." He watched as they hurried away, leaving the coffer. Locking the door securely after them, Harry followed Hal into their private quarters.

He found the prince clinging to a wall hanging, sobbing. Hands on the boy's shoulders, he asked quietly, "What's wrong, Lad?"

Louder sobs followed so Harry waited a moment. "Hal? You can tell me."

The sniffling continued. "Richard... I want him back again... Not dead!"

Harry relaxed his grip on the boy's shoulders and turned Hal around. With another little cry, the prince flung himself into Harry's embrace. "I miss him," he buried his head against Harry's chest. "Richard was my friend ... I know he was terrible ... toward a lot of folk ... especially my father. But he was always good to me..." He shook. "I can't help it. I liked him. I didn't want him to die..."

The last word was extinguished by more weeping as Harry stroked the brown hair.

"Nobody with any decency and trust in justice wanted him to die, Hal. I'm sorry, too, that he's gone. And I was one of those he often treated badly."

Hal only convulsed in fresh tears.

Lifting him, Harry carried him to a window alcove, seating himself and holding Hal like a small child. Just turned thirteen, the prince sometimes showed flashes of adult intelligence and maturity. But he was still a boy, and Harry realized that he had overlooked the depth of Hal's boyish emotions. With the inexplicable adoration of children, Hal had become deeply attached to Richard, just as Harry himself had grown close to his uncle at that age. Richard had helped raise Hal, been a kindly uncle or elder cousin rather than a despotic king. Now Richard was dead, probably killed at the order of Hal's father... Yet in all the months since Richard's death, Hal had been mute, seemingly unaffected, until sight of the crown last seen on Richard's head had set him off.

Locking the boy in his arms, Harry cursed his own blindness. Hal needed to remember Richard; needed to mourn, and, in time, put his sadness behind him. But as Hal's current guardian, in his own thick-headedness, he hadn't seen it. Of course, children were rarely asked about their feelings, and it never occurred to most adults that they might grieve deeply. Grieve they did, though, and he should have remembered that. As a boy, he had watched his mother, beautiful and distant and young, suddenly die at Alnwick, leaving a stunned husband and five children—the oldest, Harry, only eleven. No one had thought to console him and his siblings or even perceived they needed consolation, for what could children know or feel? So it had fallen to Harry to dry the tears and ease the pain of his brothers and sister, swallowing his own despair as best he could. Over the years, through strenuous physical and mental exertions, he had mastered his sorrow—along with his stutter and everything else that had troubled his early life. Growing to manhood, in chivalry, and service to his country, he found refuge and solace in every disappointment.

Even if his heart tugged at him in loneliness sometimes.

"What a muddle I've made of so much," he thought. He scarcely saw his own children and couldn't even do things right by this boy wrapped in his arms—this boy, so much like him; more arrogant and self-confident at that age than Harry had ever been, but by disposition, interests and abilities very much his junior. Odd that...

He resolved to do better.

"I should've seen how devoted you were to Richard." He lifted Hal's blotched face. "Would you like to visit his grave, in Buckinghamshire? I can take you there when you return from France, ere we go back to Chester."

Hal's eyes refilled with tears, though he blinked them away. "No. I don't like visiting graves. They aren't really the person, even dead."

Harry smiled. Without realizing it, Hal had stumbled on one of Christianity's greatest teachings. A tomb, however magnificent, however accurate the effigy carved on it, ultimately meant little. The real man wasn't there and even the bones within were not he. The real man was gone, transcending death, living anew somewhere with God.

Harry rubbed Hal's head as the boy hid his face again. Slowly, his crying ceased. "I'm sorry. I didn't mean to weep like a baby!" Hal now looked less sad than chagrined.

"There's nothing wrong with a few tears. Even Christ wept."

The boy stole another hug, then wiped his eyes and stood up. " We'd better finish with my baggage."

"You'll be all right on this trip?"

Hal nodded solemnly. "I don't want to go or wear that crown. Yet I suppose I must. At least," he brightened, "since I'm prince of England, in France no one can tell me what to do. If I only wear that crown once or twice, nobody can do anything. And if Father learns of it and screams when I return, well—let him."

Harry smiled. "By then, let's hope you'll have made him so proud, 'twon't matter."

They resumed packing. Then Hal tried on the crown, verified the fit, and set it atop a trunk without a further look.

Scooping it up, Harry returned it to its coffer, resisting the temptation to chuck it through a window. A dead man's crown was an awful burden to place on the head of a thirteen-year-old. Still, if any boy could bear it, he reckoned this was the one.

Chapter XVII
September 1400 - Northumberland

It was the stride that caught Harry's attention, from atop a hill.

Below him, a small figure walked with the long gait of a seasoned man. Yet this looked to be no man but a boy in a coarse hooded tunic and plain leggings, albeit a boy with good boots, a belt and knife. A pack, longbow laced to it, weighted his back as he glided ahead. Intrigued, Harry watched as he disappeared down the road. A runaway bond-boy, perhaps; a disenchanted lay-brother escaping some monastery; or tender-yeared thief, freed by a jailer who might otherwise have felt pressured to hang him. Or maybe a junior archer, unattached to any lord. If so, "there's always room in my ranks."

But that could wait. On horseback, he'd soon catch up. Meanwhile, his bread and cheese remained untouched.

A few minutes later, he tossed his lunch crumbs to the sparrows and smiled. 'Twas marvelous to be back in his own country, away from royal obsessions with Scottish fealty and whatever mischief Henry might stir in Wales, for after his futile Scottish incursion, the king was off to wave the royal flag there—while insisting the justiciar of North Wales remain behind.

Rising from his boulder-cum-table, Harry glanced at his horses: Redesraven and Brutus, a destrier no longer nimble enough for war but too useful (and appreciated) for slaughter. They grazed placidly, so he strolled to the nearby stream. Hands cupped, he drank and then stretched out on the bank. Shallows rippled over stones, and water bugs inscribed airy circles on the surface. As easily as their wake, his cares vanished, too, ephemeral as a dragonfly's footprint, a leaf borne on a cloud. Meadow warmth welcomed his body, and his heartbeat reverberated against the earth, which seemed to answer with a pulse of its own. Solace born of solitude flooded over him.

After a time, his journey resumed.

The vagabond's track was obvious, continuing by road before veering into brush and woods. Dismounting, Harry unstrapped his sword from the saddle and buckled it on, leaving the horses.

From the woods, the boy had followed a path strewn with sheep dung before meandering into a blackberry thicket. A space opened between two well-laden bushes, and Harry stepped through into a glade.

The wanderer sat on the ground, alongside a pile of blackberries. The boy reached for some, only to drop them in alarm. Springing up, he grabbed his bow, notched an arrow, and raised it. "Halt!"

Smiling as he shook his head, Harry took another step forward—and dodged a shaft at his feet.

"Stop." The voice quavered from within the boy's hood. "Or I'll put one through you."

"Peace, I mean no harm."

The boy seemed not to hear, drawing a second arrow. A moment later, though, his hands shook, almost imperceptibly but enough for a trained eye to catch.

Stock still, Harry felt a twinge of uneasiness. An archer who couldn't control his weapon might shoot unintentionally and lethally.

The youth spoke again. "Your sword. Take it off. Throw it here."

"I've a very bad arm for throwing," Harry replied. "I'll need to come a couple steps closer."

The youth nodded, grip tightening on the bow.

Harry advanced, more than a couple of steps. Just as the next arrow seemed ready to fly, he stopped, raising his right arm. "See, lad: My sword-arm is nowhere near my hilt. I'm going to remove my sword and throw it to you. I'll use my left hand, so I'll be clumsy. Hold your fire."

Again, the boy nodded.

Right hand aloft, Harry fumbled at his belt with his left. Taking several more steps, he leaned low and tossed the sword. Sheathed, it fell short, as Harry had planned.

But the boy lowered the bow. Retrieving the sword, he dropped it behind him.

Only a short distance separated them now.

"Come no farther till you tell me who you are and why you spied on me from that hill and followed me." The boy's fingers retightened on the bow. "I'll have answers, or you may regret it."

Harry's patience eroded. "You'll have answers? No. Tell me who you are and why you skulk alone, armed, like some damned reiver, where my writ runs. And take off that hood and show your face!"

"Why?"

Harry bristled. "Impudent pup! I've a mind to tan your hide!" He bounded ahead.

Abandoning the bow, the boy reached for his knife. He was fast but no match for Hotspur.

Bounding ahead, Harry seized the boy's hand, still struggling to draw the dirk. Forcing him to turn, Harry pulled him up against his own taller body. They faced the same direction as his left fingers clamped around the boy's wrist. The dagger fell to the ground.

Harry flung his right arm around the struggling torso. "My God!"

He froze as his right hand discovered the slenderness of an indented waist, and, lower, the unmistakable curve of pelvic bones, as he also felt the pressure of small breasts cupped against his upper arm. "A maiden!"

Gently, he spun her around, releasing his hold and taking a long step back.

She pulled the hood off, revealing red hair, and looked at him, half smiling, half confused. "No maiden, but a grown woman, who'll wager she's seen near as much of life as you, whoever you are."

He flashed a wry smile. "Harry Percy. Formally: Sir Harry Percy, Warden of the March, Justiciar of North Wales, Justice of Chester, Knight of the Garter—and various other things not worth mentioning."

Her luminous eyes lit up. "Hotspur," she said softly.

"The very one—though, at present, my spurs feel less hot than foolish." Stooping, he picked up her knife and handed it back. "You?"

"Ciarry DeCorbett Fitzwyatt. And even without titles, that's quite enough. Itinerant scribe and teacher, late of the Abbey of Saints Hilda and Kentigern."

He was unsure he'd heard her name correctly but comprehended the rest readily enough. Inexplicably nervous, he rattled off recollections: "Sort of Gilbertines—your abbey, I mean. They—you—tried to revive the idea of men and women living in common, 'neath one roof, working, praying and dining together, as in the days of Hilda and Kentigern—and Gilbert, later. The house some said was blessed with sages but others said harbored Lollards."

"Yea. We followed the Rule of St. Benedict, so we sheltered wayfarers who came to our door, even Lollards."

He nodded. "But that wasn't your whole mission."

"No. We taught in villages and parish schools—there are more now for girls as well as boys. We had a farm, too, and other duties. Mine included being abbess-elect. I was never recognized officially, though; we never got church approval for our community."

He seemed to listen eagerly, so she went on. "Eventually, some of our number left to join established orders: Benedictine, Cistercian, Franciscan. We disbanded and I started a pilgrimage through the North. I hope to visit Lindisfarne, Holy

Isle. Then I'll probably seek out a nunnery, one in need of scribe or notary."

"To take the veil again?"

"Perhaps. I'd lief live among them as a laywoman first, till I can discern God's will. I hope to find a suitable convent by winter."

Realizing she had summarized most of her recent life, she blushed. "I'm sorry, My Lord. That's more than you wanted to hear."

"No, I like listening to your voice. 'Tis an improvement over mine and my horses', which is all I've had of late. But tell me your name again. Ciarry?" He pronounced it like "Kerry," like the Irish county or the village in eastern Wales.

She nodded, and he explored its resonance aloud.

"Ciarry DeCorbett Fitzwyatt. Almost melodic." He smiled again; then their eyes locked, and neither said anything.

How petite she was, he thought, at least a head shorter than he, with a thin figure that wore the boyish garb well but otherwise might have been considered wanting. He noted the fine shape of her head, the hair that shone like flames, cropped close like his or that of a man on an old Roman coin. Her face had a broad brow, pert nose and lips, and firm chin. But her eyes were large, and of a shade he'd never seen before, a deep sable plum: the hue of heather turning from violet to the deeper tones of autumn, of the darkest cherries or rarest purple thistles, of the Welsh mountains against a midnight sky, the color of things he loved. And he realized that a man could lose himself in those eyes, yet find the key to infinity there.

He contrived temporary escape. "Excuse me, Lass ... Lady. But I've forgotten my horses. I'd best fetch them. Might you wait?"

"Yea."

He strode off.

As soon as he disappeared, she brushed her fingers through her hair, too short to have been mussed, even in the brambles. Nervously, she hoped she hadn't been blushing and then blushed at that. For all her learning, she might have been an awkward girl again.

Once, she had despaired of her looks: Carroty locks that defied the ideal (didn't the Madonna always have flowing blonde tresses?) freckles, bony shoulders and limbs. At least in the convent of her childhood and her own abbey later, beauty had been unimportant, and preoccupation with either its presence or absence a silly vanity.

Now, she had more immediate concerns, too. Here she was, with a man who could've been a simple forester yet was anything but; who was, in fact, the celebrated Hotspur. Surely a man so famous—victor in battle and joust, heir to one of the largest domains in England, holder of the posts and titles he'd tossed off so casually—surely such a man would appear only in the finest armor on a magnificent charger or in the velvets of a wealthy courtier, or amidst a retinue that swept others off the road as he thundered through the realm. Yet here he'd stood, alone, suffused not with pride but shyness, fixing her with a quiet, engaging smile, looking at her with those deep blue eyes. Never before had she seen him, yet he evoked an odd sense of familiarity as if in some hidden corner of her soul she had always known him.

Fire pounded her temples and raced through her veins.

The greatest knight in England, yea, in all Christendom, they called him. *Un chevalier par excellence, non pareil, sans peur et sans reproche.* She knew it to be true; knew too that she trusted him. And perhaps could soon love him—if she didn't already.

He returned with the horses.

"I've erred, My Lord." She forced her voice to stay calm. "I am crossing your land, armed, a thief who steals berries. I apologize and pray your leave to continue my journey. But if—"

He raised a hand. "No, Lass. I was about to seek your forgiveness. I accosted you. And you were right: Seeing you from the hill, I followed you. I'm not even sure why, save I was curious." He shrugged. "Folk have long said I'm impetuous. However that may be, if you accept my apology, I'll gladly grant your right-of-way. But you don't need permission. These roads have long been open—and our borders oft a veritable sieve, leaking cows and sheep and men, back and forth of a night."

She laughed.

"Nonetheless, better than my word, as warden of the March I'll give you a warrant guaranteeing protection. I'm a little surprised you got this far without mishap, your talent with the bow notwithstanding."

She started to thank him, but he broke in again. "No, maybe I won't give you a warrant—unless you truly wish to travel alone. Wouldn't recommend it, though. It's dangerous for a woman, disguised or not." He shook his head, amused. "I should probably arrest you, lock you up—for your good and my peace of mind. But I'll set you on a safe path if you wish.

"Otherwise," he looked shy again. "I beg you to allow me to accompany you for a few days. And you can tell me a more: Where you acquired your archery, and how someone so small can walk so fast."

Surprised, Ciarry tried to deliberate, though her heart had instantly said 'yes.'"

"Would that be all right, Lass—I'm sorry—Lady?"

"Yea, My Lord! I should be most pleased with your company. Also," she paused. "Lass is fine, although I doubt I'm a lass anymore. Nor did I ever put much stock in 'lady,' even if I married a knight. Call me what you will."

"'Lass,' then." He grinned. "That's what you look like, even if you have been an abbess-elect and whatever else."

Even as he spoke, his mind raced. Married a knight. Could a husband lurk somewhere, to snatch her from him or from whatever freedom she sought? No! Even if she'd once had a spouse, they were clearly parted now. She was trying to make her way alone into whatever fate awaited. Perhaps, if he were fortunate, he could influence that fate.

Aloud, he continued. "And please: I'm not 'My Lord,' or 'Sir Anything' but 'Harry.' Believe me, I've been called far worse."

"Then Harry 'tis. And I, Ciarry."

Mutually pleased, neither could admit it. So he retrieved his sword while she darted over to admire his horses. Brutus had wandered off after berries, but Redesraven ambled toward her. Letting him sniff her outstretched palm, she was met by avid licks and nibbling at her ears. Caressing the sleek neck, she planted little kisses down his mane. "What a marvelous creature!" she crooned softly. "So strong and comely."

"Aye, and his horse isn't bad looking either," Harry joked, coming up alongside.

Strapping his sword on, he became serious. "Listen, Ciarry, the next time you order a man to disarm, don't overlook his knife. I've still got mine. I doubt you even noticed."

"I did." She glanced at it, sheathed on his right side, opposite the sword on his left. "But I thought it too trifling for concern."

"I've killed men with that knife. When I grabbed you, I could have killed you, too. Remember that, Lass. If you're ever in even the remotest danger, take naught for granted."

"Does that mean I should beware of you, too? Most folk would say it's dangerous to be alone with a man I've scarcely met."

"And they'd be right. But not in my case." Solemnly, he faced her. "One thing I must say now, ere we travel farther: I would never hurt you. And I'd die before I'd let anyone else hurt you. You must believe that."

He spoke with such conviction that any qualms would have vanished—if she'd had any.

"I do believe it."

"Then let's away." Cheerfully, he reached for her pack. "My God, what's in here? Half the building stones from your abbey?" He set the pack down, regarding it dolefully. "I can't believe you carry that much and walk, much less walk quickly."

Ciarry laughed. "I'll not burden you with the details; you look quite burdened already. It doesn't contain stones, but something much better: Books. Likewise, money."

His eyes widened.

"The property our community had was mine, willed by my late husband, Walter Fitzwyatt, when he died."

My late husband when he died. Aye, he'd heard correctly!

"He had long promised to let me endow a religious house. But he drank away most of his patrimony and part of my dowry. And he spent many another coin wenching and gambling. Nonetheless, I got a small share in the end, including a manor. That's where we established our abbey. When we disbanded, it was still in my name. So I sold it to Lanercost Priory for a worthy sum. A share of that money is sewn into my pack. The rest Lanercost's prior holds for me."

"In good stewardship, I hope."

"Yea. He has use of one-third for five years. At the end of that time, he must repay the full amount, plus a small gratuity. I can reclaim it sooner, but risk not getting the full amount—and a nice sum indeed, it should be, well worth the wait."

"Any second thoughts about the abbey?"

"Sometimes I miss the farm: the land, the animals and orchards, the joy of planting crops and seeing them to fullness. 'Twas a little like being God. I loved it, despite the bad weather and losses we periodically suffered. To be sure," she smiled ruefully, "the labor was arduous."

He nodded. "Struggling to till and plough, or weed and harvest, before rain or hail. Days spent in too much sun, or in an ice storm, looking for livestock, or helping ewes in early lambing. And if you keep milch cows and make cheese, lugging all those heavy pails…"

"You know it well." It seemed surprising, in someone of his rank.

"I have farms and have farmed. 'Tis in my blood, or maybe my muscles." He laughed. "Left to my own devices as a boy, when my father knew not what to do with me, I followed our farm steward about. He put me to work—rightly enou'. He didn't need the high lord's son mewling and getting in his way. Then when I spent time with my uncle—Thomas Percy—he assigned me to work on his properties. Someday, he said, I'd have to manage my own, so I'd best learn how, from the bottom up, long before I came to hold sway from the top down."

"Your uncle was wise."

"Aye—and is. He made sure I had a few blisters from rakes and shovels, too, so when I later took up serious practice with sword and lance, my hands were primed, having hefted heavy tools as a boy."

With a pang, she eyed her own palms, berry-reddened, scarred from cuts and calluses. "Sometimes I think mine will always look like a harpy's, the legacy of fieldwork. Even so, it was hard to give up farming. Yet in the end I'd little choice."

"Why?"

"We made important decisions as a community, by vote after discussion. So it was in this. When it became clear we would never get official church approval, it seemed best to disperse."

Harry frowned. "Couldn't Archbishop Scrope help? He's a good man."

Ciarry paused, hesitant to get into ecclesiastical politics. "The real problem was Bishop Merks. We filed the proper documents with him, more than once. Nothing happened. His clerks said he had no objections to our abbey. Yet he never provided official authorization. Since he rarely was in Carlisle, 'twas easy for him to ignore us."

"While ignoring everyone else, too." Harry looked toward the hills, lush with late-summer green, except where wildflowers blinked toward the sun. Grouse scratched unseen in the weeds and a glimmer of another stream snaked through the lower valley, promise in every serpentine turn. "Merks never could see the merit of this land." He faced her again. "What of Scrope?"

She sighed. "He was indeed kind, sent some of our documents to Rome directly, with his blessing. But there they remained, gathering dust. Word finally came that the pope thought we should have Merks' assent first."

"Those lackeys in Rome probably wanted bribes—Merks, too," Harry suggested.

"Perhaps. I wasn't about to oblige. 'Tis not right. Besides, all our money was committed to our community and alms-giving."

He nodded.

"Merks fell from favor; yet we still got nowhere. Finally, I took it as a sign that perhaps I'd been conceited, wanting to found my own house. Perhaps we all should've entered established orders from the beginning. Yet, I don't rue it. We did good things and, I think, served God."

"Doubtless. But couldn't you have stayed at your manor? Even if it weren't an abbey?"

"I couldn't have managed alone; I would've had to hire servants and farmhands. It seemed better to move on."

"Thus you did." Harry marveled at the proficiency with which she had handled her affairs. "And now I've tracked you here."

Sinking to the ground, he kicked off his boots. Why rush? Even if they traveled together briefly, their path would inevitably lead to a parting. Better to drink in each moment, while he could. "You act like a boy to guard yourself and your treasure?"

"Yea." She, too, settled on the grass, popping a couple of berries into her mouth.

The juice turned her lips a deep red, making them even more tempting to kiss. He beat down the urge.

"If I made my way as a woman, I couldn't travel safely alone," she explained. "Nevertheless, I look much as I did at our abbey. We women cut our hair short, complementing the men's tonsure. My tunics are the same, too. But as a boy I pull on leggings instead of a skirt. Also, I take occasional shots with my bow, to look like an archer and warn off any who may think me an easy mark."

Harry helped himself to berries. "What do you do at night? Inns?"

"I try to avoid inns, uncertain ones anyway. I look for an abbey guesthouse, or a church or hamlet where the women might take me in. I don't always appear as a boy. I put on one of my skirts—I carry a couple with me—and cover my head. If asked, I just tell the truth: that I'm from a nunnery, newly disbanded." She glanced at her bow. "Should anyone ask about this, I say it belonged to my late husband and I value it. Which is true. Usually folk accept me. Many walk the roads these days. There's scarce a family or parish or estate that hasn't known deaths from plague or war against the Scots or French, and fiefs have escheated, pastures been abandoned, owners called to take over larger holdings elsewhere."

"Aye." He had seen it: His mother, dying unexpectedly, leaving properties scattered hither and yon; his stepmother, Maude, bequeathing him many of her lands and her DeLucy crest, quartered alongside the Percy lion on his coat-of-arms; men under his command, from foot soldiers to lords, over whose biers he had prayed and whose mothers, sisters, wives and children he had comforted and sometimes still supported; the craftsmen and artisans he'd helped place elsewhere as opportunity arose. Aye, the North had witnessed much. A young woman with boyish hair and a past as an ad hoc nun wasn't all that unexpected.

Ciarry's voice broke through. "...Thus, looking like a lad served me well—until now! But I'd never crossed paths with the laudable Hotspur before."

"And he's the poorer for that. And it has naught to do with your money!"

Reddening again, she looked away.

Seemingly oblivious, he wriggled stockinged toes. "We'd best be away, if you intend to travel farther afore evening."

"Yea." In truth, she didn't care whether she traveled farther or not; she was content just to be with him. Nonetheless, she scrambled up, while he slipped his feet back into boots. She extended a slim hand, to pull him up, too. He took it, and as they touched, he felt her nerves race—and he didn't want to let go, wanted to draw her into his arms. But he released his hold.

She turned. "My blackberries. I don't want to leave them." No bucket available, she dumped them into her hood, where they nestled in the thick, dark cloth.

They set off at an amiable pace, horses trailing behind. Before long, she found need to reach behind her head, to sample berries. He too, snatched a few. Again, he wanted to slip his arm around her, or brush the copper-bright strands from her brow. Instead, he began whistling a Celtic air, learned in Eaglesham. Somewhere, a magpie answered, softly, then exuberantly, picking up his notes and carrying them off, one by one, to serenade the breeze.

———

They traveled in companionable ease, sometimes in silence, more often talking easily. As they walked, he pointed out sites of interest—ancient standing stones, a Roman road, a cross from St. Cuthbert's days, a barn where he'd captured Scots raiders after a wild chase. That prompted her to ask about his exploits; so he led her on a tour of his career, from Northumberland to Aquitaine to Cyprus, back again to the Borders, and on to Cheshire and Wales, over more than two decades. Later he found himself talking about his empty marriage, acknowledging his relief that the pretence was over, telling her that Elizabeth dwelt in London with a courtier, in a blissful relationship that was wedlock in everything but name.

"Then she's truly blessed by heaven to know love like that." Ciarry's voice choked, her face wan.

Wanting to comfort her, he feared an inappropriate move or comment. Instead he reached to the verge, plucking a half-dozen yarrow blooms. One by one, he tossed them onto her head. The first few fluttered to the ground as she walked along. But he persisted until she laughed and stopped.

"What're these?"

He glanced skyward. "Doubtless blessings from heaven..."

Smiling softly, she collected them, tucking them onto her belt.

They continued down the road.

―――

"Where did you wish to stay the night? Shall I seek shelter for you at a farmstead?" Harry pointed. "There're a couple beyond that ridge. I could return for you in the morn. Or would you prefer to bide with me, though I can offer naught but an open sky and blankets for cover?" He glanced overhead. "Should be clear enough. And you needn't worry. I have more than one blanket. I'll not bother you. I swore to protect you, after all."

"Even," he admonished himself, "if that means protecting her from me." Whether she wanted to be protected was another matter, of course, if one he dare not consider yet.

"I'll stay with you, Harry. I've had enough of mummery, switching from lad-to-lass every evening. "And, mostly," she went on silently, "I couldn't leave you, even if only till morning."

He smiled. "Then we'd best make camp."

A few minutes later, he led her down the faintest of trails, through a copse into a lea sweet with grass. "Wait here. I want to make sure there's fresh water."

He was soon back. "A sweet, bubbling stream. The Lord's served us well."

"The Lord and your instincts."

He shrugged, undoing Brutus' packsaddle. "A necessity, when you're a wandering soldier. As to another necessity: supper. I'd best ride on a bit. There's an alewife at one of those houses I mentioned. Along with her beer, she puts up fine cheese and smoked ham. I should be able to buy some. Otherwise, I'll have to borrow your bow and go hunting. Or we'll have to empty my saddlebags and eat oats. But those're better in the morning."

He released Brutus into the field. "Will you be all right, alone?" Already, he seemed to have forgotten she had traveled solo for days. "Keep your bow close, and don't be afraid to use it. Who knows who might be abroad."

Ciarry seated herself on a stump. "Then let's hope no brother of yours shows up. One Lord Percy a day is plenty." She vaguely recalled tales of a sibling, Rafe, nearly as skilled a warrior as Harry.

His face clouded. "I have no more brothers. Three, I had, all younger, all gone, years afore their time: Tom, dead of fever, campaigning with John of Gaunt in Spain, these thirteen summers past. Rafe, killed at Nicopolis—perhaps in battle, perhaps afterward, I never knew. He once survived terrible wounds, fighting under me at Otterburn, only to die in the Balkans."

Ciarry shuddered. She knew of the Nicopolis campaign, one more crusade in centuries of conflict between Byzantium and its allies and often fanatically religious invaders. Many of the best knights of England, France, Hungary and elsewhere in Europe had fought at Nicopolis, where they killed nearly thirty enemy for each knight who fell, until, overwhelmed, the remaining knights surrendered. In the aftermath, the conquerors had marched the prisoners out, unarmed and nude, and slain nearly all, heedless of chivalry, morality, or even the bounty of ransoms. A few survivors had eventually limped home with the news.

"I'm sorry."

"Aye..." Bittersweet gentleness filled his eyes. "...Then there was my youngest brother, Alain, dead as a child. I scarcely had time to be brother to him, or to my little sister, Margot, also gone so soon."

Voice fading, he mounted Redesraven. "I'll be back anon."

Knees drawn to chin, hands on her legs, feeling both stricken and inexplicably happy, she heard his hoofbeats diminish. "What an extraordinary man ... what thralldom he holds me in."

She wanted to stand before him, naked—intellectually, emotionally, spiritually, and, yea, physically, too—saying only "I am yours, Harry, in all things, in all ways, for all time. Make of me what you would..." An outlandish notion! Yet her feelings far exceeded any she'd ever had for a man, or even God. If she felt such overwhelming yearning or love for someone, shouldn't it be for God? Especially God. But while her bond with the Almighty had always been close, what she experienced now differed.

Seeking wisdom, she prayed. No lightning bolts of insight followed, but a pervasive sense of well-being comforted her, telling her that whatever she felt for Harry came with God's approval; that He, above all, understood; that perhaps He had brought them together.

She rose. "I'd best do something useful, see to a hearth."

Discovering a small depression in the field, she ringed it with stones, then scavenged for wood.

"Good, Lass!" He arrived as she laid the last log on her pile, his face lighting up as he dismounted. Items emerged from his saddlebags. "Gammon, cider; cheese and bread. But let me tend to my horses, ere we dine."

"Of course." She headed for the stream and washed her face and hands, letting her wrists linger in the coolness, as if to chill her racing pulse. Slowly, she made her way back; already the campsite seemed as much a home as any she had known. Spreading the provisions on a scarf, she watched as he groomed Redesraven, talking to the horse softly. Then he retrieved Brutus and repeated the procedure. Finally, he led them to the creek, before turning them loose to graze through the night.

A set of flints kindled a fire. Cutting the meat, cheese and bread, he handed her the first portions. The cider he split between two metal cups, the kind soldiers hung from belts and used for dipping from wells.

"A toast to you, for sharing my road."

She tipped her cup against his. "And you, for safeguarding mine."

They drank happily.

Twilight deepened as they ate and the fire ascended, stealing the shadows from the gloom. A moth fluttered and an owl hooted in the trees. Stars sparkled to life, one by one, until the whole wide sky seemed naught but darkness and diamonds.

Never had Ciarry felt so at peace: with herself, with another, with Providence, with the firmament itself.

Harry saw the warmth of the blaze, mirrored in her hair; the slender outline of her body; the lights that rose in her dark eyes whenever his smile touched her face. For long moments, he feared to speak, half expecting his voice to trip itself in the old stutter, afraid he might destroy this enchantment before he had a chance to truly comprehend it. Slowly, he began. "Tell me of this Fitzwyatt you were wed to, Ciarry. He seems rather a lout."

"He was, in many ways. But to tell you that, I must tell you how I came to be his wife. My father, Fergus, was of Scottish and Norman heritage—some ancestor arrived with the Conqueror. Father was a castellan for one or another of the Douglases. He was a knight but unlanded, youngest son to the Corbetts, or DeCorbetts, as his line called themselves."

Harry nodded. "Originally of Teviotdale. I've periodically run across them—literally, probably."

"No doubt," she remarked dryly. "My father got an Irish serving girl with child. He apparently had many such dalliances, with more than one woman, though I never heard of sisters and brothers." She shrugged. "But how would I know, or how would he necessarily know? However 'twas, I was born in Douglasdale. My father did acknowledge me but sent me at an early age to a convent near Coventry. His cousin was sub-prioress there."

"Still, he named you, right?"

"No, my mother did, for the county in Eire whence her folk came, Ciarrai, and for the saint on whose day she bore me—or one of them, since there are two, both abbots. I never knew on which Ciaran's feast, or in exactly which year, I was born."

Harry smiled. "Your name fits. You were an abbess. And both Ciarans loved the land and animals, or so the legends say. You do, too, I think. I heard the way you talked of your farm. And my saddlehorse wanted to slobber all over you."

She laughed. "I do like the beasts. But I'm hardly a saint."

"An angel then. And now I know why, despite birth and blood, you sound neither like a Scot nor an Irishwoman."

"I suppose. Anyhow, I thought to join the convent myself, though some of the nuns said I had an uncommonly independent streak. If so, 'twas their doing—teaching me to use my mind, telling me all are equal in the sight of God, running their estates as well as any lord."

Harry laughed. "E'en so."

"I learned to read and write, English and Latin, and do arithmetic," she added. "I helped the cellaress with ledgers. Also, I served in the library and scriptorium. That—copying books and reading them as I copied—was best of all."

Her voice warmed at the memory, and he realized that in those moments, at least, she must have known happiness.

"But when I was about sixteen, ready to become a postulant, my cousin and father decided to marry me off. My father's rank and my education had given me, or them, more clout in the marriage mart. I had no say. So I was packed off to marry Walter Fitzwyatt, a distant kinsman, from the other side of my cousin's family. He was considered a good catch."

"How so?"

"He was a landed knight, with a small castle in Lancashire, a fief of John of Gaunt. But from his mother he also had a manor in his own name, the one I eventually acquired. I lived as his wife for ten years. It seemed like a hundred."

"I suppose it was one of those matches that pair maids with men hoary enough to be their sires or grandsires."

"No. Had he lived, he'd be about your age, I reckon. He dissipated himself young, though, with drink, gambling, wenching. I think he bedded every woman in his household, including me, of course, and many outside his walls."

Harry winced.

"In the end, he pulled his dagger on his gambling companions once too often. And he wasn't nearly as good with a knife as you. One of them got the better of him, when all were in their cups. They carried him home wounded. For days, I nursed him. Still, he died. And it sounds disloyal, but afterward I was glad of it."

She took a sip of cider. "Most of the rest you know."

He regarded her in silence, while her blood churned erratically, burning her cheeks, as she chided herself silently: "Now I've said too much. He'll think me cold, self-serving."

Yet it wasn't criticism that filled his thoughts, but a debate over whether to take her in his arms and tell her that he understood. Such a move hardly seemed appropriate, though, given her marriage to a man who had taken gross advantage of her, and others. So again he forbore.

"No one would blame you for being relieved, Ciarry.' Tis too bad this Walter couldn't rid the world of a troublemaker faster by dying sooner. If I'd ever come across him, there's a good chance he would have!"

He softened again. "No bairns, Lass?"

She shook her head. "Thrice, I conceived. I lost each babe, afore its quickening. Walter began to ignore me, months on end, as if tired of me. And I was more than tired of him. It wasn't all a loss, I suppose," she sighed. "It led to our abbey. Also, I ran Fitzwyatt's household, honing my knowledge of accounts and writing. In time, that helped our abbey and may serve me again someday.

"Besides," she recalled, "while with Fitzwyatt I took up archery. Afore I grew too old for such pastimes to be seemly, I practiced with the boys of the castle. That's also where I learned to walk so fast. In the few hours I could spare from chatelaine's duties, I'd wander the hills, by myself. And I rode like a man, not with a sidesaddle. That was wonderful. I had a fine palfrey, for a while." Her voice softened with regret. "Unbeknownst to me, Walter sold it one day to meet a gambling debt."

Harry's anger flared.

"Take no heed of it, Harry. He paid his price in the end."

"Aye, I suppose. And if you'd married a good man, you'd not be here and I'd have to keep my camp to myself." He brightened. "That again would be my loss."

Lowering her head, she hoped the flickering firelight hid her emotions. "I'd best turn in. It's been an unusual day."

"Aye." He rummaged in his gear, producing a sheepskin rug, a towel, and a thick wool blanket. Carrying them just beyond the hearth, he spread the sheepskin on the ground and the blanket over it. "For you," he said, rolling the towel into a pillow. "I'll put mine on the other side."

"Thank you." She eased onto the blanket, suddenly aware how tired she was.

"Here." Dropping her pack at her feet, he disappeared. "Good night."

She stripped and pulled on her woolen nightgown, glancing apprehensively over her shoulder. But he couldn't be seen, nor could anyone else. Wrapping the blanket around her, she wondered what he was going to use for bedding; after all, she had his rug and probably the best blanket.

After a minute or two, she peeked out and saw him arrange his oilskin on the ground, Redesraven's saddle blanket as a mattress, and another horse blanket on top.

She wormed under the covers so she couldn't see him, couldn't keep herself awake watching him. At first it did little good; thoughts of him intruded, anyway. Finally, exhaustion conquered excitement and she fell into slumber, uninterrupted even when she turned over, slipping her face from the covers, toward the unseen stars.

'Twas he who remained awake, feeding the fire, aware that he was entering *terra incognita* but had never felt more certain, nor more exultant. After a while, he strolled to the stream, watching moonlight trip silver-gold over the water, listening to a nightjar's plaintive call, closing his eyes as the breeze tickled his cheek and he pretended it was her fingertips.

"Why this lass, and why now?"

Was it merely that he was alone? Unlikely; he'd always been alone. Things were no different now. Besides, he rarely felt lonely.

A recollection stirred, something Kynge had said, something about monks. Aye, that was it: That he lived a life as ascetic as that of any anchorite, a hermit who dwelled behind a church in a hut, part of the community but separate from it. Well, perhaps he did live like that, albeit a peripatetic anchorite.

And Ian's other comment? That he needed a woman.

He smiled. In reminding Ian of his betrothal pledge—however imposed on a small boy—he hadn't mentioned the other vows he'd made: On joining the Order of the Garter as an adult; earlier, in his initial dubbing as a knight; and as a layman-monk with the Praemonstratensians at Alnwick Abbey. His Praemonstratensian vows, formally made at age twenty-three and renewed every five years, bound him to something less than the monastic confinement and obligations of priest or brother but something real nonetheless. And in both monastic and chivalric vows he had promised to uphold virtues like chastity. To be sure, that didn't mean lifelong virginity or endless celibacy. But it did mean no promiscuity, no sexual coupling in mere lust or infatuation, no intercourse not grounded in genuine love.

And love had been the one prize he'd never won. A knight was supposed to be ardently and gallantly in love, even (given the realities of a jaded age) with someone other than the wife acquired in childhood. Nor was a physical bond with the beloved forbidden, if the love was authentic and selfless and uplifting.

Love perfected and inspired a knight, helped him find himself and all that was worthy and ennobling, helped him find God. It wasn't that a man was a failure, lacking it, only that love added the extra dimension. All this was what Ian had meant, in suggesting Harry needed someone, someone linked to him in mind and heart and spirit, in true love.

And he'd tossed it off, doubting he'd ever know what true love was.

"Why this lass, and why now?" he asked again of God, fate and himself. "She has none of the attributes most men fancy. Hell, she's got about as much shape as a scrawny sapling. Though she is pretty, in a different way. She's not like some women otherwise, either. It doesn't matter one whit whether I'm a man of supposed money and standing or some itinerant horseman. Oh, she knew Hotspur all right, but because of my reputation for deeds and honor. And she's too intelligent to be subservient to some man, high lord or not. She's got her own ideas and spirit—probably too much for her own good, or that of any man fortunate (or unfortunate!) enough to be besotted by her. She's self-reliant and damned proud of it."

A broad grin crossed his face. "Admit it, Harry. She's just like you. Only better, purer, nobler."

The champion had finally met his match.

He wanted to laugh with her, to console her when sorrow stole into those expressive eyes; spend hours talking to her, testing his wit against hers and basking in her wisdom—and taking pride in it, too. He wanted years in her company, walking the valleys, riding the hills. "I'll have to find her a man's saddle. She'll never be content riding sidesaddle. Nor I content unless I can go cantering across the moors with her."

He wanted to look at her in evenings over the fire, or linger with her over supper, while wind buffeted the baileys, and snow piled in little drifts along the parapets, and the barn cats burrowed into the hay, curling their tails around themselves in snug satisfaction. He wanted to kiss her and feel her delicate body warm and willing in his embrace, to lie naked with her on featherbeds and hear the rain splattering the eaves, or the trill of the lark in the wood.

Above all, he wanted to be with her.

Returning to camp, he almost skipped. "A mere slip of a lass has vanquished me, taken my heart hostage, held it for ransom. Yet never has a knight been happier in defeat—or more willing to go on losing!"

Chapter XVIII
September 1400 - Northumberland

After belated sleep, Harry awoke brimming with even more high spirits than usual. Grabbing razor and brown soap, he headed for the brook, doffed his clothes, and plunged in, swimming to warm up before scrubbing and finishing with a shave.

Hair glistening, second-best towel on his shoulder, he retraced his steps—only to turn aside in amusement as Ciarry roused herself, disheveled by sleep. Pack in hand, she stumbled past him, in her nightgown and some consternation, bound for the water.

She returned refreshed and dressed again as a boy. But why not, he thought. 'Twas certainly easier to walk in leggings than a long skirt.

"Breakfast, in finest Borders style." He stirred a pot of porridge. "Like the Scots, we Northumbrians cherish oats and carry them in our saddlebags, for man and beast alike."

He had also boiled water for a morning infusion, a concoction to which Kynge had introduced him years earlier. "My chaplain swears by it: herbs, berries, stuff from the East–God knows-what."

"'Tis wonderful." Ciarry tasted it, then eagerly drank more before turning to her porridge. "The oats, too."

Soon they set off again.

She wasn't sure where they were bound. It didn't matter; she only wanted to be with him. "Tell me more of France," she suggested. "I heard of your exploits at Brest. They say the Duke of Brittany, France's ally, had long besieged it but you miraculously broke through."

"'Twas naught."
"Truly?"
"Naught."

Slowly, questioning eroded his reluctance, and she mentally pieced the story together, like a chronicler:

The Bretons had ringed Brest with siege towers, trying to beat it into submission. But they hadn't counted on Sir Harry. Deputized by the Privy Council to save the town, an English prize, he led a fleet of ships across the Channel. Off the coast, he ordered his boats to steal toward the harbor at midnight, directing all aboard to maintain strict silence. Nor would he allow candles on the decks, but from the high ropes and masts, he hung scores of lanterns. Watching from halfway up the rigging of his flagship, he waited until they neared. Then, he had the sailors light all the lanterns simultaneously.

Startled guards at the Breton siege towers and tents looked on, wonder becoming fear. On the water was nothing but darkness—except for pinwheels of fire, dancing above the waves, drawing closer, burning like devil eyes, phantasmagoria from hell. Then English ships took shape. Small boats filled with fighting men pulled off, rowing toward shore, the foremost containing a tall knight in gleaming armour with the lion rampant and cadency bar of the heir to Northumberland.

Landing on the beaches, Harry and his men overran the Breton camp and began toppling the wooden siege towers—sawing underpinnings of some, as desperate Bretons threw themselves off the storeys and staircases above, falling to their deaths or surrendering, bruised and crippled. Two more towers the English set afire; still others they captured in hand-to-hand fighting. Taking heart, the men from Brest descended from the walls and joined in. Pinched between the English and townsmen, the Bretons yielded.

Harry maneuvered through the confusion and smoke, accepted the Breton captain's sword, and commanded that all but one remaining siege tower be torched. Finally, he stood alone before Brest's gates and knocked on the massive door. As townspeople crowded the parapets above, it swung open. After a few steps inside, he fell to his knees. Reversing his grip on his sword, he raised it high, its hilt and bar shining like a cross beneath the night sky. There, he called out his thanks to God.

For three days, the town that had faced possible starvation wined and dined its rescuers since, along with soldiers, his ships had carried stores to replenish granaries and cupboards. He strengthened the remaining siege tower, adding wheels so it could be hauled around like a moving peel tower to confront other would-be invaders.

But none appeared. Brest's nightmare had ended.

And the audacious Sir Harry, her Harry—if she dared think of him that way—had done it.

"No wonder they cooked for you so willingly."

"Aye. The countryside was marvelous, too. 'Tis hardly surprising English kings have turned lechers o'er France. Though I guess Aquitaine and our other holdings are rightfully ours."

Ciarry sighed. "I should like to go there someday."

He almost said, "I'll take you." It was on the tip of his tongue, the kind of thing a man says to a woman he loves and hopes to make part of his life. He couldn't say it, though, couldn't make idle promises. "Yet how easy 'twould be to go on walking with Ciarry, forget duty and sail with her, sell my skills as a free-lance, live out the rest of my life with her," he mused. "But it never could be..." Even so, how grand to have found someone who caused him to spin such dreams.

She caught his enigmatic smile. "What are you thinking?"

"That we've walked enough for a morn."

In another quarter mile, he led her to a thicket that yielded to large, wide trees whose canopy covered a floor of grass dappled with warmth. Sunlight fingered wildflowers amidst the green and spattered a creek beyond with gold.

"Oh, Harry! I've never seen any place lovelier."

"Aye. In the spring, too, 'tis beautiful, covered with bluebells. It's as the Gospel says, 'not even Solomon in his grandeur was robed like one of these.' And there are thousands of them. There's a spot on the other side of the water where we can build a fire tonight," he added. "We might as well stay here. I must leave this afternoon and probably won't be back until evening."

They continued to the stream, or burn, as he called it, a bubbling froth. But it wasn't deep, so he pulled off boots and stockings and rolled his leggings to his knees. A hand on each halter, he led his horses across.

"Can you make it?" He called from the opposite bank. "Or should I come and ferry you over?"

Ciarry's desire to let him carry her warred with her sense of independence—and the latter won. Barefoot, she started across. The water felt cold but good, and she paused, stirring pebbles on the bottom with her toes.

"Now we'll have the cleanest feet for miles around," he quipped as she waded ashore.

They shared the remaining bread and cheese and lingered briefly before he again climbed into the saddle. "One of my lieutenants, Thomas Knayton, is posted nearby. I arranged, afore I met you, to confer with him this afternoon." He crossed the stream again. "Bide safely. I'll bring supper."

She watched him disappear. "Now, time for a proper bath."

Clutching towel and toiletries, she wandered downstream. A distant gleam beckoned, enticing her toward a large, placid pool, dammed off from the stream by rocks. It lay in bright sunlight, wisps of steam rising from the surface. A hand test revealed unexpected heat. Uncertain, she surveyed the woods.

But she was alone. Only birdsong and fluttering leaves broke the silence. Disrobing, she piled her clothes on a boulder and grabbed her soap. Softer and creamier than what Harry used, it was a luxury from a fair, a treat for herself after the sale of her property.

After a few steps into the pool, she felt a current coursing from underground. A rare thermal spring! Delighted, Ciarry immersed. First she washed her hair, sudsed herself, and rinsed. Then she relaxed, half underwater, eyes closed, letting heat seep into muscles, soothing, lulling her, until she felt one with the forest.

Twaccck! Crack!

Branches snapped. Brush crunched.

Her heart pounded. Fighting to stay calm, she considered options: Run ashore, dress, and hope to evade whatever was out there? Hurry ashore but leave her clothes, concealing herself in the woods? Stay as she was? Or hold her breath—in all senses—and hide underwater? Yea. Gulping air, she dove.

Only when her lungs burned did she surface, gasping.

"There you are!" Harry hailed her from the bank.

"You!" She retreated into deeper water, only her head visible. "I thought you'd left."

He laughed. "I had. But on my way to the road, I found the prettiest flowers. So I thought you should have some to compensate for being deprived of my company all afternoon." From the empty cider jug, a profusion tumbled: red poppy and yellow saxifrage, lavender-blue vetch and purple heather, white campion and pink thyme. He smiled boyishly. "Sorry, Lass. I shouldn't have frightened you."

"I thought you were a bear or wolf."

"Perhaps I am. But since you raise the point: You take great risk, bathing alone. I'd better stand guard."

"Well then..." She tried to maintain dignity. "I was enjoying myself. I think I'll resume." Shutting her eyes, she blocked him out, hoping to symbolically dismiss him as well.

A couple of minutes later, she looked up. "How long were you here before I knew?"

"Not long. And when you heard me 'twas because I let you hear me."

She blanched, diving again. When she came up, he was still there.

"Are you really here to protect me? Or just waiting till I come out so you can see me naked and laugh yourself silly?"

He reddened. "I ... I think... that ... that I'd better just rest here till you're finished." Leaning against the boulder, he stretched his legs out. But he was too restless for a nap, and, anyway, he didn't need one. "This has gone on long enough," he thought. "I want her to be sure. And I think she feels the same. But she seems hesitant yet—a timid little tadpole. Maybe if I join her in a swim, she won't feel odd about being naked with me, whatever we end up doing or not."

Rising, he began divesting himself of garments.

Ciarry watched as his body emerged—lean, fit and strong, perfectly proportioned from long legs to firmly muscled chest, powerful arms and commanding height. Soon he was down to his under-linens, scant V-shaped briefs tied at his waist. Suddenly ashamed of ogling, Ciarry dropped her gaze.

"It looks so inviting I decided to join you." He shouted to her averted head. "May I?"

"Could I stop you?" She didn't look up, aware that if he came close her restraint would dissolve. Mostly 'twas gone already.

Splashing heralded his entrance into the pool.

She paddled deeper.

But for a few minutes, he ignored her and swam underwater, abruptly surfacing to flip onto his back, spouting water from his mouth like a fountain, cavorting like an otter.

She paid no heed. But when the sounds of his antics stopped, she worried he'd gone under. A moment later, he shot from the depths and then approached her with smooth, swift strokes. He paused waist-deep, only a few feet away.

"Ciarry."

Extending a wet hand, he placed it on her shoulder.

Soft, unhurried, his touch melted her willpower. He slipped back into the water to be more at her height, and she reached out, hands on his broad shoulders. His body tensed beneath her fingertips and he gripped her upper arms. Shyly, they smiled at one another, pulled closer.

Sounds from the brush flung them apart.

Racing to the bank, Harry grabbed his belt and pulled his sword.

"Get down," he yelled back at Ciarry. "Underwater."

She complied.

Naked, sword in hand, he faced off toward the intruder.

"Halloo-oo-o! Sir Harry Percy? Harry—that you?"

It was Knayton.

"'Aye, Tom. Here, at the burn."

Knayton pushed past a tree, stopped, burst into laughter. "Well, you've greeted me on many an occasion and in many a circumstance. But never like this! I see you've found my favorite bathing hole."

Sheathing his sword, Harry dried himself with Ciarry's towel. "'Tis good to see you, Tom, I *think*!" He tossed the towel toward Ciarry in the pool.

Head low, she grabbed it and tried to tie it on underwater.

Belatedly, Knayton noticed her. And it was his turn to blush. "I seem ... to ... er... have interrupted something. I'd best be going."

Harry draped his arm across Knayton's back. "Good idea. But only as far as my camp. You must've passed it. Fetch a clean towel from my saddlebags. I'll explain later." He pulled Knayton close. "I'd introduce you to the lady now—and mind you, she *is* a lady—but she'd probably kill us both."

Knayton hurried off. Dressing, Harry turned toward Ciarry. Huddled at the dam, cheeks aflame, she said nothing.

"She's totally humiliated," he thought. "What an obnoxious ass I've been. Why couldn't I have left her alone, made sure she was all right, watched over her from afar—or found Knayton afore he found us?"

Hindsight was futile.

Ciarry likewise chided herself. She'd been flaunting her independence, carrying it to ridiculous lengths, compelling him to find her, leading to embarrassment for them both. She wondered if he'd ever understand or let her make amends.

He attempted a smile. "Oh Lass, I'm sorry. I've been a barbarian. Can you ever forgive me?"

"Only if you forgive me." She edged closer to the bank. "If you've been a barbarian, then I've been an idiot, causing you trouble."

He laughed. "If you're going to beg pardon every time you get into mischief, then I'd best give you absolution now for the rest of your life!"

She smiled, and their eyes locked once more.

Knayton reappeared, bringing not only a towel but a blanket. Harry laid them on the bank and encouraged Knayton to vanish again. As his friend slipped away, Harry addressed Ciarry.

"You can come out. You could stay, but you'd still be at risk. And I hesitate to go off while you're alone."

"I know. I'll come out."

He faced the trees.

She scrambled from the pool, toweled dry, and dressed.

"I'm ready." Picking up the jug of wildflowers, she selected a sprig and handed it to him. "For the best guardian angel I could want."

He kissed the dainty petals and slipped it inside his shirt, close to his heart. Then he threw blanket and towels over his shoulder, leading the way back to camp.

Later, riding alongside Knayton, he began explaining.

But Knayton intervened with a knowing grin and hand on his arm. "You need tell me naught, Harry. It's written all over you. Mere mention of the lass makes you look like a lovesick bard. Long overdue, I say. May you ever be happy together. Now, if you can tear yourself from thoughts of her, let me tell you what's been happening here in your absence."

―――

Ciarry determined to do something useful lest she fall into more misadventures. Besides, the activity would keep her from remembering those idyllic moments in the pool.

Chores first, she decided, proceeding to the stream to scrub her dirty clothing. Back at camp, she debated. By now, he had laundry, too, stuffed in an old grain sack. Do that also? Or would it be too intimate a gesture? No, 'twould be a kindness from one traveler to another.

So she lugged his bag to the water and washed each item in turn. Afterward, she hung up everything—most of his garments on one tree, hers on another, stockings sharing a low branch, towels waving from a limb between.

That much accomplished, she set up a fire-ring and gathered wood and chunks of peat long abandoned in a field. Finished by mid-afternoon, she realized she anxiously awaited his return.

His love and desire matched hers, she was sure. But whether they'd stop muddling and admit it was another matter. In any case, this magic journey couldn't continue indefinitely. "At best I have another day or two of his company; then he'll be gone, back into the mists of his beloved mountains, back to his duties, armies, and danger. Like as not, I'll never see him again. And, despite all he says, it is I who shall be the poorer. Nor do I even have anything to give him, to wish him Godspeed."

All she had was money, which he would refuse and consider an insult anyway, and her books. But he would never accept those, either. "Nothing else do I have, except–"

Unbuckling her pack, she collected her Psalter and tools: Wooden board; piece of parchment; quill pen, and stoppered phials of ink. She opened the Psalter to its inside cover where, in a small, precise hand, she once had inscribed the injunction from Ecclesiastes. Carefully, she began copying it onto the parchment. When finished, she opened her other phials and added a border: green ivy; red, blue, and yellow flowers; tiny bees and ladybugs. Next, she tucked stems and serrated leaves into each corner and blended red and blue ink into purple for Scottish thistles. As she set the sheet out to dry, she read it through:

> *To everything there is a season, and*
> *a time for everything under heaven:*
> *A time to be born, a time to die.*
> *A time for killing, a time for healing,*
> *A time for tears, a time for laughter.*
> *A time for searching...*
> *A time for losing, a time for keeping,*
> *A time for silence, a time for*
> *speaking.*
> *A time for war, a time for peace.*
> *A time for love...*

"From this day forward, for him let it be a time of peace–peace for his soul even amidst war," she prayed. "More than that, I dare not ask."

Another delve into her pack produced Piers Plowman, a lengthy poem she'd never read in its entirety, and she curled up on the blanket. After a couple of hours, she rose to store the now-dried parchment. It would be her surprise for him whenever they parted.

He cantered into view a few minutes later, laughing when he saw the laundry. "I'm grateful. And while you've seen to that, I've brought dinner." Dismounting, he displayed it: Two fat trout from the pond at Knayton's garrison, more bread and cheese, a basket of late peaches, and wine.

"Tom says he's become an ale-man," Harry informed her with a grin, "and that otherwise, he never would've bestowed Bordeaux on me." Actually, as he knew, Knayton was as fond of wine as ever, but had insisted that Harry raid the cellar, the better to celebrate newfound love.

Again, Harry cared for the horses before tending to the fire. Once the blaze had diminished, he finished cleaning the fish, cut a couple of green sticks, arranged them over stones, and set the trout to grilling, while she laid out the rest of the meal.

As darkness fell with restful reticence on a waiting earth, they ate. Harry picked up a wine bottle, removed the wax cover and plug with his knife, and poured equal portions. "I toast you: For not booting me from your life this afternoon." He lifted his cup. "You'll have an even harder time sending me off now."

Ciarry laughed lightly. "Sooner or later, the Scots will probably do that. Or you'll go sallying forth to Lord-knows-where. Then the next thing I'll hear is you've won another astounding victory."

"Let's pray I win." His grin faded. "Truth is, I can be summoned at any time. I've fought many a battle, more than enough for any man. Doubtless, though, much as I wish otherwise, I'll have to draw my sword again. And probably again and again after that." He shrugged. "But I'm a soldier, bound to England above all else."

She knew he was warning her: That his life involved war and might end in it; that even if he loved her, duty would always come first, taking him away for months and perhaps forever; that she had a rival, England itself, but that it was the only rival she'd ever have and one she'd best accept now because she could never supplant it.

Yet, without that devotion to the nation, he would not be the man he was, not the man she already loved.

"You'd be lost if you weren't in the saddle, roaming the land, leading your men, fighting with every ounce of strength for all you hold dear. England abounds with tales of how, time and again, when everyone else slumbered, you remained and stood vigilant." She smiled. "Henry Knighton even put that in his chronicle. Others say the same."

"In truth?"

"Aye!" She unconsciously mimicked his speech. "'Tis not just your vigilance or prowess that they mark, either."

"No?"

"No. 'Tis your sense of justice, too. Do you think no one knew what happened last summer at Chester with those mobs or earlier this year with those men suspected of high treason? Nor are those the only examples."

"My uncle must've have been bragging about me again!"

He was joking, but she continued, utterly serious:

"You were born to ride and rule, Harry, not as a king but as something even more important—a good knight, a good commander, a good governor, for 'tis on them that rule really devolves. Kings only think they have charge."

"Perhaps..."

"'Tis true. You'll ever be charging forth, courage and integrity at the fore. That's how you earned your nickname years ago; doubtless, that's how you'll be till you die. You couldn't do otherwise. Nor would I ever want you to. And..."

Embarrassed, she abruptly stopped.

"Alas, you know me too well!"

Tears stinging, she stared at the fire. If it had been difficult to rein in her emotions before, it was nigh unto impossible now. "Must be obvious that I'm falling in love with him—no, that I've already fallen in love," she admitted silently. "Anymore, I've no idea of where to turn, or where to go, for the only one I can see is Harry, the only one I want to turn to is he. And only God can extricate me now."

Equally silent, he got to his feet, simultaneously enraptured and ensnared, like a captured animal—the bold Percy lion, caged. Walking a dozen paces beyond the fire, he sought wisdom in the skies from the Big Dipper and North Star. They watched over his North and perhaps had guided him to her. For long moments, he drank in the night air, feeling the promise of all that lay ahead, the glow of the flames behind him and the radiance of her presence.

When he returned, he came up behind her, resting his hands on her shoulders, saying nothing.

Instinctively, she stiffened, her heart catching in her throat, her slenderness trembling beneath his touch. Reaching back, she closed her hands over his, and he kissed the top of her head.

"Ciarry…"

He pulled her up to face him, the hands that had wielded sword and knife in battle infinitely gentle now. Looking down with eyes more intense than all the stars combined, he wrapped her in a fierce embrace. "Please, Lass, let me just hold you awhile. You don't know how I've yearned to take you in my arms but been so afraid that I might wrong you, or hurt you, that you'd think ill of me. Oh Ciarry, I love you, as I've never loved anyone before. Never."

Loosening his grip, he saw the joyful response in her eyes.

Her hands slipped around his neck as if she'd never let go. How wonderful to hold him! How she had wished it, wanted it, all the while been almost scared of it, of what it could do to her. But there was no fear now.

Upraised, her face begged for a kiss.

Softly and quickly, he bestowed one, then another. Her eyes closed, and this time, he kissed her with all the vigor and insistence building inside him for two days.

Breaking away, they smiled at each other almost shyly, and then she fell back into his arms.

His tongue tasted her lips and penetrated deeper.

Clumsily, she tried to respond.

But he was rather more experienced at this than she, even if his experiences lay years behind him.

Leaning down, he rested his face on her shoulder, closing his eyes, lost in an ecstasy he had never thought to find. "I love you, Lass, love you so very much, and I'm not sure what I'll ever do if I have to leave you."

She retreated a few inches, taking his hands in hers, her eyes meeting his. "You'll stand tall and go through the world strong, Harry Percy, as you always do, but even more so—because now my love goes with you, always." Her head rested against his chest. "And I do love you, Harry! And I shall forever love you, no matter how much time or distance comes between us, no matter how far off you must go, or however long I must wait. I'll love you nigh unto eternity; no, through a hundred eternities."

"I know." Tentatively and then more rapidly, he began running his hands over her body and stroking her hips. Slipping his hands under her tunic and belt, he squeezed the smooth domes of her buttocks and felt the corresponding thrust of her lower body against him.

"Ciarry..." He began another round of kisses, and this time, her tongue was ready for him, pushing hard into his mouth, just as her petite body pressed harder against his. They clung together, his hands tracing lines of happiness across her back. Unbuckling her belt, he eased it from her waist. Slowly, he pushed up her tunic and undershirt beneath. "Oh Lass...." White and firm, her breasts waited, nipples erect.

Lifting her arms, she let him pull the clothing over her head, and he knelt, his face buried in her bosom. Tenderly, he kissed each breast in turn.

"So small and dainty they are. But big enough to satisfy me." He seemed almost amazed at his discovery. "And even before I touched them, they stood at attention, like soldiers being arrayed."

"You command them, My Lord. They were just saluting their captain."

She kissed his forehead as he knelt before her, his hands straying further. Lifting each of her feet in turn, he removed her boots as she leaned against his shoulder. Still kneeling, he unlaced the drawstring that held her leggings snugly around her waist. Eagerly but unhurriedly, he pulled them down and helped her step out of them. Then he untied her underbriefs at each side and eased them from her waist.

Naked, unashamed, she stood before him.

"Oh Lass, you're so lovely, so very lovely." Her pale, slim body caught the fire's glow, counterpart to her fiery hair, which shone like burnished bronze. She was like a wood nymph, a mystic faun, a sprite, standing beneath the stars, all-knowing and innocent at once.

With a shout proclaiming his good fortune, he pulled her back into his arms, his hands caressing her, up and down, up and down, from neck to thighs. They kissed heatedly, and then his hand wandered over her hips and into the little crevice between her legs.

Already, she was moist, throbbing within. As his finger explored, she moaned and rocked back and forth. Falling into his arms for support, she writhed and then shook forcefully, lightning leaping along her every nerve, exploding in her head. When she thought she could neither bear the sweet torment any longer nor allow him to stop, her body heaved in one last rippling wave. Limp, she fell against him.

Delighted, he crowed. Never before had he sent a woman into such a torrent of pleasure. But then, he'd never been in love before.

Recovering, she embraced him, smashing her hips against his, feeling his arousal in every pulsebeat.

With a moan, he forced himself away, toward his baggage. Retrieving the fleece rug, he unrolled it at the edge of the fire and unfolded a blanket atop it. In another moment, he'd yanked off his clothes.

Lifting her, he carried her to the makeshift bed and tenderly laid her down.

She reached out, and with a quick kiss, he fell onto her. Body enveloping hers, he thrust inside her, again and again, then harder still.

Involuntarily, she whimpered, a thin line of blood trickling across her thigh, streaking the hand he rested against her there. Alarmed, he started to withdraw. But her hands on his hips pushed him back in place as she kissed his chin and lips. Closing his eyes, he resumed until his insistent probing found its rhythm. Muscles tightening, he surged into her with one final push, shouting, sweat rolling down his back. Then his whole frame seemed to collapse, and he sighed, covering her face with tiny kisses.

Her arms tightened around him, his head on her breast and her hands stroking his sleek dark hair. Finally, aware he had no chance of renewed vigors, for now, at least, he rolled away. Leaning over, he kissed her once more.

"I love you, Ciarry. I love you!"

"And I you!" She pulled him nearer, wrapping the blanket around them.

"Yesterday," she confessed, "when I first saw you, I knew you were wonderful. Then you threw your sword at my feet, and I was sure you'd see my heart landing at yours. 'Twas I who surrendered afore I even knew it."

He kissed her again.

Dawn found them sleeping peacefully, still wrapped in each other's arms.

Their third day brought cloudless skies, with a stop at a tavern to buy supplies. But with evening came a storm, lashing the oilskin cloaks they hastily pulled from their packs. Sheltering in a barn uphill from a pond, they crawled into the straw to delight in each other anew. Finally, they slept, lulled by the rain on the roof and sweep of boughs outside.

The sun rose warm and strong for their breakfast.

Returning from washing the dishes afterward, Ciarry found Harry shaking out a saddle blanket.

Smiling, he beckoned her. "I've a serious proposition for you."

"What? Another, so soon?" He had just surprised her at the pond, embracing her, threatening to dunk her if she resisted too much, finally planting a kiss atop her head and leaving her in peace.

"Not *that* kind of proposition," he laughed. "Truly, 'tis serious. When we met, you said you planned to find some convent while you considered your future. Now, possibly, your intentions have changed?"

She reddened. "As yet I know not what to do. An alternative might be marriage. But after being with you, I could never do that. I've no kinsman or demesne lord to help broker a match anyway."

"Nor," she thought, "could I ever ask you to be my lord for purposes of arranging one."

"So perhaps a convent is best," she went on aloud, "till I find a position somewhere, as a scribe or teacher or notary. I can read and write Latin as well as English and some French, too." She deliberated. "Also, I know animals, crops and farmstead management. And I can handle accounts, keeping them straight, income accruing and debts promptly paid."

"Then we must put you at the Exchequer," Harry jested. "God knows, those are skills Henry and his clerks seem to lack."

Seated on the ground, Ciarry drew her knees up. "In truth, after meeting you, I've been so happy and distracted, all I'd decided was to keep on walking, with or without you, until I could see my way clear."

He joined her on the grass, sketching a crude map on the ground with his knife.

"We're approximately here." An inscribed circle marked the spot. "Over here is a farm I own, in upper Coquetdale." A rectangle took shape. "Things are somewhat wild there—not the folk, the terrain. Yet 'tis beautiful. And the farm could produce a good yield with constant oversight, which it doesn't get now. I'd like you to take it over. That is, I want to give it to you, to hold in your own name, if you wish, or as my tenant, if you prefer."

Her dark eyes filled.

"Probably the best way is a combination of the two," he continued. "Then I can address legal questions, should any arise. But it will really be your holding, Ciarry, your farm. Yours."

Joy flooded her face, though she choked back tears. He had just given her tomorrow.

While she had known he would not cast her off, she had assumed that, at best, he might make her one of his scribes. But that could arouse resentment from his current aides (like young Hardyng, of whom he spoke with such brotherly pride), at least until they came to accept her. Moreover, if she suddenly appeared in his household, outsiders might consider her naught but Lord Harry's whore.

Alternately, she had feared she'd have to take a position someplace distant, far from him.

Instead, this sounded perfect. She would be in his beloved North; his comrades could come to know her gradually, as the new owner of one of his farms, as well as his friend and confidante.

"You would do this for me?"

"Aye! Mind you, though, it'll require hard work. But you've already been mistress of your abbey farm and Fitzwyatt's lands. So I doubt not you can manage this place and do it well. And I hope you'll be happy, too."

"You know I will."

"Aye, but hear the rest." He thought aloud. "The house: Unfortunately, it's no manor. In truth, it's a bit of an oddity. It began as a peel tower, but the Scots burned it and pulled off the top floors, afore Neville's Cross."

"Neville's Cross ... that battle where they were trounced in Edward's reign."

"Aye, in 1346. After that, 'twas long forsaken. Then I came of age and claimed some of my family's properties. I found a new tenant to repair it. But he only rebuilt three floors, though he improved the root cellar—and the kitchen, as I recall, adding ovens."

"Marvelous."

"I reckon. Now, what else? Oh, it's crenellated. The most recent owner wanted to do that, and I agreed. He completed it not long ere he died."

"Killed? Fighting off Scots from his crenellation?"

"God forbid," Harry chuckled. "No, of apoplexy over his supper one night. And I should explain: He owned part of the property outright, but for the rest, including the house, he was tenant to me. And everything defaulted to me when he died. Your legal arrangement with me could be similar.

"Also," Harry nervously polished a boot with a finger, "with the house or tower or whatever it is, there's an orchard and fields for peas, hay, barleycorn and oats. You'd have a fishpond, too; last time I looked, it had nesting mallards as well. And there's a burn in the woods.

"But I can't tell you the acreage; I can't remember." A shoulder rose in a careless shrug. "Likewise, there are numerous sheep and cows in the meadows. Again, though, I'm unsure how many I own and how many belong to others with grazing rights."

Seeing her rapt attention, he went on. "You'd have neighbors—a homestead and mill not far off. The closest village is Foxbrigham, about two miles distant. The nearest market town is Rothbury, seven or eight miles away. There's also a castle at Harbottle, and peel towers at Alnham, Clennel, Tosson and Thropton."

He added a few squares to his earthen map.

"Right now, the farm is looked after, loosely, by a fellow on the adjacent farmstead. He has two sons, about fourteen and sixteen. The younger one is partly crippled. He's good with the animals and works like the devil, but there's a limit to how much he can do. And the older boy and father are busy with their own place. So they mostly ensure my house and byres haven't gone derelict or been torched by reivers.

"There *is* the threat of reivers, as there is nearly anywhere in the North. But if I do my job as warden properly, they should never get that far.

"Otherwise," he added, "I can't tell you too much, except that I want you to have it." He anxiously awaited her reaction.

Her thoughts spun round and round as they had so frequently of late. But there was little to weigh. First, he had offered her love; now he was offering her a life and something beyond him to love, something ancient and tangible and real, something to fight for, and nurture and make her own.

"Oh, Harry! Of course, I'll take it over for you, in my name or otherwise, it matters not. But you must let me pay something, as tenant-fee or farm-fee or purchase. I can't agree otherwise."

She loved him. But she would not be kept.

"You and your pride," he teased. "All right, pay me. But no more than a shilling."

The amount seemed ridiculously low, but clearly, he didn't care. So she accepted and reached into her pack for three groat coins—one shilling, or one-twentieth of a pound. Dropping them into his hand, she laughed. "Never did I foresee such a transaction when I began this journey." Voice fading, she was close to tears. "I... I know not how to thank you..."

"Say naught!" He kissed her brow. "At least not till you see the place. Then you can change your mind if you wish."

But they both knew she wouldn't.

"Come on," he got up. "We've a long walk, but we can still reach your farm today."

She stowed her belongings and checked the shelter to make sure they'd left nothing behind. In her momentary absence, he tucked the coins back into the lining of her rucksack. As far as she was concerned, she'd paid him. And if she later noticed she had a shilling more than she had expected—well, he could tease her that her arithmetical skills weren't as keen as she had claimed!

"You know I have ulterior motives," he said as they set off. "I'm selfish. I can't bear the thought of losing you or not seeing you often. So I've found a way for you to be near—as near as you ever could be, anyway, to a wandering knight who's scarcely in one place very long. Soon I must ride to Berwick. Then I've got to return to Chester and Wales. I don't know how much I'll be around these next few months."

"Would that it were otherwise, but I understand."

"Aye. But at least you'll be in Northumberland, and I'll be able to see you whenever I do return. And wherever I go, I'll carry your heart. No person, and no miles, can take that from me."

His fingers found hers, and they walked another mile. But, when the road slipped from a cleft, he dropped her hand. Climbing atop a rock that overhung fields far below, he opened his arms wide, embracing the view.

South and east, the land rolled gently, some meadows bright green, others a deep mossy shade, several more golden in hay or grain unharvested, a few farmsteads and hamlets tranquil in their midst. To the northeast, the ground sloped upward, and the road disappeared between ridges. Beyond loomed the Cheviots, the desolate and incomparably beautiful mountains he loved. On the horizon, a wispy cloud floated, and the blue sky faded to lavender while a couple of hawks looped in graceful orbs.

"How marvelous this land is!" He exulted from his rock. "How fortunate I am to have it to come home to. Someday," he laughed, rejoining her, "I'll end up here for good, cool my spurs in my dotage, become a yeoman farmer myself."

"Never. Though I might pray otherwise, I think you'll never be content with a placid life."

"Maybe," he shrugged. "But I should at least have the satisfaction of dying here. A sage once predicted it, when I was a hostage under Montgomery."

"Aye?" She already knew of Montgomery and Harry's long stay in Scotland.

He nodded. "At Montgomery's urging, I participated in a tourney—wearing his colors, of course. And I did quite well for the House of Montgomery. Afterward, a group of us, all young knights, ready to raise hell, were roistering with wine and ale and bragging. An old priest happened by our tent and heard us—not difficult, considering the racket we must've made. So he barged in, bidding us remember the sins of pride, greed, and so on."

"Rather dour."

"Actually, he was quite amiable, much given to predictions, though. We plied him with wine, and he visited awhile. For some reason, he singled me out, saying I was very valiant and would have much success on the field. And he said I'd eventually die near Berwick."

"Truly?"

"Aye. As he put it: 'Your sword will drop from your hand and you'll fall mortally, hard-by Berwick.' Or maybe it was, 'hard-by *a* Berwick.' Anyway, if I have to die somewhere—and all men must—then far better it be 'hard by Berwick,' here in the North. Probably when I am so old, I can scarcely lift my sword!"

A tremulous smile crossed her lips.

"You think me foolish, Lass."

"No. It's just that if the prediction was that you'd die 'hard-by *a* Berwick' or even 'hard-by Berwick'—well, that could be anywhere. In the language men once spoke in England, years past, 'Berwick' meant any farm structure or enclosed place, like a barn in a fenced acre or a walled barley field, beyond town or castle. Perhaps that's how your Berwick-upon-Tweed got its name."

"'Twas supposed to have been named for bears."

"Perhaps it was: a 'field of bears' and barley, too, but still a wick like many another. Perhaps that old priest was only being astute. He knew you were a knight, likely to end your days on some field. Since most battles are fought outside towns, it only makes sense you'd fall 'hard-by a berwick,' or even just 'hard-by berwick.'" She paused. "But ... perhaps not your Berwick-upon-Tweed."

Crestfallen, he paled.

Within moments, though, ebullience returned. "You're right. It just means I could die anywhere. But so can anyone, so it means naught." He noted the shadows in her eyes, lit by joy minutes earlier, and drew her close. "But let's not talk of silly auguries on such a glorious day."

They continued hand in hand.

In time, he disappeared behind a stand of trees to urinate and then strolled to a brook to refill his canteen. As he finished, he heard frenzied bleating. Crossing the meadow, he found a disconsolate sheep trapped in a ruined hut, into which it had fallen after leaping through the sole window from the higher ground outside. Normally he would have left it to eventually force itself upward and out. But today, he felt benevolent. Stepping down into the hut, he scooped the sheep into his arms, lifting it through the window. It bolted with another loud bleat and no hint of gratitude. Smiling, he made his way back to the road.

And became vexed. Ciarry was nowhere in sight. Neither were the horses.

"Damnation!"

He could see down the road ahead and—turning—behind him. Nothing. Nor was there any sign of her to the right or left. But foot and horse prints continued ahead. Trudging on, he heard a whinny beyond a thicket. The whinny was followed by another. Looking down, he could see the tracks veer into the brush on the verge.

He set off.

Behind hawthorn scrub, up a small hillock, an old apple tree grew, gnarled but elegant, inured against the bite of northern gales. Branches shook. Below, Brutus and Redesraven chomped apples in equine insouciance. They lifted their heads on his approach and then blatantly ignored him.

He spotted the small figure on a limb, halfway up the tree. Standing at the bottom, he pretended to scold. "Now that you've ruined my horses, or at least their diet, you may as well come down."

A face peered through the leaves. "Want an apple, Harry?"

"No!" He feigned anger. "I'm stronger than Adam. I'll not be tempted by any woman with fruit from a tree. Though, God only knows, you tempt me to plenty that I once never would've thought possible."

Ciarry tossed a couple of apples, red and aromatic.

Despite himself he picked them up, storing them in his belt pouch. "I think you must be guilty of compounded felonies by now. First blackberries, now apples. And I've just sequestered the evidence. As warden, I order you to desist. Or I shall have to take drastic action."

"How? Climb up after me? I'm lighter than you, remember. If you tried, you might break the branches and fall." She shifted on her perch. "However, I'm coming down."

He reached out to help, but in a pique of self-assertiveness, she refused him and jumped, landing amongst hawthorn prickles. Untangling herself, she laughed, rubbing thin red scratches. "Serves me right for being so high and mighty. Or, perhaps high in the tree but not very mighty at all."

They returned to the road, the horses following.

After a few minutes, she pulled ahead once more. Walking backward, she faced him. "This day and this country move me to poetry."

"How so?"

> *Just peg my heart to the hawthorn tree,*
> *for I'm fairly pierced with grieving.*
> *On the morrow they're going to hang me high,*
> *the warden caught me reiving!"*

With a gleeful shout, she started running.

Laughing, he caught up. Swinging her into his arms, he carried her like a child. Her knees bent over his right arm, his left arm under her shoulders, he danced in the middle of the road.

"Oh, Ciarry, I do love you! I can't explain how you make me feel—so happy, so like a boy, so full of life and so able to see it and know it, as I never have afore." He kissed her. "And I'll not say more. But I love you." He began twirling on his feet, faster and faster, in a dizzying blur. Their laughter filled the air until, shrieking and fearing he would falter and drop her, she implored him to stop.

Laughing once more, he set her down. He was inclined to find a secluded glade and spend the afternoon making love and lying naked in the sun. But he wanted her settled before duty stole him away. So he contented himself with holding her hand as their trek resumed.

They paused on the lane above, surveying her new domain, nestled among trees and fields of emerald and ochre below the purple of the Cheviots. Of greyish stone, the house was a squat square with a toothy roof, a massive door in front, arrow slits and narrow windows around its perimeter. Built into a slope, it sported a fine cellar dug deep into the earth. A stone wall rimmed house, yards and outbuildings, with a pond beyond. A couple more roofs were visible a quarter mile away. Surrounding everything, though, was naught but countryside—mountains and meadows and forests laced by streams bubbling toward the Coquet. For a moment, Harry almost regretted his decision, for the tower looked lonesome and almost foreboding. Yet, beams of afternoon sun burnished the pond and set a halo of red gold around Ciarry's head.

"How splendid!" Scurrying down the embankment, she raced through the open gate in the wall to the house and up the stair to its door and down again, then around to the barn and outbuildings and finally to the pool, where a lone deer, surprised in its late afternoon drink, bounded away.

At last, she returned to the front, where he waited and took her hands. Falling to her knees, she tried to understand this vast and wonderful thing that had happened, this vast and wonderful place that claimed her.

Vainly, he sought to raise her. But she continued clinging to his hands.

"Oh, My Lord, my love..." Her tears fell on his wrists, spilling onto his boots and splashing the rough ground below. "You gave me your love and now you've given me this, your land—given it to be mine, though I'm scarce worthy. I've felt sadness and loneliness all my days, like I yearned for a place I'd never been before. Now I know where it is: here."

He kissed her head.

"I would serve you always, Harry! I swear to you my fealty, my steadfast friendship, my devotion. I bind myself, to stand ever with you and for you and to work alongside you, for you are my lord." She smiled through her tears. "Above all I give my heart to you: *dominus mei, defensor mei, amicus mei, et amor mei.*"

At first, he could only bestow another kiss. Then he found his voice. "And I vow that I am and always will be your lord, your defender, your friend, your love. *Mon coeur se recommande a vous...* My heart commends itself to you."

He finally succeeded in lifting her into his arms. "Welcome home, Lass!"

The End

ABOUT THE AUTHOR
Liz Sevchuk Armstrong

I live in New York state, in Cold Spring, a small village on the edge of the Hudson River and foot of the Appalachian Mountains. It's about an hour from New York City but surrounded by forests, mountains, and meadows, as much of it is either part of the state park system or federal government land. Before arriving in Cold Spring when my husband's job location changed to New York City, I spent 21 years in Washington, D.C., mostly as a political-national affairs reporter for U.S. and international daily news organizations, where my responsibilities included covering the White House, Congress, and Supreme Court. When the journalism business started to tank and I got laid off 5 months after taking a new reporting job, I went to graduate school, while continuing to work part-time as a news editor, and obtained a degree in medieval history, where my specialty is British political and military history. For my required graduate research project, I studied the conflict between Sir Harry Percy—Hotspur—and King Henry IV, which led to my Epic of Hotspur series.

www.ingramcontent.com/pod-product-compliance
Lightning Source LLC
Chambersburg PA
CBHW051418290426
44109CB00016B/1351